L-R: Zohra Ansari, M.A. Ansari, Halidé Edib, Sarojini Naidu

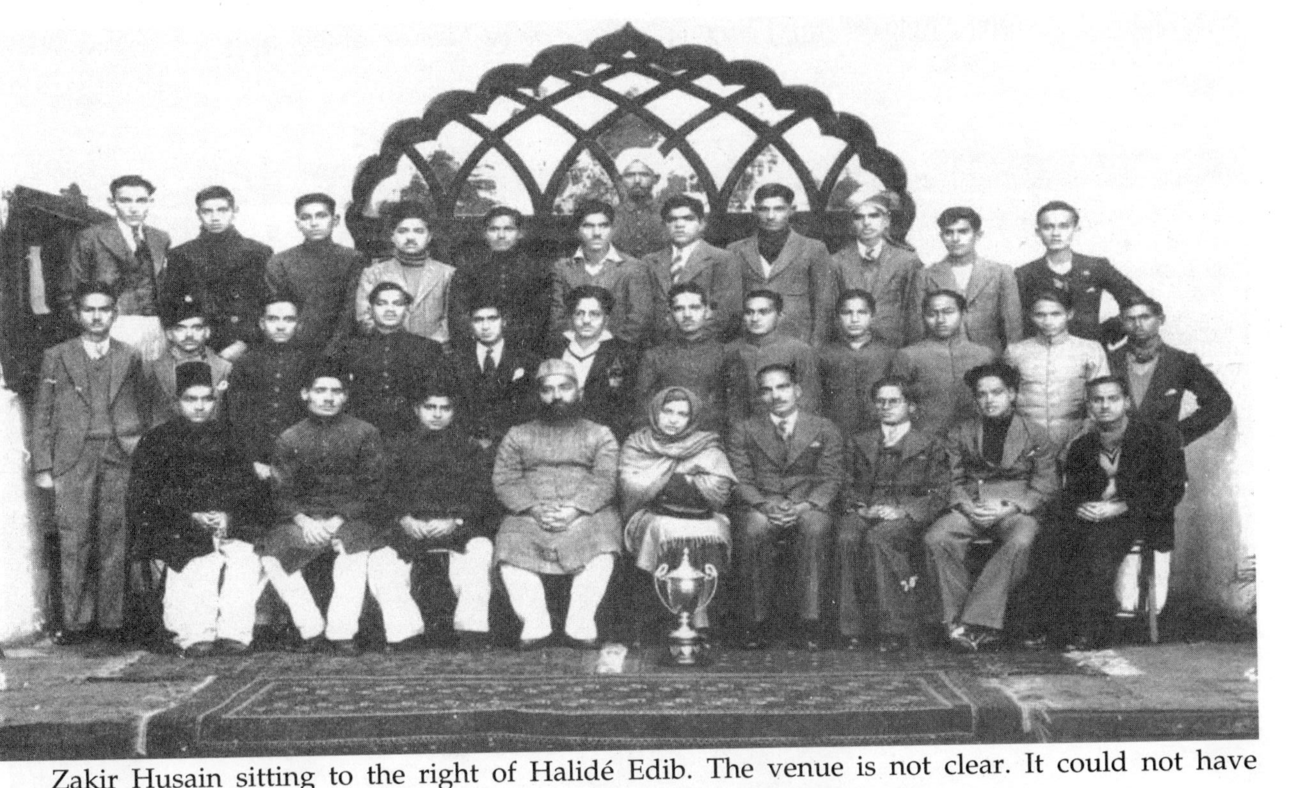

Zakir Husain sitting to the right of Halidé Edib. The venue is not clear. It could not have been in Jamia, where the *mehrab* at the back was not a part of any of its buildings.

East Faces West

Impressions of a Turkish Writer in India

Halidé Edib

Introduced and Edited by
Mushirul Hasan

Academy of Third World Studies
Jamia Millia Islamia
New Delhi

AAKAR

First Published 2009

ISBN: 978-81-89833-51-0

Published by
AAKAR BOOKS
28 E Pocket IV, Mayur Vihar Phase I, Delhi 110 091
Phone : 011-2279 5505 Telefax : 011-2279 5641
aakarbooks@gmail.com; www.aakarbooks.com

Type Setting: Line Art Graphics, Delhi-91

Printed at
Mudrak, 30-A, Patparganj, Delhi 110 091

Contents

Editor's Note

'The message of the East, the message of Asia, is not to be learnt through European spectacles, not by imitating the voices of the West, its gunpowder and atom bomb. If you want to give a message of importance to the West it must be a message of love, it must be a message of truth. Asia has to conquer the West. You and I are the inheritors of a message of love. You can re-deliver that message now in this age of democracy, in the age of an awakening of the poorest of the poor. Then you will complete the conquest of the whole of the West. ... The West is today pining for wisdom. It is despairing of [the] multiplication of atom bombs because such multiplication must destroy not merely all the West but the whole world. ... It is up to you to deliver the whole world and not merely Asia from wickedness and sin. That is the precious heritage which your teachers and my teachers have left for us.' (Stephen N. Hay, *Asian Ideas of East and West: Tagore and His Critics in Japan, China, and India*, Bombay, 1970, pp. 287-88).

This was Gandhi's message from the 'East'; but it echoed the thoughts of many social reformers, thinkers, creative writers and other public men. The themes elucidated by Gandhi in the above statement has been of considerable relevance in public discourses. It was debated at length in the aftermath of the 1857 revolt by those who apprehended the virtual destruction of a way of life by the intrusion of colonial rule. Consequently, the reformers amongst them proceeded to set their house in order with the aid of religious texts, the Vedas or the Upanishads.

After the Revolt of 1857, the elites connected with the erstwhile Awadh court had good reason to mourn the eclipse of their benefactors. Recalcitrant rajas and nawabs, some of whom had revolted against the British and were consequently humbled, bemoaned the passing of an era. The *ulama* and the *mashaikh* spent sleepless nights worrying about the future of Islamic tenets in a society dominated by Western ideas and institutions. (Such apprehensions had, in fact, led Maulvi Fazl-i Haq Khairabadi, a reputed scholar, to take part in the 1857 revolt).

It is hard to imagine anyone in Lucknow or its environs not being influenced by colonial rule or by the effects of 'the Great Western Transmutation'. Some were haunted by the prospect of Western thought undermining the moral and spiritual basis of their society. They had no cause to celebrate Great Britain's political hegemony in an area that had broadly remained insulated from the changes taking place in parts of Eastern and Western India. But most were prepared, albeit grudgingly, to make the colonial government work, seek adjustments within existing institutions, and secure benefits from the newly-created administrative and bureaucratic structures. They were inclined to arrive at a workable *modus vivendi* with the new rulers and carve out new channels of aspirations and spiritual creativity. Hence the growth of schools and colleges, the bold steps taken by some forward looking Muslim personalities, the incentive to join the 'heaven born', and the clamour for a share in decision-making bodies.

The Nadwat al-ulama, founded in 1894, symbolised this spirit of compromise. Its founder, Shibli Nomani, was sensitive to the winds of change. Lucknow became the locale for synthesising the traditional system of learning with Western methods. The Firangi Mahal, also in Lucknow and a reputed centre of Islamic education, reflected the same spirit of compromise. In sum, sections of the Muslim educated classes, particularly in Delhi and its environs, did not interpret East-West relations in conflictual terms. Instead, they talked of an Anglo-Muslim rapprochement and welcomed the flow of liberal and scientific ideas from the West. This was the message from the Delhi College and from the M.A.O. Çollege, Aligarh.

By the turn of the nineteenth century, only a few hard nuts remained to be cracked. But the colonial government thwarted their challenge through conciliation and compromise and a policy of balance and rule between what they conceived as the two great communities, the Hindu and the Muslim. Members of landed families and of service communities, principally Kayasthas and Kashmiri Pandits, were integrated into the extensive administrative apparatus with Lucknow as the focal point. Traders and commercial men benefited from the infrastructure created to serve imperial interests.

In the nineteenth and twentieth centuries, scores of reformers, writers, poets and statesman contributed to the debates on the idea of the West and its legitimacy in the colonised countries. Raja Rammohun Roy was one of the foremost thinkers on the subject, followed by Syed Ahmad Khan, Altaf Husain Hali, M.K. Gandhi, Rabindranath Tagore and Mohammad Iqbal. The debates on their intervention goes on ceaselessly, and is nowadays reinforced by theories on the 'clash of civlizations.' Even though the old theories of interpreting the 'East' and 'West' as separate, homogenised and antagonised entities have been persistently questioned, it is important to revisit the debates to discover the 'real West' in its historical and contemporary settings. We need to know more about the 'Western' view of the 'East' not because it is necessarily fair or accurate but because it is for the most part ill-informed and dangerously influential. This does not mean creating more boundaries or perpetuating Western or non-Western myths, but understanding the cluster of images and ideas of the East and the West. In our part of the world, in particular, we need to explore the West that neither celebrates nor defames it but unfolding issues in a holistic manner.

Among the Asian countries, Turkey has been in the forefront of the debates on East-West relations. From the time of the Tanzimat, the rise of the West was closely scrutinized and interepreted in multiple ways until Mustafa Kemal Pasha's major and decisive project of Westernization triggered intensive debates. It must be emphasised that his project was in accord with the views of, for example, Ziya Gokalp (1876-1924), the chief ideologue of Turkey's creation as a modern nation.

We are introducing a new voice to the existing debates, the voice of Halidé Edib, who played such a critical role in defining Turkish identity in a colonial context. In 2002, I introduced *Inside India* as a record of events and as a portrait gallery of personalities. Now, in 2009, we are re-issuing *The Conflict of East and West in Turkey* with notes on major events and personalities. The book was first printed in Delhi by the Maktaba Press in 1935 and translated into Urdu by Abid Husain, the scholar at Jamia. Muhammad Ashraf in Lahore brought out the second edition.

My introduction to *Inside India* covers the details of Halidé Edib's career. Mohammad Mujeeb's essay, translated by my colleague Nishat Zaidi, places her life into perspective. As the host at the Jamia Millia Islamia, where these lectures were delivered, he saw her at close quarters and admired her manifold qualities. Likewise, the essay by Dr M.A. Ansari, Jamia's Chancellor, is a warm tribute to Halidé Edib's contribution to the freedom struggle in Turkey. It is also a tribute to a well-known writer, a fiery orator, and a reformer.

I am currently engaged in writing a full-length intellectual biography of Halidé Edib. I hope to cover the debates triggered by her lectures.

I have not made any changes in the text. I have retained the spellings all through to retain the flavour of the original English translation. The notes are intended to help the reader. I have added the English translation of an article by Mohammad Mujeeb, a friend of Halidé Edib. The article appeared in the magazine *Jamia* in 1935.

The justification for reprinting is two-fold. First of all, the debate on East-West encounter goes on ceaselessly despite the massive transformation of the world which includes the breakdown of borders and boundaries. Indeed, even though the 'East' and 'West' are not unified and homogenised entities, it is not recognized as such. Halidé explains why this is so. My second reason for re-issuing *conflict of East and West in Turkey* is to introduce a segment of Turkish history–'one of the great melting pots of the world'. Finally, these lectures shed light of Halidé Edib's cultural attainments and her intellectual outlook. She represents, as M.A. Ansari stated in his preface to the book, 'a harmonious fusion of all that this best in the East and the West of today'.

I thank Mohammed Javed Ansari for laboriously working over the typescript and Dr. Javed Ahmad Khan, Reader in the Centre for West Asian Studies, for his assistance in editing the text of these lectures.

January 2009 Mushirul Hasan

Preface

This book is an adaptation of the Extension Lectures Halidé Hanum delivered at the Jamia Millia Islamia in January and February last. These lectures have been organised with the two-fold object of forming contacts with representative personalities of the outside world and of enriching our own experience by studying the problems and the ideals of other peoples. Halidé Hanum's visit fulfilled this object admirably. Her own cultural attainments and social and moral outlook are a harmonious fusion of all that is best in the East and West of today; and the lectures tell us all that we, as the inheritors of a culture and the builders of a future society, need to know of Turkey—one of the great melting pots of the world.

When I first met Halidé Hanum at Constantinople in 1913, she was anxious to come to India and tell us the truth about her country, for Turkey has borne the brunt of European calumny, deliberate and organised, just as she has had to withstand the fiercest onslaughts of European imperialism, and the most treacherous blows of unscrupulous diplomacy. But I am rather glad she did not come then, but now, when the battle is over and she can look back with confidence and pride on her own rich and varied experience and the invincible spirit of her people. She did not come to us with a grievance and a passion, but with an intimate and accurate knowledge of men and affairs, and the true wisdom born of sober reflection, forgiveness and under-standing.

The bare facts of Halidé Hanum's life are a matter of general information, and it would be superfluous to repeat them here. What we need to remember is that she is one of those in whose life two ways of thought, two methods of social organisation came into conflict. Her early years were spent in a typically Eastern household; her education and the problems of her time brought her face to face with the West. It would have been easy for her, like so many educated women of the East, to deny her own culture and assert the actual if not moral right to accept what standards she liked. It may also have been possible to take refuge behind self-adulatory prejudices and close her eyes to the new duties and responsibilities. But rather than live out her life with an inner futility masked by cultural accomplishments and fine manners, or a social and moral atrophy decked out in the guise of ancient and established virtue, she flung herself into the thick of the fight, and has emerged victorious. She has grasped the fundamental values of the West, freedom, organisation, efficient social co-operation; and her active life of service and guidance has made her treasure all the more highly the pearls of great price, which we are told, may be found only in the East—inner quietude, spiritual harmony, the realisation of a unity beneath all diversity, a love beyond all hatred. She has achieved great distinction as a novelist and social philosopher; she has been a professor and an educationist who helped to organise the system of public instruction; a speaker of immense courage and power, when it was necessary to raise her people from the depths of stupefaction and misery and move them to heroic effort; she has done the work of a news agency and commission of enquiry; she has worn military uniforms, and served at the headquarters of the nationalist army, with the din and the smoke of a grim battle around her. She has also been a rebel against customs and traditions that fettered life; she has fearlessly denounced men and policies in the name of brotherhood, justice and truth. She has loved and served her people, but with a large-heartedness that could look beyond them to the greater human family; she has thrown herself heart and soul into the struggle of her nation for life and liberty, but never ceased to be aware of the world-wide moral and cultural conflicts of which it formed a part. She speaks, therefore, with greater authority than any person living on the fundamental problems on whose solution will depend the future of the East.

Yet I believe this book will prove quite provocative. East and West being attitudes of mind rather than geographical terms, it is impossible to define them in a way that will be acceptable to all. No doubt, as Halidé Hanum says, over-emphasis on spirit and on matter are the basic distinction between East and West, but contrary tendencies have been sufficiently in evidence to lend plausibility to arguments against this generalisation. And particularly in the East of today such arguments are likely to overstep the limits of a purely academic and objective discussion. Everything that tends to expose the inherent weaknesses of Eastern peoples is resented, because it tightens the stranglehold of Western imperialism or confirms the moral and intellectual domination of the West. But the main contention of Halidé Hanum, that the East has succumbed to Western aggression owing to its inability to organise its material and social life cannot be challenged. And if she maintains that this has been one of the fatal consequences of the over-emphasis on spirit, she states no less clearly that over emphasis on the material side of existence is proving equally disastrous for the West. In any case, criticism coming from such a hero of a hundred fights as Halidé Hanum should be considered more of a lesson than a reproach.

In her definition of East and West I do not personally think Halidé Hanum differs from the generality of sober thinkers, Eastern or Western. But her opinions regarding pan-Islamism and her detached, objective discussion of religion and religious matters will hardly meet with the approval of the vast majority of Indian Moslems. It is in respect of this that a few explanations are necessary.

It is difficult for anyone not an Indian Moslem to realise what pan-Islamism means to the Indian Moslems. Ever since the Moslems came into India, more than seven hundred years ago, they have kept open house, in the widest political and social sense of the term. Arabs, Egyptians, Syrians, Turks, even Tartar immigrants, have been given full opportunity to earn the just reward of talent and merit. But the pan-Islamism of the twentieth century is something far deeper than the friendliness, the democratic spirit and the desire to enlist the finest talent, even though it came from China, in the service of the state, which the open door system implied. It is something similar to the attempt made in the sixteenth century to combine the naval power of the Indians and the Turks against the common enemy, the Portuguese. It is a sentiment of which the prayers for Turkish success in the Tripolitan and Balkan wars, the Relief Fund, the Medical Mission and even the Khilafat movement were but weak and faltering expressions. It is not a sentiment inspired by interest, policy or worldly wisdom; it has no definite practical end in view. But strange to say, it is just for these reasons that the pan-Islamist sentiment has been one of the Indian Moslem's most sacred and exalted passions. It is because he is helpless, because all his co-religionists are equally helpless, because Western imperialism is aggressive and everywhere successful, that he has become a pan-Islamist. And because Turkey alone of all Moslem countries is free, because the Turks alone have power to defeat enemies not overwhelmingly strong and the manliness to prefer death to slavery, the imagination of the Indian Moslems converted them into as convinced pan-Islamists as they themselves, and placed on their shoulders the burden not only of defending their hearth and home, but the honour of Islam and all Moslem peoples as well. The Turks could not, of course, be expected to appreciate this quaint romanticism and chivalry, or endure such oppressive affection. When they declined the honour that had been thrust upon them, the Indian Moslems' dream-world crashed upon their head. They could not think objectively or subjectively. They just could not think and could not believe.

Time has no doubt healed their wounds, and, they do not now reflect on the matter in the light of sentiment alone. But their world is still bleak and desolate and the wrecks of their dreams lie around them. The pan-Islamism that was once an ideal is now a vague grievance; what was once a hope and an inspiration is now a sorrow. God is still in heaven, but the world has apparently lost its balance. For the hero of the Islamic community has now become the Prodigal Son.

Yet, however tragic the situation may be for the Indian Moslems, it cannot be gainsaid that their Moslem brethren have been more directly responsible for the surrender of the pan-Islamist ideal than the Turks themselves. The Indian Moslems were guilty mainly of a confusion of issues; and except that there were Indian Moslems in the British forces in Mesopotamia and Palestine, one may even say that they have been consistent in their friendship and ready to help as far as their position as British subjects allowed them. But the non-Turkish Moslem subjects of the Ottoman Empire were openly and heartlessly treacherous. I cannot here go into the discussion whether their grievances were genuine or manufactured for the purpose, but their attitude would have convinced the most zealous Turkish pan-Islamist that there was no possibility of co-operation between them and the Turks. The Ottoman Empire is now gone and its non-Turkish Moslem subjects have all got what they wanted or what they deserved, so we may as well admit that the abolition of the Caliphate was a matter of sound policy, for the Caliphate involved the Turks in pretensions which may have given them a certain prestige, but which also exposed them to the jealous wrath of their enemies and the shiftiness of selfish friends.

Pan-Islamism in India was not in the main political. With the vast majority of Indian Moslems its appeal was purely religious. And thus a discussion of pan-Islamism inevitably leads to a discussion of religion, and to the second charge disillusioned Indian Moslems bring against the Turks. The Turks, they say, may have had some justification for the abolition of the Caliphate. But why should they have renounced their religion, their culture, indeed, everything that was distinctive and unique, and forced upon themselves an alien culture and way of life that can never, perhaps, become peculiarly their own?

Halidé Hanum could not have had Indian sentiment in mind when planning her lectures, and she has not therefore attempted a direct answer to this question. She has treated her subject objectively throughout, and made no exception with religion. She has shown us very clearly how, up to the time of Abdul Hamid, in spite of a conservative and reactionary element, religious and political sentiment worked harmoniously to one end. Abdul Hamid's tyrannical suppression of political thought, his proscriptions and persecutions, destroyed in the intelligentsia this harmony of different impulses and sentiments. It was he who converted reformers into rebels, he who spread the wild and reckless belief that the past was a vampire preying on the Turkish soul, and there would be no future unless the past was killed. If Abdul Hamid's tyranny had been followed by a generation or two of peace, the rest-cure might have undone some of the harm. But instead there came war upon war, charging the atmosphere with impatience, intolerance, panic and suffering. There was no time, it seemed, to argue and convince. The people could not grow out of one condition, one attitude, into another. There was no alternative to force. The concentration of all power in the hands of a single dictatorial party made matters easy for the few who held that everything old, everything Eastern, everything alien to the materialism, the mechanisation of life, which had made the West so formidable, would impair the efficiency and endanger the unity of the state. The Turkish Republic became secular, and made religion into one of its most strictly supervised departments, legislating for it with the same authority as in purely secular matters. This is not, as Halidé Hanum says, what one would understand from a separation of religion and the state. But those in power in the Republic will have it so.

Halidé Hanum has, in her restrained and objective manner, stated all the criticisms that can be urged against the cultural and religious attitude of the Republic, and as one privileged to know her personal opinion, I can say that it has caused her the keenest sorrow. She is too dignified to make a futile show of emotion, and besides knows her people too well to be misled by superficialities. The Turkish people, whatever the policy of their state, are as sincere Moslems now as before, and Halidé Hanum may even be right in expecting a religious revival of a nature that will have a healthy and stimulating effect on the whole Moslem world.

But I feel that Indian Moslems should also understand that their perspective is very faulty. They have a tendency, as have all those who are isolated or insular in outlook, to identify not only their beliefs, but also their manners and customs, with the prescriptions of their faith. Religion and social life are no doubt inseparable, and a society that altogether overlooks the religious element is sure to drift from one vicious whirlpool to another. But the position of a society that lacks the judgement to distinguish between conservatism and stagnation is equally insecure. Religion is the permanent basis of life, but the true religious spirit does not seek to shackle life in order to preserve a theoretical consistency between fact and belief. It endeavours rather to discover fresh sources of inspiration, which are really nothing more than fresh points of contact between the personality of the founder of a religion and of the follower across the gulf of time and altered social conditions. Rigid conformity to the letter, because it breeds a logic-worship that has no sympathy for the natural and the living, may be as injurious to society as frivolous disregard for truth. There can thus be need for reform even when the law is all written down. This reform would not imply that there are shortcomings in the faith or its law. True and healthy reform never does. Nor should we suspect an insinuation that the faith and the law was meant for a less civilised people, for though manners, habits and environment may change, the fundamental needs of man remain the same, and the voice of a preacher of truth is not lost in space and time.

I believe we should accept Halidé Hanum's assurance in regard to the religious spirit of her people all the more readily because she would not have hesitated to assert the contrary, if that were nearer the truth. That she has treated even the religious question objectively is indeed a novelty for us, because with us religion cannot be detached from sentiment even for scientific purposes, and religious opinions always have the air of finality. But Halidé Hanum's intention is to inform, not to preach. She has surveyed the most important facts, in matters of disagreement and difference she has given the main arguments of the discussion. The Indian Moslem public would have doubtless preferred something akin to a harangue to Halidé Hanum's sober, dispassionate treatment. I will only say that Halidé Hanum's knowledge, like her personality, is too great to be comprehended in one or many books. Her restraint is the stillness of deep waters. They must be catastrophic events indeed that stir her to the depths.

As I have already said, this book is an adaptation of Halidé Hanum's lectures. Her numerous engagements prevented her revising them while she was in India, and the publishers were unwilling to risk the delay involved in her taking the MS back with her and revising it at leisure. The work of revision and editing was therefore entrusted to Professor Mujeeb, of the Jamia Millia. Owing to the absence of Dr. Zakir Husain and the pressure of work on his other colleagues, Professor Mujeeb had to read proofs and deal with the press as well. Some errors and omissions may have escaped his scrutiny, which I would beg the reader to overlook.

M.A. ANSARI

Delhi
5th June 1935

Khaleda Edib Khanam*

M. Mujeeb

(Translated from Urdu by Nishat Zaidi)

Most of the educated Muslims in India are familiar with the name of Khaleda Edib Khanam— some of her books have also been translated into Urdu. She has published her autobiography and a detailed account of the Turkish freedom struggle in two volumes in English. I hope that the publication of her extension lectures in Jamia would help spread her message and ideas. And even those who do not know English would benefit from the knowledge and philosophy of Khaleda Edib.

Khaleda Khanam is among those chosen personalities whose life history is synonymous with the national history. Not just because she faced what the nation faced but also because she took national and public duty as her personal duty and her own needs and concerns could never be separated from her public life. Family problems and tragedies made Khaleda Khanam's early life a typical instance of Turkish women's struggles. After 1908, when she started writing essays, she felt the impact of public life so much that her own life and the lives of her countrymen became one like the waters of two rivers—like a river merging into the ocean.

Khaleda Khanam's father Edib Bey held a high position in the royal palace and lived like other affluent Turks. He

---

***Jamia*, Delhi: March 1935,vol.24, no.3,pp 196-211.*

was so broadminded that he had Khaleda Khanam study in an American school and did not force her to follow local customs and traditions. Yet he was not influenced enough by the European social philosophy so as to dislike or reject polygamy. And although Khaleda Khanam's mother was not sold to Western social values, she could not concur to continue in her husband's house as his first and special wife. As soon as Edib Bey married again, she left him to live with her parents. This hurt her so much that she soon fell to tuberculosis. Khaleda Khanam was very young when her mother died. All she remembered of her mother was her mother's sad face and her big eyes. She also remembered that her mother's face showed signs of happiness only after she had already died.

The grief of a dead mother is often a child's legacy. Khaleda Khanam remained sad most of the time in her childhood. She never liked to play with other children of her age and was not an enthusiastic and cheerful child. Her grandmother understood her well. And it was due to her care that Khaleda Khanam's childhood was spent in peace if not in exuberance. Edib Bey loved his children; he loved Khaleda Khanam the most but his care really bore fruits only when it came to her education. Khaleda Khanam studied at home for some time before she was admitted to school. In 1901, after finishing her college, she married her one-time teacher Saleh Zaki Bey. They married with mutual consent but temperamental differences led to clashes and, finally, after nine years of his first marriage, Saleh Zaki Bey married the second time. Like her mother, Khaleda Khanam also did not like to share her husband with another woman and compelled Saleh Zaki Bey to divorce her. By this time, Khaleda Khanam was already introduced to the academic circles and she got herself actively engaged in various academic pursuits. She could not bear the sorrow of the abrupt end of her family life.

After a few of months of illness, she embarked on a new life altogether—a life where she hardly had time to remember her past and feel sad about it.

At that time, Turkey was going through a revolution. And people who had even a little bit of concern for the nation had devoted their entire strength and life to the nation. After 30 years of oppression by Abdul Hamid, in 1908, the party of 'Young Turks', which was known as a party devoted to "unity and progress", demanded constitutional government from the sultan. As most of the members of this party were army officers, the sultan, out of fear, immediately ordered parliamentary elections. Thereafter, the zest of building a new life completely swayed the Turks. There was a clamour for reform, unity and progress all around. New institutions and parties were being formed. Newspapers were being started. Saleh Zaki Bey was himself a professor in the university. The political and intellectual leaders of the nation were mostly his old friends. Khaleda Khanam observed *purdah* to the extent that she even avoided meeting people other than the close friends of Saleh Zaki Bey. However, these very close friends managed to convince Khaleda Khanam to take part in constructive efforts. In a newly started newspaper, a section was devoted to women's issues and its editorship was handed over to Khaleda Khanam. She quickly caught the imagination of the Turkish women. The popularity of her articles, her sincere style, and most of all, her dedication made her so reliable that many women started seeking her advice. This made Khaleda Khanam well-versed with the problems of Turkish families in a way that would not have been possible with years of observation and study.

The enthusiasm and fervour of the 'Young Turks' was genuine. But they still lacked the sense of occasion and administrative abilities to handle the conventions of a constitutional government in a smooth manner. The conservative and wily followers of the sultan opposed them tooth and nail, and within a few months, overturned the new government by exploiting the early blunders made by the young leaders. The same army that had egged on its officers to establish the constitutional government now became the sworn enemy of those officers. It appeared that the crackdown against the reformist agenda would be so harsh and gory that no one would dare to talk about reform and freedom for years. Khaleda Khanam never wrote anything that could be questioned by conservatives. But under the specter of violence, some anti-reformists went after her life and honour. She had to run away from her home and country (April, 1909). She first went to Alexandria. And After spending a few months in England, she came back to Turkey in October. In the meanwhile, Mahmood Selis Pasha had salvaged the reform movement and the constitutional government. Now there was no threat to those working for reforms. It was in the same year that Khaleda Khanam published her first novel and its instant popularity inspired her to turn to writing novels with an added enthusiasm. In the same period, a senior officer of the Department of Education, Said Bey sought her suggestions and advice. He took her to inspect a girl's school and requested her to prepare a detailed report on women's education. As a result, Khaleda Khanam got involved, albeit unwillingly, in teaching. Educational philosophy was her favourite subject but she also taught history and psychology to higher classes. The dedication and efforts of the Principal of her school, Naqia Khanam, took the school to new heights. From a normal school, it became a college within three years. And a new normal school was opened in the city. In the meanwhile, many of the school alumni reached a stage where they could teach in schools and hence many primary and secondary schools were established. However, in 1913, both Naqia

Khanam and Khaleda Khanam had such fundamental differences[1] with Turkey's Education Minister Shakri Bey that both of them had to resign from their jobs. And in place of government run schools, they started working with schools under the Waqf Ministry. Sheikh-ul-Islam of the period Khiari Afandi admired them a lot and his faith in them proved right in the wake of Naqia Khanam's hard work and administrative abilities in helping the schools of Waqf grow and progress. But the Department of Education started going after Khaleda Khanam and Naqia Khanam. Within a year, all Waqf Madrasas were brought under the Department of Education. And these two had to leave.

By this time, the Balkan war had ended and the World War had begun. European enemies of Turkey took full advantage of the revolution of 1908 and early slips and weaknesses of the 'Young Turks'. In 1908, Austria captured Bosnia Herzegovina. In 1908, Krit Island separated itself from the Turkish Empire. In 1910, Italy attacked Tarabulus and in 1912, knowing its pathetic situation, Bulgaria, Greece, Serbia declared war on Turkey. In this war, due to the poor management of the Defense Department, Turks faced inexpressible defeats and hardships. The saving grace was that the Bulgarian army was stopped at Chataldja. Adreanople was also taken, but taking advantage of the quarrel among enemies, Enver Bey recaptured it. After the war ended, the party of 'Young Turks', which had regained power, once again got engaged in the reform of every department of the government and ministry. If it could have survived for 10-15 years, Turkey could have been saved from a thousand calamities. And

---

[1] Khaleda Khanam and Naqia Khanam were of the opinion that instead of educating maximum number of people, a few people should be provided the best possible education so as to facilitate the future spread of education and the proliferation of specialized madarsas. Shakri Bey, on the contrary, wanted to expand the circle of educated people to the utmost limits.

it would have been quite a prominent player in Europe. But the World War sabotaged all the efforts of the 'Young Turks'. Turks were forced to join the War and the fervor and drive for reforms was postponed until the truce.

Khaleda Khanam had taken to writing and teaching as a national obligation. She extended the responsibilities of Turkish women and of her own when she saw the sufferings of soldiers in the Balkan War. She started an institution where women could gather and discuss their personal as well as collective problems. They were free to learn European languages or learn to manage the household. The members of this club also collected money to open a small hospital with 30 beds. Khaleda Khanam herself worked as a nurse in this hospital for months. But she didn't want this work to come in the way of her other important engagements. In January 1913, her health deteriorated. She was physically frail but had a strong willpower due to which she managed to recover from her illness and became fit for work within a few weeks' time.

The shocks and reversals faced by Turkey in the Balkan War and before made it obvious that to sustain their existence, Turks had to prioritize areas to fix in their shattered empire and decide the best way forward. The Christian populace of the Balkan had seceded from their empire. Armenians, Syrians and Arabs were also thinking along the same lines—how to get rid of Turks. Nationalism was in vogue everywhere whereas the Turkish Empire had always been an international institution. After 1912, however, the nationalist sentiments started sprouting among educated Turks. And while some were busy trying to provide stability to Turkish Empire, others nurtured hope of forming a union of exclusive Turkish race. They believed that they should not try to rule over Arab, Syria and Iraq in the hope that out of the sentiments of Islamic solidarity the people of these countries will help Turks against European nations. Khaleda Khanam showed a great deal of interest in these discussions and also in the institutions and groups that were formed to carry forward and spread these debates, discussions and ideologies. During the World War, Jamal Pasha sent her to Syria to inspect educational institutions and establish a few model schools there. She performed this task with utmost dedication and sincerity. Syrians, however, were not impressed with the attempts of reform of Jamal Pasha. Khaleda Khanam was also convinced that it was no longer possible for Turkey and Syria to remain united. Gradually, she began to appreciate the view that the Turkish Empire could not remain an international institution and that the Turkish people should have the same national feelings which led European nations to the pinnacles of progress. But to her, nationalism did not mean narrow-mindedness and selfishness. She wanted Turks to form their own distinct national identity, protect their state from disruptive elements, and instead of adhering to a general Islamic social, economic and judicial order, study their own ancient history and social order and explore a social order which matched their national character and could help them in their progress. She had also started considering European social system, especially their political institutions, worth emulating as it was becoming increasingly dangerous and difficult to follow the old faith.

In order to impress the French and British, Sultan Abdul Hamid had once casually mentioned a Pan Islamic force in some context. But this idea really frightened European thinkers. Among Turks, Enver Bey was perhaps the only thinker who could see the possibility of this idea in various political institutions and movements. Otherwise, Turks and Muslims of other countries could not even imagine an alliance of this nature. And their religiosity could hardly dominate their national and political interests to allow them to accept it or implement it. In Turkey, the idea of Central-Asian unity was much more effective and much more powerful than this quasi-religious, quasi-political idea. At once point of time it seemed that Turks, Tatars of Northern Russia and the Turkish tribes of Caucasus Mountains were interested in striking such an alliance. This idea too could not withstand practical problems, though it led the educated Turks to believe that away from the general Islamic world, they held a different national unity and philosophy of life. And that it had the power to highlight their national character and help them consolidate their political system. This was the seed of nationalism that flourished later and is the breath and spirit of Turkish state today. But initially there were very few takers of this. After the Balkan War until 1918, the party of 'Young Turks' led by Enver Bey controlled the government. In the World War, Turks kept fighting for Arab, Syria and Iraq. When they faced defeat all around and were left with nothing but Constantinople and Anatolia, they obviously could not consider their state an international institution and they were left practically with no political ideology but nationalism.

Khaleda Khanam had written a political novel just before the Balkan War, titled *Naya Turan,* which represented an imagined political life of Turks in an attractive manner. This novel became quite popular to the extent that cafés and shops were opened in Constantinople with this name and everyone talked about it. This had a lasting and positive impact on the young people who were fighting for the pride of their nation in Tarabulus and reached Macedonia to die for their nation. But for Khaleda Khanam, this novel was an interesting and successful attempt at practicing the art of political expression. She had given a literary garb to these ideas. She was yet to realize her complete personality though. When British forces captured Constantinople and found Turks helpless, they forgot human values so much that they sent the Greek Army to Smyrna to dishonour and kill innocent men, women and children. It was then that Khaleda Khanam's writings and speeches became extraordinarily sharp and impressive. Earlier, she was an excellent writer, now she had become an extraordinary personality. She became the voice of a voiceless nation and its grief-stricken people and her people considered her speeches as messages from God. In the beginning, she delivered speeches in front of men under the auspices of a particular group called "Turk Aujaf" which only had Turkish people as its members. Now she started addressing gatherings of thousands. One such rally which is a cherished memory of Turkish nationalism was held near Sultan Ahmed Mosque. Khaleda Edib was in raptures. People in the rally cried, shouted and suddenly at times became silent. Fighter plains were flying over their heads, ready to bomb if the crowed showed any signs of revolt.

Speeches alone don't help nations. And at a time when the British were trying to silence everyone around, Turkish leaders could not deliver speeches anyway. Khaleda Khanam escaped from Constantinople in the beginning of 1920. And despite British attempts to arrest her, she managed to reach Ankara. Here, Mustafa Kemal Pasha, Rafat Bey, Kazým Karabekir, Rauf Bey and Noori Bey were trying to organize Anatolia's Turks to fight the Greek and the British. Khaleda Khanam established a news agency to spread information across the country. Events such as the then Caliph's declaration of *Jihad* against Ankara's government at the behest of the British, the advancement of Greeks towards Ankara and their subsequent defeat near the river Sakaria in 1922 cannot be described in detail here. Even during such tough times, however, Khaleda Khanam continued to fearlessly discharge her duties as a nationalist woman. She also wrote a book, *Turkish Struggles,* on the events of this period to remember the sacrifices of countless unheard of men and women who saved the name of the Turkish race and took it from helplessness and disgrace to a prideful place. This book did the same favour to the voiceless Turks that Khaleda Khanam's speeches did in 1919.

Mustafa Kemal Pasha entered Smyrna like a victor in 1922. Soon after this, the enemies of Turkey signed the Treaty of Lausanne to accept their defeat. Now the Turks had found a fresh ground to build a new life. The way Turkish men and women had put their life at stake to win freedom, the bravery, sensitivity and intelligence with which their leaders withstood grave difficulties and helped commanders of the army to fight showed that the Turks of Anatolia deserved a democratic government. And now the weakness of the political system would not be a hindrance in the way of their progress. But Khaleda Khanam had come to know Mustafa Kemal Pasha well enough to sense his personal aspirations. She suspected that Kemal Pasha was ready to compromise his democratic beliefs in order to achieve his objectives. This is precisely what happened after the victory. On surface, the Turkish government remained a democracy, but in effect it turned into a speechless horse which is totally controlled by its master who drives it in all directions according to his wishes. Even after shedding their blood, the people of Turkey got the same dictatorial government which had destroyed their life and wealth with oppression. And even after getting rid of their enemies, they remained deprived of the freedom that forms the foundation of a new nation. The ground for reforms which were implemented by the orders of Mustafa Kemal had already been prepared. But since the national opinion was overlooked, they appeared almost imposed. And even if it led to economic betterment, it badly hurt the Turkish character. Their creative ability for the democratic system got lost in the habit of compliance and submission to the authority.

Khaleda Khanam and many Turks around her, whose contributions were no less than that of Mustafa Kemal, left the country after the freedom struggle ended. Mustafa Kemal had expressed it in no uncertain terms that he did not want to consider anyone as his equal. He did not believe in democratic values to the extent that he did not like even a petite criticism. To challenge him or to go to people against him would have meant civil war or at least having to face lawlessness and destruction. To avoid this problem, people, who till now were ready to put their life at stake to serve the nation, agreed to accept all kinds of personal losses. Sacrificing all their hopes, they left Turkey in the hands of Mustafa Kemal and quietly went into hiding.

1
Ottoman Turks as State-Builders

The subject of the eight lectures which the Jamia Millia Islamia has asked me to deliver is the Conflict of East and West. That we are going to study it throughout Turkish history is primarily due to the incidental birth and life-experience of the speaker. As far as our purpose is concerned, this is a fortunate accident. For, although this conflict could be studied in any part of the world, in the history of any and every nation, still nowhere is it so salient and clear in some of its phases as in Turkish history, past or present. Both the Imperial Turkey of old and the present Republican Turkey are placed where the East and Wast meet geographically, namely, the Near East, an area that has bred typically Eastern and Western nations and civilisations, and has been the contending ground of all philosophical, cultural, political ideas and ideologies and human forces. Therefore Turkey is an ideal cross-section of the human world, the very best laboratory in which a student of history can make his researches on the conflict of East and West.

What is East and what is West? "All nations are of one race," says the Qur'an. It is true, for the anatomy of man is the same all over the world. Physically, man is merely the highest species, the highest rung in the biological ladder of animals. Nor does the immaterial or the invisible part of him, that is, his mind or soul, differ in any fundamental way. Everywhere his mind works differently from that of an animal in a lesser or greater degree. It is evident that he is a part of the invisible creative energy which controls our Universe. He is a child of the Thinking Universe, of God, as well as a child of the animal. That there is a difference in his colour, features, language, civilisation and behaviour in different parts of the world, is only due to climatic influences, to specific struggles, to environment as well as to historical impacts.

Let us take first Egypt, Assyria, Babylonia and Ancient Persia as types of old civilisations, for they were either within or on the borders of the Near East. Further they have had a telling influence on the later civilisations in the same area. Externally the thing that catches the eye is their dazzling splendour. The facade and the frame are of un-surpassed magnificence. Those civilisations have produced three out of the seven wonders of the world. The second impression is that all this grandeur is meant for the pleasure and use of the monarch. So colossal are the rulers of the old East that they hide from view the millions they have ruled. The masses are there to produce the capital and labour to erect those magnificent monuments for the use of the few. They are mere puppets. The term individual or nation has no significance there. Stability and the happiness of the few are the two dominant principles of those civilisations.

But the moment one tries to get a glimpse of the individual in the East behind such a facade and under such unmitigated despotism, one is agreeably surprised. The individual of the East is the possessor of a marked and unique personality. More so than the individual of the West. How has he managed it? Simply by detaching his mind from material and worldly realities. The hand of the monarch may strike and kill him as suddenly and without apparent reason as the lightning in the fields. But he thinks of it when he has to face it. The State is in the nature of Fate to him. He can never alter it. Hence very few or no attempts to rise and demand a voice in the workings and will of the State and Ruler. This sort of mind naturally turns to its inner self, to its soul. The body of such a man is not his own, the good things of the earth are not for him. Hence the spiritual values are the only values. It is no mere coincidence that the East, in which ninety-nine per cent are the owners of this sort of a mind, has been the cradle of all living religions.

The next most important thing for the man of the East is his relation to his neighbours. Behaviour has a great significance for him. He is the polite man of the world. His goal is inner quietude in life, and all that ensures peace and avoids change if fanatically observed by him. All this naturally creates in him an exaggerated attachment to tradition, and anything which is departure from tradition is hateful to him, even that which may ease his drudgery in life. In some Chinese towns men still water the streets with little pails of water; all Eastern peasants prefer the traditional plough to tractors to till the ground. Owing to this attitude of mind, even the contrast between the dire misery of the greatest number and the unashamed glitter of the wealth and plenty of the few caused next to no popular upheavals of an economic kind.

Those who are in love with the Eastern mind affirm that the man of the East possesses the only values of life worthwhile. They say that the man of the East is only concerned with the true essence of life. There is no doubt that the spiritual values are more worthwhile and more satisfying. But is this judgement entirely and wholly right? It would be, if men were merely disembodied spirits. Man being a combination of matter and spirit, this sole emphasis on the spirit has produced disastrous results in the long run. The utter discarding of material values has made of man a subject for exploitation, first by his own rulers, later by the more materialist West. The East seems to have existed only for the sake of providing cheap labour, riches and markets to the world. Such being the case, we must admit that all is not right in the East. Reduced to its simplest expression, the supreme ill of which the East is suffering is due to a lack of proportion between the material and the spiritual nature of man.

Now for the West. No golden facade of monarchs and monuments hides the early West from view. It has produced none of the seven wonders of the world. Both the men and the civilisation of the West are late arrivals.

The religion of the West came to it from the East; its philosophy and science from ancient Greece; its ideas of Government and the externals of its civilisation from Rome. Rome was the first expression of Western civilisation. Men of the West built it and built it first on the European continent. Though the Romans did not possess a single original idea, they managed to synthetise existing ideas and make a brand new civilisation.

Their first great innovation was their conception of law. In the East the law was God-made or made by the ruler. In Rome it was man-made; further, made by the consent of the governed. In practice this did not mean much always. But it created a new conception of life. The individual never had awe and respect for law to the degree of considering it as immutable as Fate. He never detached his mind from Society and State, but struggled constantly to have more and more of a say in both.

A man with such a mind naturally cannot immure himself within his soul. His mind is intensely concentrated on the material part of his being and that which he sees around himself. What he can see and hold has a greater value for him than what the cannot see; his values, except for short periods, and in the case of exceptional individuals, are material. Contemplation is an empty word for him, strife and doing the essence of life.

Christianity as a religion was expected to moderate and spiritualise the excessive materialism which the West inherited from pagan Rome. But Western Christianity had little in common with the teachings of Christ. It did spiritualise and unify the West for time under one name, but on the whole Christianity itself was fundamentally altered in the West.

The basic principle of Christianity was peace. The Christian was to turn his right cheek to the aggressor who struck him on the left cheek. But the Christian world went out of its way to strike every peaceful face under the sun.

The Christian was to give his second coat away if he possessed two coats. Such a teaching might have brought about a better distribution of worldly goods. It has not been the case. Though the standard of living of the average man in the West has been much higher than that of his Eastern fellow-man in the same state of life, still the distribution was bad enough to create an early and very intense struggle between the man who had more and the man who had less, namely the struggle between the capitalist and the worker. Though the revolt against capital has real economic reasons, still Western psychology plays a great part in it. Given the same conditions, even worse conditions, in the East, there would be no such revolt.

This emphasis on matter has produced scientific miracles in the West. Nature has been unveiled and its powers utilised for the benefit of mankind. Just as the sages of the East faced martyrdom to bring comfort to the spirit of men, so the savants of the West faced martyrdom to make a better world for man, to free him from a great many ugly diseases and bodily suffering.

Yet this source of blessing for man in the West has a seamy side. The one-sided and purely material progress has given the West an unlimited power over the rest of the world. In a few centuries, directly or indirectly, the West has laid its hands on the world. Huge continents and the millions living on them are there only to fetch and carry for the little continent of Europe on which lives the man of the West.

Those who are in love with the Western mind affirm that the man of the West possesses the only values in life worthwhile. They say that the essence of life lies in the material nature of man. Is this judgement utterly right? It would be, if man were dehumanised, or rather de-souled; if like some super-animal he had nothing but bodily appetites and needs. Man being a combination of matter and spirit, the sole emphasis laid on matter has produced disastrous results in the long run. There are ominous signs which foretell the decline, nay, the downfall of the West. To those who live in the West, the anxiety for their tottering civilisation verges on panic, and they know not where to turn to keep their materialistic civilisation on foot. Like the East of old the West is also suffering from a mortal disease. Reduced to its simplest expression, the supreme ill of which the West is suffering is also due to a lack of proportion between the material and the spiritual nature of man.

Now we will try to survey the conflict as well as the co-operation of these two states of mind, namely, those of over-emphasised spiritualism and over-emphasised materialism throughout the three phases of Turkish history: (i) State-building (ii) Culture and (iii) Social life.

Let us first consider the historic background of the Near East, where the Turks built up their State out of all the material they found ready at hand.

Ancient Greece had its cradle there. That it had been one of the most telling intellectual and cultural influences in the world goes without saying. But it was a civilisation which concentrated on the physical world; even its gods dedicated their immortal lives to the enjoyment of worldly goods. We can easily call it a materialist civilisation. Although Socrates did become conscious of a 'little demon', which was meant to be a soul, it differed from the conception of soul found in the Eastern religions.

However, what concerns us at the moment is the Greek contribution to the world in the way of political ideas and ideals: Democracy and Plato's *Republic*.

Democracy was a typically Greek institution, and the very term comes to us from Ancient Greece. The Greeks were highly individualistic, and, in practice if not in theory, regarded the state as a means to serve the ends of the individual. But Plato's *Republic*, the first great political Utopia, also comes to us from Greece, and there are principles in this great work which do not agree with Greek or with modern democracy. For its most remarkable feature is the way it sets out to show how a governing class and caste must be trained within very definite and rigid rules. Greek democracies were based on the popular vote, they never attempted to create such institutions as are suggested in the *Republic*, for they never desired to be ruled by experts and specially trained castes. It was perhaps for this reason that they were short-lived.

Rome succeeded Greece. The Roman State was a better organised structure than the Greek. It was not exclusive, but capable of ruling over the largest area possible and over the largest number of peoples. Its basis, like that of the Greek State, was material and pagan. But the Romans were realists to the end, and they had a genius for using all the available forces for the benefit of the state. Contrary to the Greeks, they emphasised the state rather than the individual. Their very name is not that of a race but that of their central city. A Roman could be of any race. He had to be a Roman above everything.

The Byzantine Empire, the successor of Rome, had a particularly Greek complexion. Rome was falling to pieces through invasions. The Greeks of Europe, driven by the Avars and the Slavs, the Greeks of Asia, driven by the Arabs, concentrated in the Imperial City of Constantinople, and gave it an administration predominantly Greek.

But the Byzantine Empire, which extended from the Balkans in the West to the Anatolian Peninsula in the east, was unable to hold both against continual invasions from outside. It concentrated on Anatolia. From the sixth century onward Anatolia was Hellenised and Christianised and its language became Greek. The original inhabitants, the Hittites, the Phrygians and other races were swallowed up by the Greek colonisation, though this new civilisation did not penetrate deeply enough into the peasant world. But, as Byzantium drew from Anatolia all its money, nobility and army, and used them in the Balkans against barbarian invasions, the country was drained, and subjected to the utmost extortion. The centre of Anatolia broke away from Byzantium, the rest followed. Byzantium continued to rule nominally, but it lost all control over its Anatolian possessions.

During this Graeco-Roman decadence the Turks came into Anatolia. From the eighth century onward Turkish invasions increased; Seljuk Turks formed a state in the eleventh century in the centre and the west of Anatolia, making it completely Turkish and Moslem, though it would be wrong to imagine that this conversion and change was effected by force.[1] The Seljuk kingdom decayed in the thirteenth century and broke up into small principalities. But the area over which it had extended remained Moslem and Turkish.

The Ottoman Turks came into this decadent Moslem and Turkish Asia Minor in the thirteenth century. Their name is not that of a people or race. It is that of their first Sultan. Like a Roman, an Ottoman could be of any race. 'Ottoman' today means an attitude of mind in state-building.

The most striking thing about the Ottomans in Asia Minor is the smallness of their numbers, the vastness of their empire and the shortness of time in which they built it up. Before a century and a half was over the Ottoman Empire had become one of the strongest world powers.

Western historians, specially those who deal with our decadent period, in which political passions ran very high, dismiss the Ottoman Empire as that of simple nomads, and explain its endurance as due to the fighting qualities of the Ottoman Turks. Ibn-Khaldun, who is accepted by the West as a great philosopher of history and a sociologist of the old Moslem world, says that no nomadic state could last more than three generations, that is, 120 years. Historical evidence confirms his statement. States built on nomadic principles have rarely lasted more than two hundred years, and very rarely that long.

The Mongols, who were both great fighters and nomads, invaded Anatolia from the north-east and passed on to the west. They did not establish anything worthy of the name of state. The Seljuks came armed with experience in state-building from Persia. Their state also did not last more than two hundred years. The Byzantines had the example of Rome, they had the learing of old Greece, a very remarkable ability for organisation, but they never managed to establish anything like the old Roman peace and order. The Ottomans could not succeed if they possessed only the physical virtues of the fighting nomad and his special but simple outlook in state-building; their task demanded a very keen and comprehensive mind and the practical ability to create a lasting and workable political system. Therefore it would be useful to survey briefly their background and to discover the sources from which they must have derived the courage to undertake, and the mental and moral power to perform their stupendous task.

The Ottoman did come to the Near East as a nomad. He had all the simple virtues, that is courage, and the practical ability of those who have to struggle against natural forces and organise their existence in the face of the ever-changing challenge of nature. This explains why the simple nomadic Turks in general managed to build states over more civilised but more passive masses. The Ottoman Turks had no experience in state-building. But from their past they had the traditions, the lore and the folk literature which passed from mouth to mouth and on which they brought up their children. These traditions are valuable not only for explaining Ottoman but also contemporary Turkish history, so we might stop and consider them for a moment.

The Turks became known to history from the fifth century A.D. onward. The Chinese annals speak of them as Tou-Kiou and the Byzantine as Turki.

To their vitality and activity between the fifth and eleventh centuries there is perhaps no parallel in world history. To realise the extent of their field of action one has just to look over the map of Asia and read the names they have given to mountains, valleys and rivers. Both they and the early Mongols are looked upon as mere hordes or nomads by the West, but they had civilisations of their own before they set out for conquest and state-building in Asia. The centres of the earliest of these civilisations were mostly in Mogulistan and on Chinese borders, and we can learn something about them from inscriptions that have been discovered in which idioms and worlds are used that occur in the Turkish spoken by the Anatolian nomads today. The inscriptions are of various kinds, some particularly illustrative of the mentality and character of the early Turks.[2] One, perhaps the most remarkable, is the history of the Turks as told by their King, Kul-Tegin.

'There was the blue sky above and the blackness below when man was created and God appointed man's ancestors to rule.

The rulers and ministers in those great and happy days were brave on the battlefield and wise in counsel. But dark days followed those happy days. Sons were no longer like their fathers, rulers and ministers were cowardly, people took to evil ways. Because of these evils the Chinese took advantage and ended the independence of the kingdom. The Beys served the Chinese, accepting rewards and titles. But the God of the Turks sent Bilke Khan, that the Turkish race may not perish.'

The inscription goes on the tell how the new ruler gathered the scattered tribes and organised them. He gained many victories, and increased the number of his people. He enriched the poor and brought his people to name and fame. Throughout the writings one sees a people attached to independence and ready to fight all foreign domination. But that is not all. They also object to internal tyranny. A new king called Meto becomes tyrannical, so much so that a great many Turks emigrate to China. Finally there is a rising and they kill Meto Khan, and Bilke Khan the Second becomes the ruler. There is a beautiful reflection in connection with Turkish emigration to China. 'The gold, the silver, the wines and the silks of the Chinese are beautiful, but they soften the Turk, he becomes lazy and dissipated. In "Uttuken", the land of the Turks, there are not such things, but there is Freedom.'

The Ottoman Turks came to the Near East with this sort of simplicity and vigour. On the borders of it they were converted to Islam. I say "borders" because the grandsire of Ertugrul was still Shaman and the conversion of the Ottomans was of recent date. Most of their names were still Day, Moon, Rock, Lion, Iron, etc., just as they used to be in their pagan days. We find them in abundance in the early Broussa period. And Islam must have appealed to them for some such reasons as H.G. Wells summarises in his *Outline of History*. The last Sermon of the Prophet, he says, 'Sweeps away all plunder and blood feuds among the followers of Islam. (It) makes the believing negro the brother of the Caliph. (These words) established in the world a great tradition of dignified fair dealing, they breathe a spirit of generosity. They created a society more free from widespread cruelty and social oppression than any society had ever been before in the world.'

The Ottomans first established their state in the north-west of Anatolia, a region not yet wholly Moslem or Turkish. In the early Broussa period (Broussa was their first capital), everything was very much in keeping with their love of freedom and the sense of social justice they derived from Islam. Their Sultan lived as frugally and simply as the rest, walked in the market-places, even acted as a judge of peace, passing judgement over cases that were brought before him. Hammer records an instance in which he pronounced in favour of a poor Christian against a Moslem. There must have been many such cases. For the young and the brilliant element of Byzantium joined the Truks voluntarily and accepted their religion, and the Greeks from neighbouring towns flocked into the state and settled there. To be under its jurisdiction was a privilege.

At the back of the Ottoman Turks was a solid Moslem Turkish mass, though politically they were separate units. Before them was Christian Byzantium and the Balkans, leading into Europe. The logical thing for them would have been to conquer Anatolia first. That would have created a strong and unified national state in Asia Minor. But in the Ottoman mind there was no desire for a national state. It was filled with the urge to advance further west, to conquer Eastern Europe and Byzantium. This was a more difficult enterprise; for the subjugation of the Balkans was a challenge which had remained unanswered since the fall of Rome. All that was nomadic in the Ottomans led them to prefer the Herculean task to one that was human and easy to accomplish. That they first conquered the Balkans and then Byzantium also shows their marked preference for the harder task. And it is again worthy of notice that Macedonia was subdued by the Ottoman Turks under commanders some of whose, like Evranos Bey, were of Greek origin. The young Greek converts who became great commanders or administrators in the Turkish State had often previously served the Byzantine Empire, yet Byzantium had been unable to pacify Macedonia. Ability and capacity in men depend rather on environment, on training and above all on the existence of faith in some particular line than on the accident of birth.

The Ottoman mind, the moment the fighting part of the campaign was over, must have seized the characteristics and needs of Macedonia and only the Romans had grasped them. The Macedonians were both volcanic in nature and heterogeneous. Hence everyone's hand was against his neighbour. Such a people primarily needed very strong, even ruthless handling. But that was not enough. There was an already established common tie between them. That was their newly-acquired Christianity, their religion, and that had to be respected. Therefore a state which would combine strength and organisation, a state which could be both autocratic and liberal would alone answer the need. This may appear a paradox, but the Ottoman worked it out.

The Ottoman system, which embodies these seemingly contradictory principles, was established before the conquest of Adrianople and Constantinople. But it evolved during and after these conquest and probably because of a better understanding of the human element at a closer range.

Now we have to look for the ideas in state-building which, in addition to their earlier and simpler training, could from the basis of the Ottoman system.

The first and the closest contact of the Ottoman Turks was with the Greeks, through Byzantine channels. Their princes married Byzantine princesses; young Turkish noblemen as well as the princes went to Constantinople for schooling. Some of them, like Mohamed the Conqueror, became scholars in Greek and Latin. Therefore there is not the slightest doubt about their having read Plato's *Republic* in the original. Further, they must have kept their eyes open in Constantinople and studied the Byzantine ideas and system carefully. And though the Ottoman Turks took both good and evil things from Byzantine civilisation, still the weakness of the Byzantine system must have aroused contempt in them. They must also have noted that the Latin and Western Christian powers from whom the Byzantines implored help did not offer any effective principle in statesmanship. Gibbon tells us how the Latin and Western armies who came to help the Byzantines looted and massacred the Greeks. The Byzantines answered in kind.

Such keen and ambitious minds as those of the Ottoman Turks must soon have discovered that from the eighth century onward Eastern Europe and Byzantium lacked order; that the peoples over whom Byzantium ruled were very different from the passive Eastern masses over which other Turks had founded states; and that the only power which had created lasting order had been Rome. Hence Rome should be an example. Its ruthless strength and its realism appealed most to the early Ottomans.

The formula which would explain the ingredients that went to the making of the Ottomans as state-builders would be this:

Ottoman Turkish strength and nomadic virtues + Islamic principles of social justice and non-discrimination of race + Greek ideas of bodily training + Byzantine organisation + Roman realism and strength + Plato's *Republic*.

In this formula the inclusion of Plato's *Republic* may perhaps appear as a far-fetched idea to some. But I am not the only student of Ottoman history and system who is struck by its influence. Professor Lybyer, the author of *Soleyman the Magnificent*, a work which I believe to be the most classical and masterly study of the Ottoman system by a modern writer, comes to the same conclusion:

'Perhaps no more daring experiment has been tried on a large scale upon the face of the earth than that embodied in the Ottoman ruling institution.' Its nearest idea is found in the *Republic* of Plato.

Plato would have been delighted with the training of the Sultan's family. He would have approved of the life-long education, the equally careful training of body and mind, the separation into soldiers and rulers, the relative freedom from family ties, the system's rigid control of the individual, and, above all, of the government of the wise. Whether the founders of the Ottoman system were acquainted with Plato will probably never be known, but they seem to have come as near to his plan as it is possible to come in a remarkable scheme. In some practical ways they improved upon Plato—by avoiding the uncertainties of heredity, by ensuring a balance of power, and making their system capable of a vast imperial rule.

Let me show in a simple diagram the fundamentals of the Ottoman system.

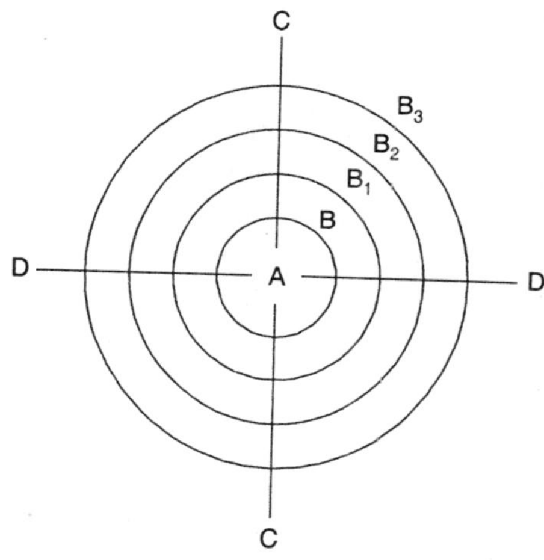

A = the Central State, composed of the legislature and the executive. They were incorporated in the civil and the military departments. In the early state the division between the civil and military was not very marked. The head of this body was the Sultan. He was the only individual in this body whose hereditary rights were recognised, but he had no divine rights. He was trained from his early youth and made to serve as a private soldier in his own army and work in the civil administration, in order to get experience before he became the Sultan.

The unifying force of this body was Islam. Each individual who entered it was first trained as a devout Moslem. But there was also a definite and absolute state-ideal—'Devlet-i-ebet-mudet'—the Everlasting State. A mystical turn was given to this ideal, which became as powerful and inspiring a conception as that of 'Eternal Rome'. And for five long centuries there was as rigid a discipline and as great, even greater, service rendered to the abstract idea of the 'Everlasting State' than to 'Eternal Rome'.

To ensure this almost religious devotion the individual had to be free of family ties, of old customs, and any tradition which could attach him to his particular human *milieu*. The individual, after being trained in all the moral and bodily requirements of the Caste, had to live within the body itself. For that reason the ordinary member of the Caste did not have a home, he was not allowed to marry. His life was almost monastic in the rigour of its discipline.

The recruitment for the governing Caste was made from among the prisoners of war and Christian children. The age was from twelve to twenty. The selection of Christians may have been due to missionary motives, but it is equally obvious that the intention was to detach the child entirely from his environment. Each region had to provide a certain number of children. The recruiting officer went to the village or the town inscribed on his list, studied the registers, asked for the children, and made his choice according to the appearance, manners, physique and intelligence of the candidates. This system is called 'Devshirme' in Turkish and 'Blood Tribute' by the Western historians. There was no force used. On the contrary, parents were over-anxious to give their children. The Moslems, who were barred from this privilege, often bribed their Christian neighbours to pass theirs as Christian boys. The boy who was selected could become a commander, a governor, a Grand Vezir.

These children came to the Palace School and underwent a very severe education. The bodily part of it was very much on the Greek or Spartan lines. The mental consisted of a training in the classics, music, Arabic, Persian and Turkish, and other subjects considered an essential part of learning at the time. Every youth, including the royal children, had to acquire proficiency in some handicraft as well. This system was as near to Plato's *Republic* as it is possible for any institution to be.

The circle B = the Islamic Nation: Moslem Turks, Kurds, Arabs, Albanians, etc. The nations were classified according to Churches. Men of the same faith and belonging to an organised Church were a national unit. This classification was adopted partly owing to the Islamic principle of non-discrimination of race and partly because, under the circumstances, no other classification was possible. Though the Moslems were of the same faith as the Ottoman Caste, they were as alien to the ruling Caste as the other Church nations.

B^1 = the Orthodox Nation. All Orthodox peoples, Greeks, Slavs, Ullahs, etc. belonged to it. Communally and culturally it was free. The Patriarch was the responsible head of the community. It was the most privileged Church nation after the conquest of Constantinople. The Macedonian Christian Majorities which enjoyed semi-independent governments had Greek governors (Fenariotes).

B^2 = the Gregorian Nation (Armenians mostly).

B^3 = the Jews etc.

They all enjoyed the same communal and cultural liberty. Outside the community and in their obligation to the state these national units came into contact with the lines C and D.

C = the Islamic Body, the Ulema with the Sheikh-ul-Islam as their head. This was another strong and very definitely trained Caste, an independent body whose primary duty was to supervise the religious and judicial affairs of the Moslems. But it also acted as a moral control over the rigid despotism of the state, because it could depose the Sultan, and no new law could be passed without its veto. Further, it was the only representative of the moral rights of the peoples, Moslems or Christian. In more than one instance it stood up against forcible conversion.

D = the Army and the civil administration, incorporated in A.

Such was the structure of the Ottoman State, with its rigid despotic facade and the inner nation circles where there was freedom of conscience and cultural and communal liberty.

Selim the Grim, the grandson of the Conqueror, first detected an inner weakness in the Ottoman State. It was like a mosaic of nations, and the Christian part of the design far outweighed the rest. So the Sultan turned his back to the west and directed his armies to the Moslem East. His cruel treatment of the Shiites during his Persian campaign, though partly due to his relentless nature, was also an attempt to unify Islam within itself. After his conquest of Tebriz he marched to Syria and Egypt and annexed the Arab Moslem world to the empire. The Moslem block was vastly increased.

This sudden change of direction in Ottoman expansion is regarded as a pan-Islamist move. But it seems to me far more probable that it was the innate desire for stability in the Ottoman mind which led Selim to attempt to create an equilibrium among the nations of whom the state was composed.

Historically the Caliphate question, for Turkey, also begins at this particular period. The last Caliph was residing in Egypt when Selim conquered it. The Caliph had lost his temporal power and was nothing but a shadow figure whose sole use, it seemed, was to bless the Moslem rulers of Egypt at their accession to the throne. General history speaks of Selim as having brought the Caliph to Istamboul, and having received the title and prerogatives of the Caliphate from him. This point needs discussion.

The first document of Selim's conquest is the *Fetihname* which he sent to foreign Powers—Venice and Persia (1517). In it there is no word about the Caliphate. If to become Caliph had been the aim of a man such as Sultan Selim, it seems to me that he would have made it known to the world with a flourish. The second historical document is *The Conquest of Egypt*, written by Hasan Tuloun. The author was a witness of Selim's conquest of Egypt, and his work is in MSS. in the British Museum, where Dr. Adnan discovered it when he was making historical researches in the MSS. part of the Library. Hasan Tuloun records the different parts of the campaign and Sultan Selim's stay in Egypt minutely, but devotes only a short passage to the Caliphate question. He says that

Sultan invited the Ulema of Egypt and asked them whether it was necessary for a Moslem ruler to be consecrated by the Caliph to legitimise his power. They answered, 'No'. Sultan Selim dropped the subject and did not visit the Caliph.

The bringing of the Caliph of Istamboul might also be a myth. The historian of the time does not mention it. If the last Caliph and been brought to Istamboul and died there, where had he lived and died? There is no single legend about that and no legend about his grave. As it is, the Turkish annals do not speak of the Caliph and Caliphate, and Selim and the Sultans after him did not take the title for a long time. The Caliphate became a living topic only in the time of Abdul Hamid II.

That Sultan Selim was a devout Moslem and believed in Islam as a force there is not doubt. The Sherif of Mecca, through his son, sent the keys of Mecca to Selim when he was at Aleppo. In the mosque, when the 'Khatib' referred to Selim for the first time as the 'Sahib-ul-Haremein-ish-Sherifein', Selim said that he was not the 'Sahib'—lord,— but the servant—'Khadim', —of the Holy Places. After this one of the important titles of the Sultans was 'Khadim-ul-Haremein-ish-Sherifein'. There is no doubt Selim attached great importance to this. When a 'Khatib' in Egypt mentioned this title, Selim lifted the prayer rug and made his *sejde* on the marble. If we remember the iron nerve of the Sultan, this show of emotion is very significant.

When Selim returned from his Eastern campaign, he proposed to have all the Christians converted by force or persuasion. He further proposed to have Arabic adopted as the language of the empire.

The Sheikh-ul-Islam, Jemali Effendi, objected. No great step such as this could be taken without a *Fetva*; and the freedom of conscience and faith accorded to the people by Mohammed the Conqueror could not be revoked. After a long and interesting discussion, around which a great deal of legend has accumulated, Selim doubted the authenticity of these liberties. Jemali Effendi produced three Janissaries, all over a hundred years old, before the Sultan. As soldiers who had served under the Conqueror they bore witness to the fact that these rights had been accorded. Selim had to give up his desire to unify the empire by forcible conversion.

The incident is significant in more than one way. First, a man like Sultan Selim, who had killed no end of Vezirs and Grand Vezirs, bows to the Sheikh-ul-Islam, that is, to the representative of the law, a proof that the institutions of the Ottoman State and its principles were at the time stronger than any Sultan. Besides, we see that Jemali Effendi, as the head of the Islamic Body, and the three Janissaries as devout Moslems, were Ottoman enough to stand by the principles of state, though as Moslems they must have very much wished to see a purely Moslem State.

With Selim the Grim the Islamising urge died out. His son, Soleyman the Magnificent, once more turned towards the Christian West, and his victorious armies advanced as far as Vienna.

The Ottoman State had been founded in 1287; its best days lasted to 1778 (Treaty of Kutchuk Kaynarja). The inner decline must have begun earlier, but it become very acute after that date. For another century and a half the Ottoman State maintained a stubborn defence against numerically superior and better equipped armies. It passed away in 1918.

No critical and constructive Ottoman history has yet been written, though there is a vast amount of official and human records on the subject. So far there has been either a compilation of data or a biased history in favour of or against the Ottomans. It could not be otherwise. For, during the lifetime of the Ottoman State, the political passion aroused was too intense to allow any historian in the West or in the East to study the subject as a whole objectively. Fortunately, fragments of Ottoman history have been written by able historians.

Now that the Ottoman Sate is buried in the past and can neither hurt nor benefit any one, its history can be studied with a fair and objective standard by any historian or a body of historians. Preferably this should be done by a body of men, for a single man's life and work would not suffice for such a colossal task. Meanwhile, one whose early youth was passed in the dying days of the Ottoman system may be permitted to speculate for a few minutes more on the subject.

To me the real significance of the Ottoman mind in state-building does not lie in its unusual combinations, its choice of contradictory principles and its method of working. Its supreme importance lies in the fact that it is recurring as a state-mind in our own time.

Human society has been a matter of growth in the world so far, West or East. The most despotic old Eastern governments let the soul of the individual alone, whatever they might have done to enslave his body. In the West governments tampered a little more with the soul of the individual, and the struggle of the individual to establish liberty of faith as well as liberty of thought is one of the mightiest epics of human history. Apart from that struggle, or because of it, governments in the West, especially in their national area, have been a matter of growth.

On the other hand, during political, social or economic distress and confusion in the West there have appeared from time to time plans, Utopias. One of them was by a feeble old man who worked among the musty and dusty old books of the British Museum. It is called *Das Kapital*. Yet until the post-war years no one in the West dreamed of applying a Utopia on peoples.

Now, however, we bear witness to the rise of dictatorships which try to apply a plan in its entirety on nations. Though they differ widely in their aim and principle, their procedure and their organisations are the same. The first parallel to this sort of mind and action appears in history with the Ottomans.

The dictatorship which resembles curiously the Ottoman conceptions in some of its phases, is Communist Russia. Like the Ottomans, Communist state-builders are of mixed origins. Race is utterly discarded. The individual who enters the Caste of Communist rulers may be of any race. What matters is that he must believe unconditionally in the Communist creed. With the Ottoman unit of the Caste it was unconditional belief in Islam and service to the Everlasting State.

The challenge to which the Ottoman system answered was the lack of order in the Near East. That of Communist Russia is the universal cry for bread and economic inequality.

In the system of selection and the training of the units of the ruling Caste Communist Russia resembles the Ottoman system still more closely. Beginning with the discarding of race (there are all sorts of people trained as Communists in Soviet Russia), the next important thing is to select the units of the Caste young, the second, to detach them entirely from early environment, custom and everything that binds them to their past. The Serai school and the Janissary Hearths as training camps and educational centres are the prototypes of the training centres of Communist youths. Both attempts signify this—to fabricate a new mind in the human unit according to state prescription. With the Ottomans this fabrication was restricted to the units within the Caste, in Soviet Russia there is the further ambition to make the new fabrication the archetype of humanity.

The result in both from the point of view of government is the same. The trained Communist Caste—civil and military—rules over Soviet Russia just as a specially trained Ottoman Caste ruled over the Ottoman Empire. Comrade Stalin has more power than Selim the Grim had. Like the Ottoman Sultan he has it in his power to kill or imprison any number of his countrymen. But he cannot, any more than Selim could, go against the fundamental principles of the state. Selim's inability to convert his Christian subjects to Islam is a glaring example of the limits to his power. The right of the individual to his religion was one of the fundamentals of the Ottoman State. Stalin, if he tried to restore property-holding, though the majority of Russia may want it, could not do it in the face of the Communist State.

The difference between the Ottoman and the Soviet systems lies mainly in their aim and scope and the greater efficiency of the Soviet, which has all the accumulated administrative experience of Europe and the equipment of modern science at its service.

But both are superimposed states with a specially trained ruling Caste. Professoor A. Toynbee in his *Study of History*, a remarkable philosophy of history, says that the Ottoman system was contrary to human nature. I agree with Professor Toynbee. It is somewhat distasteful to me that even in the limited area of the ruling Caste the Ottomans tried to fabricate a mind as one fabricates a robot. But what I feel, and what my generation feel, is not of great importance. In the West states are rising which want to fabricate not only the ruling Caste but nations wholesale. Nor is this movement without any backing from the world of learning and philosophy. Such minds as Bertrand Russell and H.G. Wells believe in planning society. One could safely say that for the moment it is only the artist who rebels against a planned type of humanity and stands for the freedom of the individual. And it is an artist, Aldous Huxley, who gives a picture of planned society in his *Brave New World*. It is no mere phantasy that in such a state all art, all great thought of the Past, is banned.

To conclude: The world of today is in a great confusion. The issue is betwen the superimposed state and a conception of growth in human institutions. The originators of a superimposed state in practice in a limited area were the Ottomans. Therefore their system is of interest for the maximalists of the superimposed state. It is also of interest to the upholders of the ideal of free and inner growth, for the

Ottomans managed to allow the masses enough elbow-room to grow communally. The point to note in the conflict of East and West as ideas in the building of the Ottoman State is that the East had the upper hand. It was Islam that made the Ottomans respect and recognise the inviolability of the rights of the spirit.

1. See Arnold, *The Preaching of Islam,* Chapters III and VI.
2. See specially Thomsen, *Les Inscriptions de l' Orkhon.* Helisingfors, 1900.

2

The Decline of the Ottomans

[Mahatma Gandhi presided over this lecture. Addressing him, the lecturer said:

A Turkish poet of old, whose philosophy of life is for all time because he stood for the permanent values, has a short poem which we often read at home. It pictures the march of a lonely caravan, a small troop of the few whose goal is not the riches of this world, who are not seekers after the spiritual joy of ecstasy as a personal end, who do not aspire to a seat of honour in heaven. They are the select guard of a value without which human society would be merely a well-ordered animal state.

"Do not think our calls in the dark are in vain," they cry. "We are the guards of the Fortress of Truth, in the Kingdom of Love". And yet they know not whether, when their watch ends, there will be another watch to replace them. They are afraid lest they hear nothing but the echo of their own voices when their hour strikes.

Once in centuries these lonely units hear the voice of a leader of souls. Then they rejoice. For it means that somewhere there is a centre where a great teacher is training and mobilising fresh forces to guard the sacred Fortress. The twentieth century is blessed in having in Mahatma Gandhi, the New Teacher, the needed servant of humanity. No lonely guard need fear lest there be no one to take up the watch. We thank our Creator for him. He is ours, and it is a part of his mission to say to any lonely private: Hold your torch high up in the darkness! When you are no more, it will pass into a younger and stronger hand.]

There are two happenings in human life the exact time of which we can never tell. One concerns the individual, and that is the moment he falls asleep. No one has ever been able to seize the moment of passage from being awake to sleep. The second concerns a nation. It is the moment of decline. No one can tell the exact date of it; everyone is conscious of it when it is in full swing.

No matter how agreeable the day's work is, a man must sleep off his fatigue, rest and recuperate in order to begin a new day. No matter how long a civilisation and a state last, or how great it is, its founders also need rest. Decline is the recuperation time, the rest-cure of nations. What the day is to the individual, a long historic period is to the nation. The decline of Rome, the Dark Ages, was a period of rest for the Western world. New nations under new names awoke and built up fresh civilisations in the West. In the homes of older Eastern civilisations, where peoples seemed fast asleep to the naked eye, in China, India and the Near East there are now signs of awakening. May it be a good morning to them all!

Another aspect of decline is in the change of rhythm, in the swing of the pendulum from one side to the other in the nation's life. For while regimes and states fall, and civilisations seem to lose their hold on a people, a series of new values arises, and an unconscious preparation for a new civilisation and a new life within the nation begins.

To the decline of the Ottoman Empire it is difficult to assign a date. Because of the great defeat and humiliation of the Ottoman armies in 1774, the casual historian sets the date at that year. But conditions which made the disaster possible were long in preparation in the 'Everlasting State'. Further, the decline was, besides being very complicated, not at all uniform. What was decline for one part meant awakening for another part. To be clear let us once more go over our diagram.

We begin with the Centre, A,—the governing Caste and its machinery.

The Ottoman dynasty produced a record number of geniuses. They were trained for the army and the civil service and carefully educated. Their active service as governors or soldiers gave them first-hand knowledge and experience of the people over whom they were destined to rule. If a Sultan happened to be a genius, his training made him a world figure, if he were an ordinary man, his training and experience made him work in harmony with the system without pulling it to pieces.

The recognised zenith of Ottoman Power was the time of Soleyman the Magnificent. He ruled over three continents, and in Europe only his empire extended to the walls of Vienna. Great Powers sought his alliance and his forces could beat the combined forces of the Western world on land and sea. But over Soleyman ruled his wife, Hurrem Sultan, known as Roxalane to the Western world because of her Russian origin. This little woman with red hair and a turned-up nose, who was not much to look at, judging from her pictures, possessed a temperament and a capacity for intrigue which could beat all the Medici ladies put together.

Hurrem Sultan had a son, a degenerate youth given to drink and to other vices. She wanted him to rule after Soleyman. But there was an heir to the throne, Prince Mustafa, the son of an earlier wife, who was a magnificent specimen of military and administrative talent. How Hurrem Sultan set out to open a breach between Soleyman and his heir, and how finally she managed to have Prince Mustafa murdered, belongs to the domain of dramatic art rather than history. But she did have her son appointed to the Ottoman throne.

It would not have mattered much if the thing had ended there, for the force and stability of the empire depended more on the ingenious way the system was organised, and great statesmen often covered the lapses of incapable Sultans. But Hurrem Sultan went further. She persuaded Soleyman to adopt the 'Cage' system for the princes, and with that she dealt a fatal blow to the dynasty. The experimental and bodily part of the prince's training was abandoned, though he was still taught the classics and given some education, and he was obliged to spend his life in the harem to the moment he could ascend the throne. The consequence was a series of hot-house princes, soft and ignorant of the conditions of their empire.

The seventeenth century is a long record of evil Sultans. When they were not soft they were intolerable tyrants, when they were the Harem brand they were vicious and incredibly corrupt. Their favourite ladies began to sell every important post in the empire. 'The fish rots from the head', we say. The civil service took its cue from the Sultan and bribery became quite a habit in the disposal of important offices. Merit, which hand been the sole measure of promotion, became a vain word. Thus the Ottoman Sultans, who had been more like the virile type of early Roman emperors, became like the Byzantine rulers. The Ottoman palace of these days was very much like the Byzantine palace. Very few Sultans died in their beds, for there were chronic military risings and dethronements, often accompanied by ass-assination.

The decline in the army, D, which was the backbone of the state system, was more fatal. The Reform Bill of Cochi Bey, presented to Sultan Murad in the seventeenth century, contains the principal changes which caused the decline.

The old recruiting system, which had been based on careful selection, was abandoned. Instead of the earlier method of levying from all the races, it was now only the Moslems who were asked to contribute. Further, in the enlistment and promotions, favouritism played a great part. The army contained not only those who had some function in it but a vast number of people who remained outside the crops, and were inscribed that they might receive the pay, or obtain the privileges of Janissaries. Among them there were even a French Consul and an Armenian Patriarch.

The Patriarch had been reported to the Grand Vezir by the leading Armenians as being a Roman Catholic at heart. They asked the Grand Vezir to send him to the galleys. The Patriarch learnt of this and managed to get himself inscribed as a Janissary in a corps, the officer of which was a personal friend of his. One Sunday, two Janissary detachments appeared at the door of the church where he was officiating, one to take him to the galleys, the other to protect him. When the officer of the first learnt that the Patriarch was a Janissary, he saluted and retired. This sounds very much like someone trying to sneak into the Communist Party or any other ruling party in the dictatorships of today for protection and privilege.

The monastic rigidity of the military order also disappeared, for the Janissaries were now getting married and interested in matters outside. The fanatical and mystical belief in the unique importance of the state was losing its hold on men's minds, though at times the ruling caste exhibited that iron discipline of which only the Ottomans and the Romans were capable. This was due only to the momentum of the early traditions. For now the nightmarish tyranny and corruption of the Sultans was fast undermining the old discipline. At times the unrest was so great that the army rose about once a month to protest against some royal abuse. Generally speaking, there was hardly a year in which it did not at least twice refuse its soup and overthrow the cauldron—the sign for rising. This might have checked the Sultans, but it did not. Rising became a habit with the army, and as the political moves of the palace and parties outside always had to be carried out with the help of the military, the army became the sole arbiter in politics.

The judicial and the religious Caste—C,—which was independent of A, but a very important part of the machinery, also began to decline. Its position as the protector of the religious liberties of the non-Moslems it retained, indeed, down to the time of Abdul Hamid II, and not only in the time of Selim the Grim, but in the seventeenth century as well, it had to protect the Christians. Again, as an independent moral power which could curb the excesses of the Sultans it no doubt brought some relief, for by their *Fetva*, the Ulema could depose the Sultan. But for this very reason they were forced to co-operate with the army and meddle with politics all the time. They were no longer a neutral judicial and religious body, and religion became a pawn in the political game.

The position and attitude of the Ulema as the sole dispensers of education to the Moslem nation, B, requires more detailed discussion.

As long as the world remained scholastic, the Moslem Religious Body did its duty admirably, and the Sulemanieh and Fatih Medressehs were the centres of learning, and of whatever science there was at the time. But when the West broke the chains of scholasticism and created a new learning and science, the effects of which were to change the face of the world, the Islamic Religious Body failed very badly in its educational function. The Ulema took it far granted that human knowledge had not grown beyond what it was in the thirteenth century, and this attitude of mind persisted in their educational system down to the middle of the last century.

The complacence of the Ulema in Turkey particularly and in the Moslem world generally had nothing to do with their loyalty to the teachings of Islam, for scholastic philosophy and theology—Christian or Moslem—is Hellenic. It is more or less Aristotelian, the teaching of a Greek, a pagan philosopher. And for this reason a brief comparative review of the Christian and the Islamic teaching seems necessary here.

The Qur'an does not set out to explain the creation of the material universe in detail. It emphasises much more the moral and social side of life. It is concerned with 'Husn' and 'Kubuh', that is, the beautiful and the ugly, which is nothing more than the good and the evil. Hence its law. Nor is the metaphysical and spiritual side of Islam at all complicated. It is based on the recognition of Unity—of a single creative Force, of one Allah. Hence the simplicity of Islam and the comparative freedom of the Moslem to accept new interpretations of the material world. But this admirable simplicity and openmindedness, which could accommodate new knowledge of matter, did not last long among the Moslems. In the ninth century, not only Islamic law, but also theology was definitely put into rigid frames by the great Moslem thinkers—the 'Mutakallemin' the philosophy of Aristotle was incorporated in the new Moslem theology, and the door of 'Ijtihad'[1] was closed.

Now Christian doctrine, which is the teaching of St. Paul and the Church Fathers rather than that of Christ, contains a detailed explanation of the material universe. This had been accepted as revelation, and its truth had to be accounted for. As Christian theologians could not prove everything by observation, they tried to do so by reasoning. They had recourse to Aristotle, for the reason that Aristotle is almost a magician in his logical capacity.

When the West began to study nature by observation, by analysis and experiment, the Christian Church was shocked. When the analytical methods led to great discoveries, the Church thought that meant the end of its authority. Hence in the West we behold an age of suffering and martyrdom for the scientist and the honest seeker after truth about the material universe.

After a bloody conflict of science and religion, the Christian Church took up a realistic attitude, and scientific knowledge was gradually incorporated in the instruction given in the colleges as well as the primary schools. The universities, which were like the Medresses of the Ulema, evolved into centres of science and new learning without losing their hold over theology and metaphysics. The consequence was that the Christian Church preserved its authority over some division, at least, of the intelligentsia; the Catholic and the Protestant priest could discuss problems of every kind with the new youth, and could be reckoned among the scientifically-educated elite.

The position of the Ottoman Ulema was quite different. They never persecuted new learning or new truth about matter. But in the first place there was nothing in the way of new thought to persecute. As long as they were the supreme educators of the Moslem nation, nothing new could be infiltrated; they saw to that, and their learning stagnated. Further, during the age of decline, they were so occupied with politics that it seemed far the easier thing to stick to Aristotle, to reasoning as the basis of knowledge, rather than venture on observation and analysis. Therefore the Medresses remained up to the end of the last century what they were in the thirteenth century. The 'Vakf' or Mosque schools, which were the sole organisation for primary education, remained similarly unchanged.

Though the state began to found high schools of a modern type in 1860, the Medresses had still a great attendance. For the Moslems, who alone shouldered the burden of defending the empire (from the beginning of the seventeenth century Christians gradually ceased to contribute to the Army) could escape from an indefinite and almost always lifelong military service only by being enrolled in a Medresse. So these medieval centres harboured a vast number of Moslems. On the other hand, the Moslem youth who after 1860 attended the state schools where science was being taught, conceived the idea that Islamic teaching was an obstacle to progress and truth, and their anti-clericalism became as irascible and as fanatical as a new religion.

In 1860 the first primary schools with a curriculum on Western lines were opened, but they were too few to cover the need. Therefore the masses remained stagnant. And change, instead of being a matter of growth and healthy development, became a thing forced from above. And it was brought about by a minority usually, who were not content to do away with the Religious Body as an educational organisation, but were also determined to undermine its moral authority.

Intellectual stagnation and the inefficiency of the educational system were not features peculiar to Turkish life, but were common to the whole Moslem world. Hence the reform movements in the middle of the nineteenth century, such as those of Senoussis, Wahhabis, Babis, etc. But the man who most clearly realised and categorically stated the decisive role a defective and antiquated system of education was playing in the decline of the Moslem communities was Sheikh Jemaleddine Afghani. He came to Turkey to propagate his teaching after a rather long and hard experience in Afghanistan. He at once attracted the attention of the most intellectual and enlightened people, who thronged to his lectures; there was quite a movement for better education, and the Sheikh was appointed a member of the Council of Education by the State. But all this was regarded with suspicion by the Turkish Ulema. The Sheikhul-Islam, Fahmi Effendi, declared the Sheikh's teaching unorthodox. In 1870, after a lecture in which he spoke on the social duty of prophets, the atmosphere became too hot for him and he left for Egypt. And the Ulema continued teaching in their particular schools after the same old fashion.

So much for the decline within the system itself. As to the position of the nations represented by the circles, conditions differed.

Educationally, the non-Moslem nations fared better than Moslems. I cannot say that the Christian nations during the age of our decline produced anything great, but on the whole they were aware of the changes in the outside world, and from a material point of view they profited by their knowledge. They were also in a position to profit, for the

Moslem peoples, especially the Turks, were almost always on the battlefield.

The difference between the economic position of the Moslem and Christian nations as well as the general economic decline of the Moslems is one of the important features of this period. The question has unfortunately not been sufficiently studied with an unbiased mind. European historians are inclined to dismiss the subject by saying that the Moslem Ottomans were merely a parasitic element, never the producers or workers. But whatever data I could gather from historical documents and annals tend to show that this generalisation is utterly baseless and contrary to the truth. As long as agriculture, commerce and industry and transport depended on manual labour, organisation and a realistic grasp of facts rather than on machinery and science, the Ottoman Empire preserved its economic prosperity, and there was a balance between its heterogeneous elements, a division of labour. The bulk of the Ottoman Turks were peasants and animal breeders, they supplied the empire with all the necessary wheat, vegetable, fruit and animals for meat, for transport and domestic use. The empire exported grains and stock on a large scale. Again, by tradition Ottoman Moslems, especially the Turks, trained every male child in some profession or craft, be he a prince or an ordinary child. Women also were trained to embroider and to weave, besides attending to the land in the rural districts. The household goods, furniture, clothing, cotton, silk and woollen textiles, leather for bookbinding or trunks, pottery, silverware, carpet and embroidery were mostly made by Moslems. Except silver, all the raw material for these industries existed in the empire. Trade and hand industry were under highly organised guilds which classified the producers and protected them, controlling at the same time all the commerce within the empire. All the means of transport, mules and camel caravans as well as sailing vessels, were also in the hands of Moslems and Turks.

The non-Moslems, though to some degree producers or workers, were in the main *intermediaries* of exports. Naturally, they reaped the greatest benefit from the introduction of machinery, while the Moslem Turks lost their hold over the sea transport, and their hand-made products, though infinitely more beautiful, were unable to compete with the machine-made goods that flooded their markets. In addition to this economic advantage, exemption from military service enabled the Christians to increase and prosper, while Moslem elements, especially the Turks, became impoverished, decreased in number and remained in ignorance. The empire in its decline, just like the Byzantine Empire in its decline, was drawing all its manpower mainly from Anatolia.

The deterioration of the empire economically was accelerated and its evils intensified by the system of Capitulations.

Capitulations were commerical and economic necessities in the Near East, and the system existed under the Byzantine Empire. The Mediterranean lands have always been inhabited by very different peoples, all of them engaged in trade and commerce. In such a world where customs varied, and the output also was of a varied nature, a certain adjustment and mutual sacrifice was necessary for the sake of all. The Ottoman Turks, the successors of the Graeco-Roman Empire, were strong enough to do away with all previous arrangements. Their ratification of all existing rights was, therefore, not only a sign of liberalism but of realsim as well, for the material prosperity of their empire depended on those adjustments. The Conqueror confirmed the Genoese rights in 1453, Soleyman the Magnificent signed a treaty of 'Friendship and Commerce' with France in 1535, and similar commerical treaties were made with other Powers later. Both sides profited from these treaties, for both sides needed markets.

But when the Ottoman Empire weakened, the Capitulations, which had been mere treaties of commercial adjustment, took on a different complexion. After each Turkish defeat the victorious Power imposed a new clause in the Capitulations in its own favour. These newly-acquired privileges were not only commercial; some of them were jurisdictional and legal. The subjects of foreign Powers resident in Turkey began to demand special and separate judicial treatment. Some of the Christian subjects of the empire acquired foreign protection Any of them assaulting an Ottoman subject was judged by the Consul of the Power sitting as a court. When an Ottoman subject happened to assault a foreigner, quite often the Powers sent their fleets to bully the Sublime Porte. Further, the Sublime Porte could not adopt any economic policy without the Capitulary Powers interfering. No tariffs could be raised or abolished without their consent, railways could not be built where they were a necessity, economically or from a strategic point of view. The worst of it was that the Powers never agreed among themselves.[2]

The Ottomans had really frightened the Powers in the early period of their history. They were aggressive and for centuries victorious in Europe. The Crusades had failed to stem their expansion. Then the European Powers had begun to solicit Ottoman alliance in their own wars. But when the empire showed signs of weakness, it became an appetising piece, and each Power dreamed of carving out the best slice for itself. The Ottoman Empire was called the 'Sick Man', whose possession and property had to be divided among the Western Powers. They began to bargain and bicker over their prospective shares among themselves. Their rivalries, alliances, a whole series of actions and policies which constitute one of the most exciting but ugly chapters of modern history, are collectively called the 'Eastern Question'.

To speed up the Ottoman decline the Powers played with the non-Moslem groups in the Balkans. They were more or less semi-independent and formed national units, and they became pawns in the international game for the dismemberment of the Ottoman Empire. The two trump cards of the Powers were religion and nationalism.

The Greek Orthodox Church, from the moment the Byzantine Empire was gone and the Ottoman Turks had begun to rule the Near East, never ceased to cherish the ideal of Byzantine restoration. The Patriarchate was its champion and propagandist. Every Greek child in his communal school was brought up to believe in it. Later, Russia became its protagonist. For the Russian Empire was Orthodox, it was young and had to expand, to find an outlet for its abundant superfluous energy. Peter the Great and Catherine the Great took up the cause of Byzantine restoration with the utmost eagerness and zeal, and Russia began to look upon herself as the rightful heir to the Byzantine Empire. But apart from this, the Russians had sound matérial reasons for wanting to capture Constantinople, as the Ottoman Empire barred them from the Black Sea and the Mediterranean. If half of Russian Imperialism was nothing but lust for territorial acquisition in the Near or the Far East, the other half expressed a legitimate desire for outlets. Russia, therefore, to hasten the downfall of Turkey, openly constituted herself the protector of the Orthodox people. Further, as a Slav nation, she put forth the idea of pan-Slavism, of nationalism on the racial principle. The peoples of the Balkans were Orthodox if they were not Slavic or Slav Orthodox. Therefore Russia could claim the allegiance of them all under a religious or national pretext.

Nationalism in the Balkans inaugurated the inter-massacre of Christians. To reduce the number of one another, so that in a given area the Greeks or the Slavs may be in a majority, they throttled each other lustily. Religion next inaugurated the massacre of the Moslems by all the other Balkan nations. For religion in their minds was the fight of the Cross against the Crescent. During the Greek rising for independence, the insurgents who entered Tripolitza, in Morea, massacred two thousand Moslems, including women and children, to celebrate the triumph of the Cross. The Ottoman Government, which thought of itself as an empire rather than a national government, in the early stage restrained the Moslems from retaliating.

In this struggle between Russian expansion and Ottoman decline, England and France have often helped the Ottoman Empire to stem too great a Slav expansion. To manipulate Western public opinion, there were propaganda centres in the West, subsidised by Russia, which made it their business to prove the case against the Moslem element and the Ottoman Government. Hamlin, the founder of Robert College at Istamboul, in his *Fifty Years of Turkey* says that whenever he read an item of news about Ottoman misdeeds, he prayed the Lord to make him disbelieve.

The Ottoman Government realised its peril and the necessity for reform towards the end of the eighteenth century. In 1774, the year of that humiliating defeat which ended in the Treaty of Kutchuk Kaynarja, they engaged Western experts for the army. But the real attempts at reform and Western penetration in a new sense began in the next century, the earlier half of which produced three great Sultans and marks the Renaissance of the Turkish part of the empire.

Selim III (1787–1807), who had not been 'caged' by his uncle Abdul Hamid the First, was a genius in more than one way. In addition to his education in the Turkish classics, he had studied carefully the French Revolution and the ideas and aspirations it embodied. The passion for political democracy which swept across Europe in those days had its fascination for him also. He did not aim only at reform; he aimed at re-creating the state on new principles.

Seeing that nothing could be done with the old army, he created the nucleus of a new army, which is called the 'Nizam-i-Jedid'. He opened several good schools, the Engineering School being one in which he personally taught. He at once drew the hostility of the old army upon himself. But his new army was pretty strong with all the officers ardently desirous of reform, and for a time his position was secure.

Selim also attempted to rebuild the civil administration on the principle of local responsibility, the people in the provinces elected their provincial councils and having a voice in the management of local affairs. This set all the governors in the provinces against him, for they had been practically absolute rulers so far. Therefore Selim had to reckon with both the old military and the civil service as obstacles to his reforms. When his new army marched to the Balkans to put down a rising the old army in Constantinople rose and killed him. They attempted also to kill the heir to the throne, Mahmoud II, whom he had personally educated, but thanks to the vigilance of a woman he was saved.

The new army marched at once on Constantinople under Alemdar Mustafa Pasha, and though too late to save their master, they managed to place Mahmoud (1807–1839) on the throne. The new Sultan, to gain time, had to abolish Selim's reforms. But a genius in his own way, he managed to recreate Selim's new army under another name and to persuade the liberal Ulema to proclaim his reform to be in accordance with the spirit of Islam. He got the backing of the people of Istamboul too. So he exterminated the old army. After that, as far as the inner reforms were concerned, it was plain sailing.

But European Powers, especially Russia, always found a pretext to declare war whenever there were signs of awakening and reform which might strengthen the empire. And so when Mahmoud's little army had hardly been in training for a year, Russia declared war. This seemed like a calamity at first. But Russia had to fight two hardly-won battles and send two numerically superior armies before she could dictate a peace, and the heroism and the fighting quality of Mahmoud's little army convinced the Moslem nation of the superiority of Western methods at once. Mahmoud's enactments for reform were now strongly backed by the people. Being a believer in centralisation, he put an end to the unlimited power of the governors. They could do nothing to an individual outside the law. He also increased the number of schools. The Medical School was equipped with professors of great renown from Vienna, and twenty-eight young Turks were sent to different parts of Europe to study. Mahmoud's enactments removed a great many official abuses, and ensured the impartiality of justice. 'For me', he said on one occasion, 'there is no difference between my subjects; I know that some go to the mosque and some to the church or synagogue, but when they are out of it they are all the same'. This Sultan was also the first sartorial reformer, for he introduced the fez and European dress in the army.

Mahumoud is called the Peter the Great of the Turks. Like all men of action, he attempted to do things which would bring immediate results. His most remarkable qualities were his incredible tenacity and broad views as well as his ruthlessness. He had to face a series of external calamities while he was going on with his reforms, yet he never wavered. The Russian wars; then the Greek rising (1826), which created modern Greece, involving, in addition to other problems, the difficult and thankless task of keeping the Moslems from retaliating after the massacres of the Moslems in the Morea; the revolt of Mehemed Ali, the governor of Janina; the revolt of Mehemed Ali, the governor of Egypt, who nearly captured the Ottoman throne; these are the most notable calamities of his reign.

With Mahmoud ended the first era of reform, and with Abdul Mejid (1839–1851) began the second and more important reform movement, the Tanzimat. In Mahmoud's time it was more or less the government which changed itself and inaugurated reforms. During the Tanzimat the reform went deeper, the people began to change, not only through schools but also through the great school of Literature, of which we will speak in another lecture.

Abdul Mejid was fortunate in having a galaxy of great statesmen to advise and assist him, of whom Mustafa Reshid was the most prominent. The new era was inaugurated by the royal decree of Gulhane-hatti-Humayun. In the presence of the diplomatic crops and a large gathering Mustafa Reshid read the royal proclamation from a high pulpit in the open. The ceremony was celebrated by guns and public rejoicings. A statue was also to be erected, but at the moment it was thought wiser not to excite reactionary opinion against the decree.

The decree gave concrete and legal form to a great many of the changes which had been brought about by Mahmoud through royal enactments. 'One can never make a revolution, one can only give legal recognition and a practical application to a revolution which has been accomplished in the actual conditions of society,' says Ferdinand Lassalle. The Tanzimat was merely legalising and creating sanctions for what had been accomplished by Selim and Mahmoud. But even a superficial study of the Tanzimat is enough to convince one that a gigantic task had been undertaken. What was accomplished in the face of great odds is extraordinary. And whatever criticisms may be levelled against the ideas and methods of the Tanzimatists, one far-reaching result has to be admitted. They laid the foundation of new Turkey, and made it possible for the Turkey element to rise and create a state over the debris of the empire in spite of world opposition.

The Tanzimatists were the second Ottoman team which consciously started to re-create the state. Let us briefly consider the ideas which inspired their reforms and the human area to which these reforms were applied.

Like the early Ottomans the Tanzimatists were mentally a mixture of East and West. But from the thirteenth to the nineteenth century much water had flowed through the Bosphorus. The East had taken a deeper root in the minds of Turks. A mystic and spiritual philosophy of Eastern origin had been evolved which had impressed itself on their literature and their personal life. Moral and spiritual values, essentially Eastern, had gained the upper hand in the life and thought of the masses. The thinkers and statesmen, even when Western in outlook, were not indifferent to the national culture. So that when they came under the influence of the French Encyclopaedists, they assimilated most readily ideas which were in keeping with their Eastern bent.

The French Revolution produced two sets of ideals in regard to State-Nationalism and Democracy. The Tanzimatists took up Democracy. Their hearts rang in passionate response to the declaration of the Rights of Man. And because with in their remembrance and their past history Islam only had made as grand a declaration, the ideal they offered to the empire had its roots in the Islamic and Turkish consciousness. The Christian part of the Ottomans, on the other hand, took to Nationalism. The Tanzimatists never realised or admitted that any such explosive and separatist sentiment could be genuine, regarding it as entirely a reaction against bad government. They were convinced that reform, good government and the preaching and practising of democratic principles would cure the non-Moslem subjects of the empire of the their nationalism. Throughout the Tanzimat period there were no terrorist measures; the new policy of 'Union of Elements' was to be carried out entirely by persuasion and appeal to interest and loyalties. Therefore all the efforts and reforms of the Tanzimatists were mostly for the benefit of the Prodigal Son of the Ottoman state, that is, for the Christian who was no longer content to remain in the Ottoman fold.

The best administrative reforms, and by the ablest men were carried out in Bulgaria, where, principally through education, an attempt was made to unite the 'elements'. In 1838, a council of education was instituted, which opened a series of primary and secondary schools. In these secondary state schools the youth of all races and religions received education. The Galata-Serai Lycee played a great part in the Tanzimat. Here young men were trained for the civil service, and all alike were obliged to learn the local language of the districts where they meant to seek a position. No doubt these measures had the desired effect to a certain degree. But whether, if left alone, the non-Moslem peoples would have with time become loyal citizens and given up their national ideals is very problematic, for nationalism is as strong an ideal as democracy. As a matter of fact, the primary education of the Christian youth had emphasised nationalism throughout centuries, and now foreign Powers, specially Russia, saw to it that the Tanzimat did not bring about a union. Wars and local risings, protests that the reforms were too slow, protests that the reforms were not necessary, all came from the Christian element. So, although the Christians profited from the material point of view through the Tanzimat reforms, its policy did not succeed on any scale among them.

There was one thing which the Tanzimatists in their attempt to make citizens of the Christians overlooked. You cannot make citizens out of people by giving them only privileges. They must have equal responsibility and duty. They must *give* as well as *take*. We rarely remain attached for long to things which yield a little profit without demanding any labour, but we can never forsake things or persons whom we have served and for whom we have made sacrifices. It is a lasting and ever new human characteristic. The Christians made sacrifices for their national ideals, the Tanzimat democrats offered them benefits : they were not to contribute to defence, they were to remain communally as separate as ever.

Though the Turkish element seemed to be losers materially from the Tanzimat reforms, I am certain that they got something better out of it on the whole. They developed and strengthened their native qualities, those qualities out of which nations are made. The Ottoman Turks were already state-builders and knew how to die for their state. Now they learnt to love their country more than their State or Sultan. The individual, out of the system as well as within the system, got a new interpretation of love of state—Patriotism. Again, independence has always been a fundamental necessity with the Turks. If they had the leisure and developed the commercial characteristics of the new West, such as the richer Levantine class had done, they might have been turned into tools and slaves of a strong and dominant capitalism. It would have been difficult, then, to make them die and suffer generation after generation for the sake of their independence, for the sake of a Turkey to be. 'The land of the West contained gold and silver, wine and silk, the land of the Turk hand none of these, but it had Freedom.'

In addition to this everlasting loyalty to the ideal of Independence, the Tanzimat introduced the idea of individual freedom, and created the desire to have a voice in the government. What this meant to the Turk, and how much he has suffered for it, will be discussed when we deal with literature. In the political domain, a movement for constitutional government developed within a nucleus of writers and statesmen known as the Young Turks.

In the later years of Abdul Aziz's rule, the old autocratic spirit of the Sultans began to raise its head. Men began to be exiled for their opinions without trial. But the benevolent despotism under which individuals led an almost ideally-free life had strengthened the Young Turkish Association; Abdul Aziz was dethroned, and Abdul Hamid II, who ascended the throne, gave the people their first constitution in 1876.

In conclusion, the conflict of East and West in this reform period (1774–1876) may be summed up in this way. The new West had entered the Ottoman world as a method in thought. Institutions were changing, but in accordance with the spirit of the old tradition. The Rights of Man were regarded as an interpretation of Moslem ideals, and the state did not observe any distinctions or discriminate in favour of any community in the benevolent institutions it tried to create. Once the Ottomans had taken peoples of other races and creeds into partnership only after converting them. Now not only outside, but also with the ruling system, the religion of a man was to be respected. The Constitution was to be revived of the right of 'Meshveret', which Islam had accorded to the man in the street.

Thus one by one new Western ideas and forms were interpreted, assimilated and incorporated in what Turkey had inherited from the old East, without the old or the new upsetting the balance in its favour. Indeed, like the state-building of the Ottoman, the Tanzimat movement might have resulted in a new blend of East and West—but for Abdul Hamid II.

As a prince he appeared intelligent and liberal; he gained the confidence of the Young Turks and their leader, the Midhat Pasha, one of the greatest historical figures of new Turkey. But Abdul Hamid himself did not reciprocate this confidence. He consented to give a Constitution only that he might ascend the throne.

An International Council consisting of the delegates of all the Powers had assembled in Istamboul, and was discussing the Bosnian, Serbian and Bulgarian questions. It proposed a Commission of Investigation and a Governor-General for all these regions. This was no doubt a blow to Ottoman sovereignty. Further, a war would be fatal to a constitutional form of government, a first Parliament in its infancy. Both seemed to Abdul Hamid excellent reasons for rejecting the proposal. He went to war and dissolved the Parliament.

The war lasted more than a year. Turkey was beaten not only in Europe but also in Asia Minor. The Russian army came to Adrianople and the preliminaries of peace were signed in January 1878. The Porte lost more than it would have done by coming to a peaceful understanding a year before. Rumania, Serbia and Bulgaria were to become principalities with borders which reached the Black Sea and the Mediterranean. In the east Russia was given Ardahan and Bayazid. This treaty was modified later at the Congress of Berlin (June 1878), which Russia also was obliged to attend. Serbian, Montenegran and Rumanian independence was recognised; Bulgaria was divided into two parts, one of which would be under Ottoman suzerainty but self-governing, and Bayazid was restored to the Turks.

The Ottoman Empire was forced to pay for its defeat, but it had managed at least to make a defensive alliance with England by ceding Cyprus. There was, however, one clause of the Berlin Treaty which had a far-reaching result. It mentioned Armenia for the first time and demanded reforms in the eastern provinces. This meant clearly that the racial and national struggles of Macedonia, with the Powers using each nation as a pawn in the game, were going to be repeated in Anatolia.

During the thirty-three years of his reign, except for the Graeco-Turkish war of 1887, the Sultan did his very best to avoid wars of any importance. He was the last Ottoman Emperor and also the last one who had a definite internal and external policy.

As a ruler of the extreme absolutist type, he must have felt keenly the transfer of power from the Palace to the Sublime Porte during the Tanzimat period. The arbitrary tendencies of Abdul Aziz's last years had failed to shift the centre of power to the Palace. The greatest obstacles to this were the type of men who belonged to Midhat Pasha's school. Though Midhat Pasha had been asked to leave the country when the Parliament was dissolved, his ideas still prevailed. The Sultan trapped Midhat Pasha by asking him to return and accept the governorship of Smyrna. Then he had him arrested and tried for the murder of Abdul Aziz. It was a sham trial of the grandest kind. Midhat Pasha was sentenced to death, but the Sultan modified the death penalty to a life sentence. This graciousness was really a clever ruse. When Midhat Pasha had been for a time out of the public view in his distant prison at Taif, Abdul Hamid had him murdered along with a few others. After that the Sultan managed, not without some difficulty, to shift the centre of power from the Sublime Porte to the Palace.

Even when Midhat was dead and his followers exiled or silenced, their ideas continued to dominate the minds of the people, and this worried Abdul Hamid. His next move was to establish a cenorship, and punish very severely any one who was found with Tanzimat literature in his possession, to read a page of which was high treason. The use of such words as 'liberty', 'constitution', 'patriotism' was penalised, and the very words were erased from the dictionaries.

The people who seemed to be attached to the ideas of the Tanzimat with an almost religious fervour were the Turks, especially the youth. For thirty years Abdul Hamid endeavoured to suppress Turkish thought through an unparalleled spy system. If Russia had its Siberia for her intellectuals, Turkey had the Tripolitan desert and Yemen. It would be hard to imagine how oppressive the reign was for the Turkish youth and how many died in exile. Those who say that the Turks do not know how to suffer for ideas should read the annals of these years.

As against the Turks, Abdul Hamid sought and found support among his non-Turkish Moslem subjects through their leaders. He heaped favours on Kurdish, Arab and Albanian chiefs, and attached them to his person. As the Tanzimat literature was in Turkish and had not much affected the non-Turkish Moslems as a people, they did not suffer from the Sultan's oppressive system as much as the Turks. And they were not advanced enough to realise that the royal favours were mere bribes to turn them away from thoughts of progress, from having ideas. Further, in this reign the burden of the military service, unlimited and extremely harsh, remained almost solely on Turkish shoulders. With his Islamic bias the Sultan was obliged to emphasise the importance of the Caliphate in his internal policy, for that would be the strongest bond of union among his non-Turkish subjects.

The other internal danger which the Sultan tried to circumvent came from the Armenians. The insertion of their name as a nation in the Berlin Treaty gave them vague but strong hopes. Russia was at their beck and call. Therefore the Armenian Political Committees began their activity. Contrary to the method of the Young Turks, they at once adopted a terrorist policy—risings and a free use of bombs. Abdul Hamid suppressed them very drastically both in the capital and in the east, where he used the Moslem Kurds to keep them down. But on the whole he was not more oppressive to the Armenians than he was to the Turks.

The lever of Abdul Hamid's external policy was the fact that after 1904 England, Russia and France had arrived at a perfect understanding over the partition of the Sick Man's goods. The Sultan was shrewd enough to the see that he could not trust any of these Powers. Only Germany could be relied upon to an extent, since it was clear that she was looking for economic, but not for territorial expansion in the Near East. The trump card in Abdul Hamid's external policy was therefore his pan-Islamism and his title of Caliph. Though a political pan-Islamism is obviously impossible because of the geographical position of the different Moslem nations, it was nonetheless a strong card, and Abdul Hamid played it well. The dismemberment of the Ottoman Empire would be difficult as long as the Moslem elements were kept together and objected to Western rule, and while Abdul Hamid lived it was almost certain that his Moslem subjects would be on the side of the Ottoman Empire.

But the security which the Sultan thus achieved for himself was fraught with greater danger to the empire than he himself, perhaps, imagined. England, France and Russia had Moslem subjects. An independent Moslem Power, such as the Ottoman State, with a ruler who emphasise the Caliphate, could become very obnoxious. Even if pan-Islamism and the Caliphate could not form the basis of any practical policy for the Moslem subjects of the said Powers, still it was to their interest to destroy even the most shadowy emblem of Moslem unity. Therefore the partition of Turkey became a psychological necessity for the Western Powers. As to why they did not do it earlier there are two possible answers. First, it took a long time to agree on the shares, secondly, the Turkish victory of 1897 over the Greeks showed that the military power of the Ottomans could not be ignored. The immediate Western answer to Hamidian pan-Islamism within the empire was to begin nationalist propaganda among the non-Turkish subjects of the Caliph.

Among the Arabs, with or without Western encouragement, national self-consciousenss was bound to come, for they are fifteen million, as large a unit as the Turks. The point at which the West aimed was to create nationalist sentiment at a stage when the Turks, Arabs and other Moslem peoples were not politically advanced enough to find a *modus vivendi* which would keep the foreigner out.

The Turks were not unaware of the peril to which they were exposed. Though in Paris there was a Young Turkish Committee, it could not influence opinion in the country except by sending in pamphlets occasionally. An organisation within the country seemed hardly possible because of the widely spread spy system and the drastic measures of the Sultan. When, after the Bulgarian insurrection, the Sublime Porte accepted a programme of reform for the three provinces, Uskub, Monastir and Salonika, with a Turkish Inspector-General and foreign experts, these provinces became relatively free, and political organisations of a revolutionary sort could be created there. A 'Union and Progress Committee' was formed, Masonic Lodges playing the part of a model, and very soon it won over the young and staff-officer element in the army.

In 1907 after a meeting between Tsar Nicholas and King Edward, which gave rise to the rumour of a new partition plan, the Young Turks proclaimed the constitution in Macedonia and forced the Sultan to accord it again on July 23, 1908. The first Parliament, freely elected, assembled in Istamboul. All the races were represented by the best of their leading men. But a counter-revolution, provoked by the inexperience of the Young Turks, the propaganda of the foreign Powers and of the Greek Patriarchate, which subsidised a part of the reactionary press, followed the initiation of parliamentary rule. It was a bloody and and ugly affair. A great many young men were murdered for the sole reason that they wore collars, the sign of an extreme anti-religious attitude of mind. Eventually Mahmoud Shevket Pasha marched on Istamboul with a Macedonian army, smashed the reactionary organisations and deposed Abdul Hamid. From now on the Young Turks really took the government into their hands.

Abdul Hamid lived confined to his home and died in 1918. His character and policy possessed hardly a single relieving feature, and if he was really mad, it must have been excess of selfish cunning that brought on the malady. For if the modern Turks and the unfortunate Ottoman dynasty were to set aside a day for national mourning, it ought to be the day of Abdul Hamid's accession to the throne.

The Tanzimat had prepared the way for a steady and unsubversive change from a despotic to a constitutional form of government. The mind of the Turk, in this period of transition, had a well-balanced pose, his tradition and culture were the basis for the infiltration of the new Western ideas and institutions. Further the Sultans, either as creators or as supporters of reform, were to remain as an integral part of the new political and social system. The monarchy might have developed into a constitutional one and the Sultan might have been a unifying and stabilising force of the political and social system. But Abdul Hamid destroyed the chances of such a peaceful evolution. The two generations which lived under his rule suffered perpetual oppression and tyranny, and a half-baked intelligentsia, extremely bitter, extremely radical and revolutionary came into existence. The balance between what is the root of a people's culture and the outside idea was now gone. Unconsciously for the majority, but very consciously for the active minority, the figure of the Sultan became as strong an obstacle to progress as the Religious Body. Abdul Hamid was unwittingly destroying the very roots of a people he wanted to preserve. To the new rulers the West may have become as great an enemy as to Abdul Hamid, but they were bound to adopt its ideas and methods wholesale. Only those methods seemed to be successful in the world in 1909. Therefore in the conflict of East and West in what was left of the Ottoman Empire, the West had a greater chance of victory.

---

1. *Lit* 'endeavour', 'seeking (the good)'. It meant in practice the right to offer opinions on questions not definitely settled by the Holy Qur'an and the Hadith.
2. *Foreigners in Turkey*, by M. Ph. Brown: *The Bagdad Railway*, by Earle, give illuminating details and data on this question.

3

Revolution and War

The first two months of the Constitutional regime belong to lyric art rather than to critical history. The collective emotion was so strong, rejoicing over the principles of liberty, equality and justice so intense, that no one in Turkey who has lived those moments can ever think of them without being profoundly stirred. It was the delirium of the French Revolution without its bloodshed. People kissed and embraced each other instead of tearing each other's throats. Never before or since in Ottoman history have all the 'Elements' believed in the same ideal and loved the same country.

The Union and Progress party, conscious of its inexperience, left the government to the politicians of the older school, imagining that they were sufficiently influenced and impressed by the new ideals to work for their realisation in the same spirit as the young men of the party. But they had reckoned without their own youthful impatience and the possibility of a counter-revolution such as they actually had to face in 1909. The honeymoon of the Union and Progress revolution lasted for two months. Then came the time to establish a united family out of almost incompatible elements, and with that the disintegration of the empire began once more.

The causes of internal friction were many. The Christians as a mass were touched by the new enthusiasm, and inclined to make common cause with the Turks, but their Church authorities and their political leaders were not. They had been something like a state within a state; now also they wanted the privileges of citizenship along with the rest, but without any responsibilities. The question of military service, from which they had been exempt for centuries, brought on the first hot discussion between the government and the Patriarchates. The very natural demand that Turkish should be taught in their primary schools led to a wild cry of protest that they were being Turkicised. Among the non-Turkish Moslems, the Arabs, Albanians, Kurds, etc., also, the leaders were against the new regime both by sentiment and by interest. It curtailed the power and abandoned the policy of the Sultan, from whom they received huge sums as subsidy, and under whom their people could shirk taxes and military service without anyone taking them to task. Even the Turkish element was not wholly for the new regime. Conservatives were justly suspicious of the radicalism of the Union and Progress party, fanatics opposed it because they had a horror of all change, evolutionary or revolutionary. Lastly, the vast number of men employed in the espionage system of Abdul Hamid were threatened with both unemployment and disgrace. The Sultan had kept very carefully classified files of all the reports which had been made to him, and not only the professional spies but ordinary men had, under the old regime, reported some neighbour for personal vengeance or for remuneration. Their dread of public exposure made the atmosphere intolerable. When the Young Turks decided to burn all the reports, these men breathed again. But once the reports were burnt, and the evidence of their past guilt destroyed, they sneaked into the new revolutionary organisation with their spirit of suspicion and spy mentality.

Some of these difficulties the Tanzimat Young Turks also had to face. But there was a difference between them and the twentieth century Young Turks. The Tanzimatists were the outcome of post-revolutionary Liberalism; idealism was the dominant characteristic of their time, and the romantic declaration of the Rights of Man was still a living influence. The Young Turks of 1908 were born in a more materialistic and realistic age, which pioneered the Great War. Romantic literature, indeed, romanticism of every kind had passed away. Its place was taken by commerical methods: the new ideal was to get rich. Economic competition and the ways and means to success were much more important now than any idealistic sentiment. But the men themselves had changed no less than the ideal. The earlier Young Turks, whether statesmen or writers, were all highly cultured, belonging without exception to the leisured and ruling classes. They were uncompromisingly idealistic. They were out to obtain lasting and not immediate results; the ways and means were to them as important as the ideal itself. Rather than employ radical methods they preferred to wait and rely on the slow effects of teaching and persuasion. The Union and Progress Young Turks were of petty bourgeoisie origin, officers or small officials. In the formative stage one does not come across anyone among them who was a sound intellectual, able to analyse and compare the old and new world. But they were nearer to the people, entirely home-made. Further, they were mostly Macedonians, possessing a temperament which combines realism and ruthlessness, and will stop at nothing in its endeavour to realise its aims. Therefore, though they also were strong idealists, they would adopt all ways and means to carry out their ideas.

When the Union and Progress party took the reins of government into its hands for good in 1909, it believed itself to be the successor of the Tanzimat. It believed that a union of the 'Elements', equal representation and a parliamentary system wall all that was needed to change the country overnight into a new one. So when they encountered stiff opposition of the kind I have mentioned above, they resorted to direct action. They swept aside all the old privileges.

The sympathy of the European press led them to hope that Europe would give them a chance to live peacefully while their hands were full with internal adjustments. Because the Tanzimatists were great admirers of the English system, though culturally more inclined to the French, because Abdul Hamid hated the English, the Young Turks relied on English support. But in no country was the press more hostile to them once they were in power. Apart from the testaments and agreements which had been made against them between the Chancellories of Europe, the English people themselves could never be really sympathetic. Aubrey Herbert rightly says that though English Liberals liked reform, they hated revolutionaries. And 'forces ranked against the Young Turks were too formidable to admit the possibility of a rejuvenated Turkey, even if the leaders of the movement had all risen to the sustained heights of the ideals which they proclaimed. Europe wanted a client, not a competitor. Officialdom was conservative and antagonistic, for the Young Turks were not conservative but experimentalists'. No truer observation has been made on the Union and Progress movement by a foreign observer.

The fear that the determined spirit of the Young Turks which stuck at nothing might after all create a strong enough Turkey and wreck the partition plans led some foreign Powers try to grab whatever they could before the internal organisation could be completed and the full resources marshalled for the defence of the country. Austria annexed Bosnia, which had been under her protection since 1876; Crete followed suit by suit by seceding to Greece; Italy occupied Tripoli. The first two matters were settled more or less peacefully. The Italian occupation did not rouse official Turkey to anything beyond a protest, but unofficial Turkey, the young officers and some doctors went to Tripoli and became the backbone of the local resistance. So when the greatest blow came, and the Balkan War was forced on Turkey, the hardiest element was away from the country.

The Balkan Wars were a dress rehearsal of the Great War. The preparation and the staging of both are due to the evil genius of Iswolski, the Russian Foreign Minister, perhaps the ablest diplomat of the late nineteenth and early twentieth century. The present world confusion is due very largely to his machinations, still one must admit that he was a patriot and gifted with an extraordinarily astute mind. Iswolski was opposed to the policy of expansion in the Far East, and after the Russian defeat of 1905, when he came into power, he set about manipulating the interests and ambitions of other European nations in order ultimately to secure the Straits and Constantinople for Russia. The most important consideration was somehow to obtain the consent of Great Britain and France. To placate England he came to an understanding with Japan in 1907, and settled all the Russo-Japanese differences, especially in regard to their sphere of influence in China. In the same year Russia signed a convention with England in regard to Afghanistan, Tibet and Persia. The former two they decided to leave alone, Persia they divided into two zones of influence, Further, Russia, to win Great Britain's favour, seemed ready to encircle Germany. But still the British were not at all inclined to approve of Russia occupying the Straits.

To get Austria on his side Iswolski met Count Aehrenthal in 1908, and suggested that Russia would accept Austria's annexation of Bosnia and Novi-Bazar if she would in turn accept Russia's domination over the Straits. The Austrian statesman agreed to this on condition that Bulgaria and Rumania also had rights. With Italy Iswolski bargained over Tripoli. Both Powers grabbed their promised slices before there was a general consent. But as England and France remained opposed to Russia's control of the Straits, Iswolski thought of an indirect plan. Russia would have Turkey smashed and driven out by the intermediary of the Balkan Powers. Then Russia would get France and England involved in a greater European conflict in which Austria and Germany would be ousted from the Balkans. These two, the Turks and the Germans, once out of the game, Russia could easily saddle in the Straits and in Constantinople.

In 1910 Iswolski resigned from the Cabinet and became Ambassador to France, from where he manoeuvred very ably the Balkan confederation. From 1909 on, pan-Slavist propaganda in the Balkans stiffened. Intellectuals in Russia suddenly developed archaeological and other interests in Macedonia, and there they propagated the idea of a greater Serbia at the expense of Austria-Hungary. In the same year Russia signed a secret treaty with Bulgaria, the fifth clause of which reads:

The realisation of the high ideals of the Slav peoples in the Balkans, which are so near to Russia's heart, is only possible after a fortunate struggle with Germany and Austria-Hungary.

In 1912 (March) Iswolski managed to persuade Bulgaria and Serbia to sign a secret treaty against Turkey. He communicated this to M. Poincare, asking him not to divulge it. Bulgaria obtained a loan of 180 million francs, which she spent entirely on armaments. Russia seemed to want nothing beyond the right to arbitrate after the Turko-Bulgarian struggle was over.

While all this was going on behind the scenes, the fears of the new regime in Turkey were being calmed by all means. In 1910 both the Bulgarian and Serbian monarchs visited Turkey and assured the Porte of their pacific intentions. The Italians invited 150 prominent Turks to Italy and assured them that Italy had no territorial ambitions and that if Turkey herself offered Tripoli she would refuse. Because of this assurance Turkey transferred her defensive forces from Tripoli to Yemen, where there was a rising. Only when the Italians occupied Tripoli did the Young Turks discover that it was the signal for a general attack.

About the same time the position of the Union and Progress party had become very precarious. The conservative element in the country had had enough of their radicalism; there was a split in the party itself. A section of the army, upholding the conservative cause, got the upper hand. The

Parliament was dissolved; after a new election Kiamil Pasha, an old statesman, came to power and formed a non-party Cabinet, also known as the Great Cabinet. The naughty boys of the Union and Progress were dismissed or imprisoned, the army which was being organised by Mahmoud Shevket and the younger and abler element fell into older and less capable hands. Kiamil Pasha himself was a statesman of the traditional pro-English type. Though it could be clearly seen that war-clouds were gathering in the Balkans, Kiamil Pasha sincerely believed that England would not allow a war. So in August 1912 he demobilised 67,000 veterans stationed on the frontiers. When war became a certainty Turkey asked the Powers to intervene, but this was too good an opportunity for the Balkan States to let slip. Seeing Turkey ready to make concessions, Montenegro declared war and the other Powers followed. The Turks had 100,000 men, all new recruits, Bulgaria had 100,000, Serbia 80,000 and Greece 50,000.

At the commencement of hostilities the Western Powers declared that the status quo would be maintained in the Balkans, no matter which party won the war. This was no doubt a provision against the possibility of Turkish victory, for when Turkey was beaten, the European press adopted a medieval crusading tone—the Crescent had been vanquished by the Cross, and there was no question now of a status quo.

The first treaty of peace was signed in London, May 1913. But the Turkish booty they had seized was too big for the Balkan Powers to agree at once upon the shares, and a second war began in which the others combined against Bulgaria. In the meantime Turkey snatched Adrianople from the enemy. In the second war Bulgaria was defeated, and a second treaty was signed at Bucharest, August 1913. Owing to the moderate atitude of England and France, and of Germany, who persuaded Austria to remain neutral, the Great War was for the time averted, and the conflict was localised.

Russia had not been able to get the Straits, but she had at least gained the knowledge that it was impossible to realise her end with the Balkan Powers as intermediaries, for Bulgaria had nearly got Constantinople for herself. Russia must await the greater conflict. In this one she had moved only a step or two further. Turkey was out of the Balkans, a greater Serbia had been created, and Bulgaria which had not been docile enough, was punished.

The Turkish defeat brought about a psychological change in the minds of the Western Powers. Russia was delighted at the Turkish defeat, but rather disconcerted by its completeness. Iswolski had written at the beginning of the Balkan War that 'a complete Turkish defeat would be disastrous to the Entente': the collapse of the Ottoman Empire must be brought about by the Powers themselves, and not by the Balkan States. The ambition and ability of the Bulgars also came as an unpleasant surprise. The weight of Russia and France's favour therefore went to Serbia. She was to be the successor of the Hapsburg Empire. Bulgaria in retaliation flirted with Vienna. France and England felt that Turkey was broken and beaten for good. Her only asset, that of being a military power of some importance, was no longer of any value. She ceased even to be regarded as a pawn in the international game.

On the minds of the Turks the effects of the defeat were naturally greater still. The direct cause of the disasters had been the senile vanity of Kiamil Pasha and his blind belief in the honesty and humanity of the West, which led him to demobilise a veteran army, and the general bungling and inefficiency of men of the old school. Their chances both as administrators and soldiers were now gone for ever. But the ignominy of defeat was not all that the Turks had to bear. The spectacle of Moslem refugees, men and women and children, fleeing from the fire and sword of the enemy; the slaying of prisoners of war, their mutilation and starvation; atrocities and massacres perpetrated on the civil population—

the first of their kind in twentieth century warfare—inflicted wounds far deeper than the defeat itself. For no voice was raised in the West against these horrors until the Balkan Powers did to each other what they had done to the Turks. Then Carnegie sent an International Commission to study the situation. In the early stages of the war Turkish women had met in the University Hall at Istamboul and appealed to European Queens to intervene from a humanitarian point of view in favour of the Moslem population in the Balkans. No answer was received. But when the same savagery was let loose on the Christian population, the anxiety and horror of the Western world was extreme. This brutal partiality was revolting to the Turks. And it was not the educated Turks only who were affected. Thousands of refugees from Macedonia passsed on into Anatolia with their tales of carnage, and this impaired the friendly relations of the Moslems and Christians in Anatolia.

Unfortunately the Balkan disaster did not, as one would have imagined, bring the Moslems of the empire closer together. To the Moslem brothers of the outside world we owe a great debt of gratitude. India helped us and showed her sympathy in every possible way. But within the empire the separatist tendencies of the Moslems became more organised and more determined.

Bearing all this in mind, there are two very grave criticisms which must be made here in regard to the inability of the Young Turks to handle the situation. When they came to power the thing that leaped to the eye was that the reduced empire could not last. It could be strong enough to resist the overwhelming forces arrayed against it only through a close understanding between the Turks and the Arabs. It is true that the Arabs were already seized with the nationalist fever, but there was an idea ascribed to Mahmoud Shevket Pasha, himself of Arab origin, which was worth a trial. It was the creation of a dual monarchy, Arabo-Turkish, with the seat of government at Alepppo. Whether it could have prevented

Moslem disintegration or not, one cannot be certain, but the experiment should have been made. Again, in the face of a pan-Slavic combination, with Russia working from behind, the Young Turks should have endeavoured to come to an understanding with the non-Slavic States in the Balkans, particularly with Greece. Both from the different declarations of Venizelos before the war, and from the Memoirs of Izzet Pasha, published since, it is evident that such a move was possible, though it would no doubt have involved some sacrifice. If the Turks had made some sufficiently tempting offer, the tragedy of the Balkans would have been at least mitigated. As it is, time has shown that in the Near East there shall have to be always a balance of power through a combination of Slavic and non-Slavic nations. Peace between the two can be kept only so long as both sides realise that the strength of the other is equal to theirs, and there would be risk in attacking it. This cardinal fact of their foreign policy the Young Turks completely overlooked.

The net result of the Balkan Wars in the sentiment and outlook of the Turkish element of the empire was the growth of nationalism. The empire was dead or dying. The last child of the Sick Man was to be the Turkish Nation-State. It proved to be an unusually sturdy child, in spite of the age and infirmity of its parent.

A historical criticism of the Union and Progress Young Turks is a difficult matter, for there is no unity in their policy, internal or external. We can, however, appreciate and estimate their work if we analyse the three different elements in their thought and ideology, the three principal political, social and cultural movements of their time with which they experimented, nationalism, pan-Islamism and pan-Turanism. We will only consider their political aspects at the moment, and deal with their other phases when discussing the literature of the time.

The nationalism of the Young Turks was a reaction against two particular results of the Balkan Wars: first, that there was no important Christian majority left in the country, and secondly, that the Arab Moslems were drifting away. In case of a final disintegration, the Turkish element would have to be prepared and organised in such a way that it could be formed into a separate nation. In its attitude towards other nations this nationalism was very pacific, wanting merely that the Turks should be let alone in the modest area which remained after the Balkan disaster. With the Arab separatists also this nationalism could have provided a convenient and reliable basis for an understanding. But the ruling section of the Young Turks had very little sympathy for it. Because it was the strongest and most widespread sentiment the Young Turkish government kept an eye on its promoters, and very few leading figures supported it.

Pan-Islamism, with Enver Pasha as the leading personality, was a movement with an organisation under the Young Turkish party. Personally, I could never make out its political platform. It was possessed with a vague desire to unite the Moslems under the Caliph, but how the numerous geographical and other barriers were to be surmounted was never clearly visualised. It could have succeeded only as a spiritual, educative and moral force, but unfortunately that phase of it remained negligible to the last. Germany toyed with it and the Allied Powers eyed it with suspicion, the nationalists were against its political aspect, but as a political force it was really always non-existent. When during the War 'Jihad' was declared, Moslem brothers still continued to fight against the Turks. And it could not have been otherwise.

Pan-Turanism was the pet political ideal of the Young Turks and Enver was again the leading figure. Its political aim was to seek unity with the Turks outside Turkey, who were and are mostly under Russian rule. It was thus an answer to pan-Slavism. Of its cultural side we will speak in connection with literature; politically it was a dangerous game. Further its actual realisation, considering the difficulties, was as remote a possibility as the practical success of pan-Islamism.

While the Young Turks discussed these political ideas and experimented with them, nationalism, with its modest and pacific outlook had the upper hand up to the Great War, and the Young Turks caried through a series of economic and educational reforms rather ably, establishing at the same time a fairly efficient administrative machinery.

The economic revival began with the abolition of Capitulations in September 1914, and the government took active steps to reorganise the economic life of Turkey. The superiority of foreigners in the economic field disappeared with the abrogation of privileges and the imposition of equal taxes. A new tariff which raised the duty on food-stuffs enriched the peasants to a hitherto unknown degree, and since it applied also to all imports which subjected Turkish products to foreign competition, it benefited all classes of Turkish manufacturers as well. The new language law (1916) made it compulsory for all foreign companies to do business in Turkish. Hitherto these companies had employed either foreigners or Christians, who were better equipped in foreign languages, but now there was an opening for the Turkish youth as well. At the same time opportunities for vocational training were increased. Professional colleges, mostly commercial, were established and schools for arts and crafts besides. A large number of boys was sent to the allied countries as apprentices, labourers, mechanics, etc. to provide the nation with skilled workmen. The first Turkish bank (National Credit), which was indispensable for big business, also owes its foundation to the Young Turks.

Another interesting phase of the new economic life of Turkey was the beginning of co-operatives and trade unions. It was a revival of the old Turkish guilds, and could have become a strong element in the new economy. Unfortunately, it was organised by strong party men, so the whole thing was smashed by the Sultan's government in 1918, when the

Young Turks were obliged to surrender authority. A similar disadvantage was that the general atmosphere and the exigencies of the situation led the government to formulate an economic policy which was definitely inclined to state control. State control and state monopolies usually degenerate into party control and graft, especially in wartime, and it happened so in Turkey.

An intense and honest discussion and close study of the population question deserves to be mentioned as one of the achievements of the Young Turks. The decrease of population through war, disease and infant mortality put an end to all illusions about the endlessness of our resources and our indifference to public health. Never had the Turks realised their weak points to the degree they did now. Anti-tuberculosis, anti-malaria, infant welfare and other relief and social activities began to be organised by the government. Our statesmen were likewise forced to face the problem of a diminishing population, a problem that confronts us even now. Long peace and a good immigration law are essential for us. Only we have to be very careful not to involve the country in political complications when choosing the elements that come to Turkey as immigrants.

The star performance of the Young Turks, however, and the one that endured, was their service to education. They built up the structure of our present system of public instruction. The University also owes its re-establishment to them. For though it was opened by the Tanzimat Young Turks, Abdul Hamid had closed it down. During the last years of his reign instruction was permitted in the theological and science sections, but the institution worthy of being called a University began with the Young Turks of the Union and Progress. Nineteen professors, some of whom were prominent men, were engaged. They had Turkish assistants, educated in German universities, and the Turkish University became a reality during the ten years of the Young Turkish regime. The best feature of its activities was the profusion of its publications, mostly translations of scientific, historical and literary works. The Academy of History also published valuable literature on different aspects of Ottoman history.

The Number of secondary and primary schools specially normal schools, was considerably augmented. A noteworthy attempt at educational reform was made by the Sheikh-ul-Islam, Hairi Effendi. He reorganised and modernised the mosque primary schools in the capital, and opened a modern Medresse, in which scientific and historical instruction was entrusted to very able teachers. The schools were taken over by the Public Instruction Department and the Medresse was closed down after his resignation.

In 1908, when the Young Turks took over the government, literacy was one per cent in a population of 23 millions. In 1918, when they left, the proportion of literacy had risen to over 20 per cent in a population of 14 millions.

In the Army and Finance Departments fundamental changes were introduced. The former, under the stimulus of German instructors and thanks to the great organising ability of Enver Pasha, became thoroughly modernised. The Interior also attempted a number of reforms, but it could never become an efficient machinery because of the perpetual political interference hampering had devitalising it.

After 1913 the Young Turks showed real maturity in their grasp of the political situation. They saw clearly that the economic rivalries of Powers in the Near Eastern market must be neutralised. They divided the concessions between the Powers as best as they could. Between 1910 and 1914 Russia, France and England came to different agreements over Turkish railways, especially the Baghdad Railway. It looked as if the commercial rivalries could be definitely adjusted. In 1914 the Turks even endeavoured to soften the traditional Turko-Russian hostility. A delegation visited the Tsar in Livadia, and a Turko-Russian Association was formed in Istamboul. The opening of the Straits was frankly discussed in the Turkish press. Similar attempts were made to come to a thorough understanding with England and France. Turkish statesmen tried with equal frankness to settle their differences with Greece, and an exchange of population was negotiated in order to solve the problem in Macedonia.

So by 1914 the Young Turks had managed to discover the danger spots, and with another generation of peace the Eastern question might have ceased for ever to be a source of international discord, if the Great War had not supervened. It was a turning point in human history, and the clash of ideas and forces which it involved deserves any labour that might be devoted to its study. For the moment we are, however, concerned primarily with Turkey's position as a cause, as a bone of contention, and as the most important cross-section of the human area during the conflict.

The real causes of the War may be regarded as belonging to remote history: one could go back as far as the reign of Charlemagne. Professor Fay, in his *Origins of the War*, a most comprehensive study, ascribes it to the 'international anarchy produced by alliances, increase of armaments and secret diplomacy'. The data is not complete, and historians are not objective enough at the moment, to give a strictly impartial account of the events which led to it, but we may briefly review the immediate causes.

Russia and Germany stand out in direct relation to the events that led to the Great War, for the imperialistic aspirations of both—pan-Slavism and pan-Germanism—were at loggerheads over the Balkans and the Near East, namely Turkey. England and France got involved, the former for fear of successful economic rivalry, the latter for the sentimental object of regaining Alsace-Lorraine. The situation of Germany was perhaps the most critical. In 1871 she could hardly feed the 36 million she had. In 1914 she had 67 million to feed. To provide for this population she was obliged to import 10 billion marks worth of grain and other accesssories and was consequently obliged to export something equivalent to her imports. Commercial expansion was a question of life and death for her. She could not find an outlet through colonial expansion, for the limited area of the East was already in the possession of other European Powers. Markets were also monopolised by others. Deprived of every opportunity for territorial expansion, Germany tried to capture the Asia Minor market. The construction of the Baghdad Railway by her had for its ultimate object the creation of a highly-developed Turkey with a greatly increased power of buying German goods. This disconcerted England because she was an economic rival; it disconcerted Russia because the opening of the Baghdad Railway brought into view a Turkey organised enough to resist Russian invasion and shatter all Russian hopes of conquering Constantinople. Between 1910 and 1914 the Young Turks had tried to neutralise the economic rivalries of European nations, and I believe they succeeded. But the forces which impelled Russia to get hold of the Straits and Constantinople they could not neutralise. And Russia meant to nip all schemes of Turkish development in the bud; to hasten, if necessary, the great European conflict which would crush Germany and give her the Straits.

It is perhaps suspected with justice that the tragedy of Sarajevo was the work of Russian agents. Bogatchovitz, a Serbian, in his *Causes of the War*, makes it pretty clear that those who worked for the greater Serbian ideal propagated by Iswolski before the Balkan War, actually were the agents of the assassination. Austria was caught by the bait. England and France, involved in the issue by previous alliances, had to join. The Great War was launched.

The Turks, as the centre of the dispute, had to think clearly and act cautiously, with a full realisation of the consequences. They had adopted a pro-German policy, because Germany had seemed the lesser evil. There is not doubt that they were aware of the strength and resources of the Allies. Moreover, the moderates of the party and public opinion were favourably inclined to the Allies. Therefore the Young

Turkish statesmen first tried hard to be accepted as allies by the Entente. But although the Entente was making every possible effort to win over the other Balkan States to its side, it turned a cold shoulder to all Turkish overtures. Turkey was deemed an inferior fighting force owing to her recent defeat, and besides, Russia, the most determined of the Allies, had gone to war principally with the object of dismembering Turkey.

A small minority of Young Turks, mostly soldiers, wanted an alliance with Germany. From the very beginning they had thought it an impossibility to be on the side of a party where imperialist Russia was a leading member. Germany, too, had favoured the Balkan States more than Turkey in the days when war had not become inevitable, but now she offered Turkey a treaty of defensive alliance, which was accepted and signed on 31st July, 1914. There are three clauses in this treaty which show the psychology of the contracting parties clearly.

(*a*) The contracting Powers agree to observe strict neutrality in the present conflict between Austria nd Serbia.

There is no doubt that both the parties longed to have the conflict localised. But if Russia went to war both Germany and Turkey would be threatened. So the next clause says:

(*b*) If Russia intervenes and takes active military measures, and the necessity arises for Germany to carry out her pledges of alliance, Turkey will be under an obligation in such a case to carry out her pledges made to Germany.

But the bait Turkey swallowed readily was in the fourth clause:

(*c*) In case Turkish territories are threatened by Russia, Germany agrees to defend them, if need be, by force of arms.

Only three men, Enver, Tal'at and Said Pasha knew of the treaty. When it was disclosed to the Cabinet, the moderate element opposed it and a few members even resigned.

A week after this secret treaty Enver Pasha went to the Russian Embassy and proposed to attack Austria and checkmate those Balkan States which were anti-Russian, asking in return for a rearrangement of the map of the Balkans in favour of Turkey. Russia did not reject the proposal at once, but she did not seem willing to accept it. Enver Pasha's strange move may be regarded as evidence of Turkey having started to play the ugly game of secret diplomacy which had been prevalent in Europe and had brought about such disastrous results. Or it may be that Enver was playing for time, or was making a last attempt to come to an understanding with Russia. However, there is little doubt that the military party wanted to join the war, no matter on which side, but preferably on the side of the Allies. They had a sentimental as well as a real reason for this attitude. They longed to wipe out the shame of the Balkan defeat: and they felt certain that Turkey could not keep out of the war and survive in case of a great Entente victory, which would mean Russia's taking the Straits and Constantinople.

Those who at the time believed that Turkey could and should have kept out of the war have mostly revised their opinion in the light of later developments. But at the time the peace party struggled and hoped to save Turkey from being drawn into the fray. A surprise was, however, sprung on them when two war-ships, which had been bought by the government but were under German command, entered the Black Sea and fired on Russian vessels. Russia declared war on Turkey (4th November), and England and France followed (5th November).

The part Turkey played in the war was against everybody's expectations. Germany, when she signed the secret treaty, counted not so much on Turkey's fighting strength as on pan-Islamism and pan-Turanism, for with the Caliph on her side, Germany hoped that the Allies would be weakened and hampered in every way by the alienation of their Moslem subjects. Events showed that pan-Islamism was not, at least at that moment, a living force. Pan-Turanism, which was to bring about the disintegration of Russia, proved equally ineffective. If Germany and her allies had been victorious, it might have been of some use in the long run. As it was, it did not help the Germans or the Turks. But this disappointment was fully compensated by the extraordinary stand the Turkish army made in the field.

The Allied press was jubilant when Turkey entered the war on the German side, believing that she would collapse in three months, and could then be divided up among themselves. Hence the main pressure of the Allied attack was on the Dardanelles, Turkey's vital point. And Turkey's stubborn resistance thus became one of the most telling events of the war, important enough to make the Dardanelles campaign one of the decisive battles, perhaps, of world history. Turkey's ability to remain in the field until Germany herself had broken down was another critical factor. Whatever doubt the Balkan defeat had created about the fighting quality of the Turk vanished. But a far weightier consequence was that the length of the Turkish resistance hastened the Russian revolution. It must have come sooner or later, but if Russia had been able to capture the Straits and Constantinople, it would have been considerably delayed.

By 1918, however, Turkey was definitely beaten, and an armistice was signed at Mudros in October. Her fate now depended on which of the four partition plans was carried out and how.

The first of these plans is called the Constantinople Agreement, and was signed by England, France and Russia in March 1915. It accorded the Straits to Russia, Constantinople was to be made a free port for Allied merchantmen, and the Holy Places were to be taken from Turkey and put under a Moslem Arab State, a matter over which Arab nationalists and the Sherif of Mecca had come to an understanding with the Allies even before Turkey joined the war. The second partition plan is called the London Pact, signed in April 1915. Its object was to bring Italy into the war by offering her Adalia. The third was the Sykes-Picto

Agreement, signed in May 1916, by Russia, England, France and Italy. It related chiefly to the Arab regions, far out of the territory promised to Russia. It was kept secret from the Arabs, so that when the Bolsheviks published it, King Hussein refused to sign the Sevres Treaty. Toynbee, speaking of it, says:

'This private and secret treaty indicates, as do the others, the way in which, anticipating the successful outcome of the war, the Allied representatives carved up an empire and planned new states, as if the countries and the peoples of the world were jigsaw puzzles, to be toyed with, shaken up and refitted as a statesman's pastime.'

The fourth plan is known as the treaty of St. Jean du Maurienne, and was signed in April 1917. In this Italy was promised Western Asia Minor and Smyrna. As Russia had collapsed in the meantime and did not sign, England and France did ot hold the treaty valid, but Italy did.

The Young Turks, after losing the war, had not only to resign power but to leave the country; they, as well as the Union and Progress party, now passed out of Turkish politics. In concluding our account of their activity, we may briefly discuss this last stage in the conflict of East and West in Turkey.

We have already stated that the Tanzimat Young Turks studied the higher ideals of the eighteenth and early nineteenth century West as expressed in political institutions. They had considered those ideals as externalised expressions of the best ideals of the East. They, therefore, met the West on an equal footing, and developed no inferiority complex. They overlooked the mechanical, industrial and commerical aspects of Western civilisation, and the West cannot be said to have achieved a definite victory over their minds. It acquired pre-eminently the position of a collaborator and wise neighbour. The Union and Progress Young Turks saw nothing but the materialistic, the industrialised, the commerical West. In that respect the East had nothing equal to offer. Therefore an inferiority complex was inevitable; also an intense desire to reach the standard of Western civilisation as evidenced in its material progress. To reach that standard they had to accelerate the establishment of the external machinery which made the West so powerful, and this, in a milieu where traditionalists still believed in the moral superority of the East, meant that they had to be overwhelmingly strong. So they swung back from constitutionalism to arbitrary methods. How they came about it must be properly considered, for the Young Turks of 1908 are the forerunners of all party dictatorships of the post-war world.

The Turkish Constitution of 1876 was very little modified when it was restored in 1908. It limited the Sultan's power to formalities and ceremonies. As Caliph he was head of the Islamic institutions, but that did not interfere with religion at all. The government was formed by the leader of the majority, and was responsible to the Chamber of Deputies. There was a consultative Senate of forty, appointed for life by the Sultan. This was the outer form of the administrative structure. Side by side with this the Union and Progress party had a General Assembly, elected by the annual Congress, and its clubs in different provincial centres. On the whole its earlier aspect did not differ from that of any other party. But with the beginning of the Great War the Union and Progress party clearly showed that it had given up the idea of a constitutional government, such as the Tanzimat Young Turks had worked for. The Assembly, which had censured the war policy of the government, was dissolved. Its place was taken by a central Council, which was not elected by the rank and file of a properly assembled Congress, and it turned into a full-fledged secret Cabinet. Party commissars were sent to each province, and they became the moving power behind the nominal governor. Non-party officials could not afford an independent attitude. The power thus passed into the hands of a highly-organised minority in the party, and in consequence the state machinery began to lose its authority and vitality.

There is no doubt that the embryonic dictatorship of a single party as inaugurated by the Union and Progress Young Turks was a powerful and highly-centralised organisation. But it was not at all the kind out of which a democratic or constitutional state could evolve. It allowed of no second party, that is, there could be no second trained and responsible group to take over the government if the administration of the Union and Progress broke down. That and the moral paralysis of the administrative system were the most glaring evils for the moment.

Though the Union and Progress Young Turks were inferior to the Tanzimatists in their intellectual and cultural attainments, they were more ingenious and original in the way they produced a pattern for party dictatorship in the world, and were nearer to the Ottomans in being the pioneers of a new method. But even a cursory comparison will show that in this respect the early Ottomans were definitely superior, for in creating their incomparable system they were able to preserve the vitality of the administrative machinery; and in spite of absolutism and tyranny this machinery endured, because their state was above the ruling Caste. A single party is apt to confound the party interests with those of the state, ignoring the people who are outside it and usually monopolising the material and moral goods of the country. To be rich you must be in the party, to be deemed patriotic you must also be in the party.

The only point the Union and progress Young Turks scored over the early Ottomans is that they did not follow any readymade pattern, such as Plato's *Republic* was to the Ottomans. But they also went for inspiration to the West. They lived at a time when, side by side with the individualistic trend in Western society, there were signs of the birth of new state ideal. Their political philosophy is summed up in a verse of Keuk Alp Zia, the most remarkable and synthetic thinker the Union and Progress movement has produced: 'There is no Individual but only Society; there are no Rights, but only Duty'. The idea of the verse is taken from the French sociologist E. Durkheim, and it embodies a sentiment that has provided many a slogan to all dictatorships. It was on the strength of some such impulse that the Union and Progress leaders attempted to build up their clumsy but original pattern of a system of government that was to become fashionable in the post-war world. And thus the West had the last word in determining the sentiments and principles that went into the making of the Union and Progress creed.

4

The Turkish Republic

However fervently I may hope and pray for it, yet today I dare not affirm that war as an institution has passed away from human society. But in 1918, after the slaughter of 20 millions of mothers' sons, after the suffering in the war-stricken areas, after the horrors of deported populations and inter-massacres, after a general uprooting of humanity, there was a universal desire for peace. The victors and the vanquished longed for it with the same degree of passionate sincerity. And never has there been a time in human history when the peoples were more disposed to lay the foundations of a new era on an equitable and human basis.

The Turks had perhaps been the greatest sufferers. They had been ten long years on the field, and the internal tragedy of inter-massacres and revolutions had bled their country white. They were ready to pay a high price for peace. But even a high price has a limit, and that limit was defined by the declarations of Western statesmen before the armistice. Mr. Lloyd George on January 5, 1918, had stated that the homelands of the Turks and their capital would be left to them. Turkey knew that she would lose two-thirds of her possessions, but where the Turks were in a majority, they expected to be left alone to evolve their new destiny. They were confirmed in this hope by the pronouncements of President Wilson. 'Every territorial settlement involved in this war', he had declared once, 'must be in the interest of the population concerned, and not as a part of any new adjustment or compromise of claims among rival states'. And again: 'The impartial justice meted out must involve no discrimination between those to whom we wish to be just and those to whom we do not wish to be just. It must be a justice that knows no favourites and knows no standards but the equal rights of the several peoples concerned'. He among all the old statesmen seemed to have sensed the strong human current for peace. And in the style of Shakespeare and the spirit of the New Testament, he enunciated his fourteen points; Fourteen Commandments, four more than those of Moses. But unlike Moses he had no power to enforce his commands. He had wandered in and out of a world council, laying down the law for those over whom he possessed no authority. Peace was made by statesmen of the old school; all of them very able men and patriots in the pre-war sense, but all of them too short-sighted to read the writing on the wall, too hardened to respond to the new wave from below; above all too blind to understand that the post-war patriot must create peace and security among his neighbours if he wishes his own beloved land to be safe.

With the Armistice the Allied forces occupied Istamboul, Cilica and Chanak. The Turks began to disarm. For six months the Turks believed that the occupation was going to be temporary and that it would end with the signing of the peace. But the sight of a disarmed Turkey with all its internal desolation and helplessness at once revived the age-old appetites expressed in the secret treaties. 'Like wolves about a camp-fire the Powers were prowling at the threshold with hungry eyes. For Turkey is rich by nature and Imperialism is greedy,' as Arnold Toynbee says in his book, *Turkey*.

The condition of Turkey was indeed desperate. The Union and Progress leaders had left the country, their organisations lacked leadership, and there was no opposition party to take their place and represent the people. They had allowed none. This, as I pointed out in the last lecture, is one of the curses of a single-party government. It inevitably identifies itself with the country; so do its opponents, and ultimately everyone fights the sections of the people which they believe the rival party have represented. After the occupation, both the Allies and the opponents of the Union and Progress were trying to punish the naughty boys of the Union and Progress in the persons of innocent Turkish people. For the naughty boys had left and there remained only some useful and vital elements which had sympathised with or supported some phase of the Union and Progress reforms. Unfortunately there were very few leading figures who had not belonged to the party some time or other.

Meantime the government passed into the hands of the Sultan, who dissolved the Parliament. As it had been more or less a puppet Parliament, this did not matter much. But the Sultan did not order fresh elections. So the government remained in his hands and he in the hands of the Occupying Powers and their Forces. In his Cabinet from time to time he had men of unquestionable patriotism and ability, but the moment they showed signs of unwillingness to be the blind tools of the Occupying Forces they were dismissed.

Before offering peace terms to Turkey, the Powers had come to a dangerous decision. It was to create a Greek Empire in the Near East which would include Eastern and Western Thrace and Smyrna and the hinterland. This would, they thought, keep the Straits open for the benefit of the Allies; it would also keep out the Turks, the Bulgarians and even the Russians. They had, besides, resolved to establish an Armenia in the east from Samsoun to the Caspian Sea, and from the Mediterranean to the Black Sea. Not only Turkey but Persian and Russian lands were to contribute to this new Armenia.

They were not in a great hurry over the eastern part of their scheme. There already was an Armenia which Turkey had recognised. Therefore the East was suspicious of this new Armenia. Besides, Kiazim Kara Bekir was there with a regular Turkish force of about 15 thousand, the territory was beyond the range of the guns of the Allied fleets, and the dauntless spirit of the frontier people was another great drawback. But the landing of Greek armies in Smyrna was possible even at that moment. It was indeed a favourable moment, for the Italians, who wanted Smyrna, had retired from the Peace Conference. Arnold Toynbee calls this sort of Allied action picking each other's pockets. The Allies gave notice twenty-four hours before, saying that they would land their forces in Smyrna, which was an ugly pre-varication if not an actual lie. They landed the Greek army on May 15, 1919.

There was an instantaneous change in the Turks. They stopped disarming and the people passed to action at once. Arnold Toynbee, whose fairness of mind as a historian and sense of justice as a man makes him an honour to the human race, describes the landing in his *Western Question in Greece and Turkey* in these terms:

'On 15th May, 1919, a destructive force was let loose in Western Anatolia, as sudden and apparently incomprehensible in its action as the eruption of a volcano. One morning, six months after the close of the European war, civilians and disarmed soldiers were massacred in the streets of Smyrna; whole quarters and villages were plundered; then the rich valleys in the hinterland were devastated by further arson and bloodshed; a military front came into existence, which cut off the ports of Smyrna and Constantinople from the interior and ruined the trade. As the war continued, capital investments like houses, bridges and tunnels were steadily destroyed, human beings conscripted, deported or otherwise driven away, if they escaped murder. In fact a wholesale ruin and extermination of its inhabitants began over an area which extended with alarming speed.'

In the reaction of the Turks to this treatment there is one thing which the world must never forget. The reaction came first from the people itself. All over the country vast meetings were held to protest against the action of the Allies; the front in Smyrna was created by the people, peasants and highlanders, women included; officers escaped from Istamboul and helped to organise guerilla warfare. Later, two forces converted this psychological upheaval into a successful war of independence; the vast number of ordinary and unknown people who could sacrifice their lives and were gifted with an astonishing ability to organise, and the genius of the few leading figures who knew how to utilise this material as well as moral force. As a witness and a humble participant in this extraordinary historical drama, I feel we should, after acknowledging the service and the ability of the great, attribute the success that was achieved to the psychology of despair and the determination of the people to die fighting rather than to allow themselves to be slaughtered like a flock of sheep. Bearing this in mind we will go over the struggle very briefly.

At the moment the struggle began the Occupying Forces on Turkish lands numbered 100,000. On the other side was the army in the East under Kiazim Kara Bekir Pasha, a small armed force under Ali Fuad Pasha in middle Anatolia and dispersed and half-disarmed regiments here and there. The rest were guerilla forces and they were inadequately armed.

The Allies, uneasy about the situation in the East, had induced the Sultan to send Mustafa Kemal Pasha there as the General Military Inspector to hasten the disarmament. There had been communications and contacts in secret between him and the commanders at Istamboul. On July 19, 1919, Mustafa Kemal, Refet, Ali Fuad Pashas and Raouf Bey met at Amassia and signed the Amassia Protocol, which is the foundation and the first constitutional document of the present Turkish State. Its gist is this: The central government is in the hands of foreign Powers; the Turkish people by their action have shown that they are resolved to resist foreign domination; the activities and the forces of the people must be united and organised and a representative Congress must be assembled to discuss and determine plans of defence.

The first Congress (Erzerum, July 23, 1919), which met under the presidentship of Mustafa Kemal Pasha, decided to elect a representative body which could take—in case of necessity—the place of a temporary government in Anatolia to carry on the defence, to attach all the defence groups to one Anatolian centre, and to prepare a National Pact over which the whole nation would agree. The Congress at Sivas (September 4, 1919) worked on identical but broader lines. Anatolia broke away from the Sultan's government and took the civil as well as the military administration into its hands. The Sultan, frightened at the development, dismissed Damad Ferid Pasha's Cabinet, which was considered a tool of the Allies, and formed a Cabinet with nationalist or pro-nationalist ministers and ordered the elections. The country returned a vast nationalist majority to the Parliament, which met at Istamboul in January 1920. Its virtual leader was Raouf Bey. The Commanders, including Mustafa Kemal Pasha, remained—fortunately—in Anatolia.

The first act of the Parliament was to issue the National Pacts in its final form. It was not different from the first draft made at Erzerum. It demanded that the lands where the Turks were in majority, and which had not been occupied at the time the Armistice was signed, should remain Turkish; the fate of the areas occupied at the moment—mostly Arab—should be determined by a free vote of the people. It proposed to open the Straits and the Bosphorus to commerce, provided that the security of Istamboul and the Sea of Marmora was ensured. The minority rights of the Moslems in the neighbouring countries were accepted as a basis for determining the rights of the minorities in Turkey.

This Pact was communicated to the Allies when they had not yet publicly announced the peace terms they meant to offer Turkey. They had two alternatives. They could accept the Turkish terms, which were nothing more than what they themselves had offered to the Turks before they laid down their arms; that would have ended the war. Or they could attempt coercion and carry out their partition plans. They chose the second course.

On March 16, the Allied forces staged their famous coup d'etat. They landed more troops in Istamboul, raided the houses of all nationalists and dragged people out of their beds. They also raided the Parliament and a number of nationalist deputies, including Raouf Bey, were sent to Malta. Malta was already full of Union and Progress or what were supposed to be Union and Progress men. The Allied Occupation Centre further proclaimed martial law and issued proclamations that anyone who gave refuge to a nationalist would be sentenced to death. To prevent the escape of the nationalists into Anatolia they armed Christian bands and put them on the roads leading inland. But Turkish bands also collected at once to help the refugees to escape. Both arms and men slipped through in spite of the Allied watch-dogs.

The Government of the Sultan instituted an extraordinary Court and passed death sentences on the nationalists. Mustafa Kemal Pasha, Ali Fuad Pasha, Dr. Adnan and myself were in that first list. Further, the Sheikh-ul-Islam issued a *Fetva* that every Moslem who killed any of the seven on the list could be sure of being rewarded with heaven. It is very regrettable that for the first time a Sheikh-ul-Islam should have thus identified himself not only with the foreign occupation of the country but also with injustice and tyranny. It was a moral lapse for which the guilty Sheikh-ul-Islam suffered the keenest agony for the rest of his days.

Meanwhile Mustafa Kemal Pasha, who had come to Angora some time before, asked the country to send fresh representatives to replace those who could not or would not join the Nationalist Parliament that was to meet in Angora. It was to be a Constituent Assembly.

The Constituent Assembly, which held its first session at Angora on April 23, 1920, formed itself into a government known as the Government of the Great National Assembly. It was the first government in the East created by the people and acting for the people. In that process of giving and taking which we have called the conflict of East and West this is one of the best gifts that the West made to the East. For the first time in Turkish history, and at the most critical moment, the entire responsibility of governing the country fell on the shoulders of a simple Anatolian majority, and the people's representatives who now took charge were confronted with tasks as arduous as those of the handful of Ottomans who, in the thirteenth century, laid the foundations of the empire which endured for seven hundred years.

The Government of the Great national Assembly can be compared to the French Convention. It combined the legislative as well as the executive authority. The President of the Assembly corresponded to the head of the Government, the Vice-President to the Speaker, the Executive to the Cabinet. Each member of the Cabinet was elected by the Assembly separately and was personally responsible to the Assembly. This constitution is worth study, for it was one of the most democratic forms of government known to history.

The most difficult period of the Government was from April to June 1920. It had to establish judicial and civil administration throughout the country. This was comparatively easy, for there was an established administrative machinery left over from the Young Turkish period. The central structure was harder to build up, for few would or could join. But the real danger and difficulty arose from the civil war. The defence of middle Anatolia depended wholly on the Irregulars. Though there were idealists among them and they were undoubtedly the pioneers of the national movement, still it was difficult for the leaders to maintain discipline among the rank and file, and they oppressed the people at times as cruelly as the Greek Forces. Further, the Sultan had, with Allied money, armed thousands of his non-Turkish subjects to fight the Nationalists in Anatolia and given them the high-sounding name of the Caliphate Army.

This was one event which turned the tide in favour of the Government of the Great National Assembly. The other and far more effective one was the Sevres Treaty, which really amounted to nothing less than a sentence of mutilation and death on the Turkish people. It gave Smyrna and the hinterland and Eastern and Western Thrace to Greece; it created an Armenia that would extend from the east to the south down to Cilicia, swallowing up the Kurdish regions; it handed over the ports to the Allies, the Straits with Istamboul and the eastern and western coasts being under Allied control; it placed the finances also in the charge of the Allies, with the Capitulations restored for the exclusive benefit of the victors; no fleet or aircraft, no army, but only a land-force of 15,000 (which would include the gendarmerie), could be maintained by Turkey. Indeed, if the treaty were executed, Turkey would have become altogether an abstract term, for even the arid bit of land in middle Anatolia had been divided into Zones of Influence. It was, however, only the Sultan-Caliph who sealed his doom by signing this treaty and equipping the Caliphate forces. The Turkish nation would not submit to extermination, by treaty or by force of arms. While the Allies and the Caliph were engaged in the diplomatic formalities of the Sevres Treaty, the National Government created a new army into which the irregulars were incorporated. Certain bands resisted and their resistance coincided with a Greek offensive. But the tiny army inspired confidence in the people by defeating both the Greek army and the Irregulars at Inn-Eunu, and henceforth they supported the new government unconditionally.

Conferences were, however, held from time to time in London during this period to settle the Anatolian affair. We may leave them out. They gathered always after some Turkish victory and their aim was obviously to give the Greek army time to recuperate.

The decisive battle between the Turkish and the Greek forces was fought at the Sakaria. The Greeks, after defeating the Turks at Eskishehir, captured all the railways and marched on Angora. The situation was most critical, but both the Assembly and the people rose to the occasion. Mustafa Kemal Pasha was made the Generalissimo and given some emergency powers, Ismet Pasha became the Commander of the Front, Fevzi Pasha, the Chief of Staff, and Refet Pasha, the Vekil of National Defence. The difficulties were enormous. Men, arms and ammunition were to be brought from the east, over 400 miles of roadless desert and mountains under the worst possible weather conditions. But the will of the thousands of patriotic men and women found a way. All available means of transport were offered to the state, and where no other means were available, human backs did the duty. Workshops were improvised; whatever was left of the railways was torn and turned into weapons.

The Greeks had 80,000 well-equipped soldiers, with a splendid park of 200 cannon and an inexhaustible supply of ammunition. All the railways were at their service, and they could run lorries over the comparatively better roads of Western Anatolia. The Turkish army consisted of 25,000 thousand men with rifles belonging to four different categories, from Mauser to old Martini, only six cannon by way of artillery and very limited ammunition.

The heroism of the Turkish front is beyond description. The losses within the 23 days of open battle amounted to 16,500, a vast number of which consisted of officers. No one turned his face from the battle-field, though Turkish attacks were very little protected while the Greeks attacked under cover of very superior artillery. Kiazim Kara Bekir Pasha sent a wire to Mustafa Kemal Pasha during the battle which expresses the sentiment of the Army at the moment: 'Until a single fighter is left on a single hill-top, the resistance will continue'. There is a beautiful passage in a speech of Mustafa Kemal Pasha which also reflects the general feeling.

'As the President of the National Assembly, I declare openly before you that we do not want war: we want peace ... (But) if the Greek army supposes that it will make us give up our legitimate right, it is mistaken. It is perfectly natural that we should be defending our country's existence by arms against attempts to wipe out its nationhood. There can, indeed, be no more justifiable and reasonable attitude than this. Gentlemen, I assure you that we will continue our offensive pressure on the Greek army till not a single soldier is left in our lands.'

The Turks won at the Sakaria. Clair Price, in his *Rebirth of Turkey*, reveals the full significance of the battle:

'The Turkish victory on the banks of the Sakaria radically changed the political complexion of the Near East and the Middle East. For two hundred years the West had been breaking down the old Ottoman Empire. But on the Sakaria river it encountered the Turk himself, ... and the tide turned. History will one day find in this obscure engagement on the Sakaria one of the decisive battles of our era.'

With this victory the new Government was securely established. It broke the backbone of the Greek army and it divided the Allied front. France made peace, recognised the Government of the Great National Assembly and withdrew from Cilicia. Italy retired from Adalia. So far only Soviet Russia had recognised the Angora Government. It was of immense moral and material value during the struggle to feel ourselves safe in the east when we had to concentrate on the western front. Kiazim Kara Bekir Pasha, by his campaign in Armenia, which led to the annexation of Kars and Ardahan and a definite peace with Armenia, also contributed greatly to our success, for we could draw freely upon the forces of the east for the battle at the Sakaria.

In August 1922, a year after Sakaria, the Turkish army took the offensive under the command of Mustafa Kemal Pasha and cleared the country of the entire Greek forces by its march on Smyrna. The Turkish nation had passed victoriously through its ordeal by sword and by fire. The Powers decided to call a conference at Lausanne to settle the terms of peace.

But they invited both the Istamboul Government and the Government of the Great National Assembly, and before going to the conference the anomaly of the two governments had to be settled. After an exciting and long session the Assembly voted the separation of the Sultanate and the Caliphate; it abolished the Sultanate, making Istamboul a province with a local government (November 1922). Sultan Vahideddine having taken refuge on an Allied warship, the Assembly elected Abdul Mejid Effendi as Caliph.

The Lausanne Conference opened in November 1922, and ended in July 1923. The Treaty of Peace signed between the Government of the Great National Assembly and the Allies confirmed all the clauses of the National Pact.

The world may rightly and justly admire the great names who have brought to a successful issue the struggle of the Turkish people for life and liberty. But the world knows nothing about the superhuman sacrifice of the host of unknown men and women lost in the struggle. It would beg all to remember them when they pray in their temples and mosques, those martyrs of both sexes and all ages who suffered and died that their nation might live in peace and honour. Such unknown heroes shall ever be worthy of the prayers of all peoples.

On October 29, 1923, the Great National Assembly constituted itself a Republic and established the Cabinet system. The life of the new Turkish State could be divided into three periods:

(1) 1920–1923—This is the period of the Government of the Great National Assembly. Though there were no parties with names, still there were three groups representing three kinds of opinion in the country—Radicals, Conservative-Liberals, and the extreme wing of Conservatives, who were in a minority. The last was spoken of as the Hoja Group. On questions of national importance they voted unanimously, in other matters they did not hesitate to express their differences. The Assembly was one the strongest any country

could ever produce. One who reads the verbatim reports of the discussions would really be surprised to see how these men, the majority of whom consisted of the simpler, less educated element, had the wisdom and the common-sense as well as the patriotism to know when they could agree to differ during such a critical time as this. The abolition of the Sultanate was voted by them all. This is very significant. It meant that all shades of opinion at that moment were decided on the form of government Turkey would have in the future. It was not to be a Sultanate.

2. 1923–1925—In 1923 there was a new election. The Hoja Group or the extreme wing of the Conservatives dropped out. On October 29, 1923, as has been mentioned, the Assembly constituted itself a Republic and established the Cabinet system. In March 1924, it abolished the Caliphate. It can be said that both the Republic and the abolition of the Caliphate were passed by a representative majority. The absence of any reaction among the people is noteworthy, for it proved beyond doubt that the Caliphate no longer commanded the allegiance of the Turkish people. This subject is perhaps too important a thing to be discussed hurriedly by a lay person such as myself, but I shall just mention the obvious reasons for this revolution in Turkish sentiment. As a force of inter-Islamic unity within the Turkish Empire the Caliphate had proved itself ineffective. Abdul Hamid's policy of using it as a political bogy to frighten the West produced disastrous results. The 'Jihad' proclamation during the Great War was a farce. Further, Vahideddine's troops, fighting under the name of a Caliphate Army against the people who were defending their honour and their existence smothered whatever respect and love for the institution still remained in the minds of the people.

In 1923 the People's Party was formed, but almost everybody in the Assembly belonged to that party. Yet it was evident that though on fundamental things they all agreed, there was a decided difference of opinion on many matters.

There was a progressive and liberal group who were at the same time strong constitutionalists and a radical section. What they were all agreed on was that they must proceed with the reforms till a thorough Westernisation in education and the state-system was achieved. The progressives believed that this could be done by constitutional methods, the radicals thought that their ends could be realised only by means of a party dictatorship and through drastic measures. However, there was no split and they continued their work of reform till the end of 1925.

In March 1924, the Assembly passed a series of laws which completed the separation of religoin from the state. The office of the Sheikh-ul-Islam was abolished, a presidency of religious affairs was instituted and placed under the Prime Minister. The 'Evkaf' were confiscated by the state and handed over to the Finance Department, the Medresses and the Tekkes were closed down and visits to the graves of Sultans and Saints prohibited. All these measures were passed by a properly representative body with two shades of opinion, liberal and radical. It meant that the separation of religion and the state, of which we will speak in some detail later, was one of the generally-accepted necessities. An obvious defect of the act, however, is that though it freed the state from the interference of religion, religion itself fell under state tutelage. The earlier believers in separation had hoped that religion would become free to develop on spiritual lines and to play its old and appropriate part in the moral education of the people, that is, to concentrate itself on the moral and philanthropic side of Turkish life. After the measure, the Moslems are the only community in Turkey who are under state tutelage in reagard to their religious life, while the Christian and the Jewish Church is entirely free.

In 1925 the Assembly split into two parties, Progressive Republicans and the People's Party. The Kurdish revolt of the same year which brought into existence the revolutionary tribunals also led to the disappearance of the Progressive

Republicans. After 1925 the Republic has been ruled by a single party, that is, the People's Party.

The radical phase of the reforms began after 1926. The measures which may give a new orientation to Turkish thought and a new complexion to Turkish society are the adoption of the Swiss Code (1926), and of the Latin characters (1928). Of the latter we will speak in connection with literature. The first demands a fuller histroical review, for therein one sees in what way the Turkish Moslem differs from the other Moslem brothers in the present way of thinking.

Islam is a code which aims at regulating all human relationships. In any Moslem state it is the unique law. The Ottoman Turks took it as such and entrusted its enforcement to a strong and independent judicial organisation. It was more or less the same with the other Moslem States. But while the others kept it in its earliest form, that is, they remained faithful to the idea that the Sheriat was the expression of God-made law, the Ottoman Turks began to add to the Sheriat; God-made law was supplemented by man-made laws under the name of 'Canun'.

In the early sixteenth century Soleyman the Magnificent enacted the 'Canun' which was an embryo of the later criminal and commerical laws. This 'Canun' was incorporated in the Sheriat; the Sheikh-ul-Islam continued to be the administrator of justice and the Sheriat Courts were the only courts.

In the beginning of the nineteenth century, when the Tanzimat reformers began to think in terms of the new West which the French revolution had created, they made starting changes in the laws and the judicial system.

The French Penal Code and the French Commercial Code were adopted wholesale. But they did not stop at that. Between 1869 and 1877 a colossal work of codification was undertaken, the result of which was the famous Ottoman Civil Code. In appearance it was occidental, that is, it was divided into articles and chapters and it was promulgated under the authority of the state. But in spirit and in substance it was Islamic. And it became the Common Law for the Ottoman subject, whatever his creed or race.

As Islam is more than liberal and demands that the religion of a man should not be interfered with by the state, the family law of each community, marriage, divorce and inheritance, remained within the jurisdiction of the comunal church. Moslem family law remained in the charge of the Sheriat Courts and under the jurisdiction of the Sheikh-ul-Islam. But the Tanzimat created the Nizamieh Courts and instituted a Ministry of Justice. So the law of the land, except that of the family, was administered by non-religious State Courts from 1856 onwards. In the Courts of First Instance, Courts of Appeal and the Courts of Cassation Christian and Moslem judges sat side by side.

One could analyse the beliefs of the Moslem Ottoman Turks in regard to law at the end of the nineteenth century thus : Commerce and trade are subject to change; the laws that deal with them must be left to the state, so that it can amend them or adopt any new law which seems suitable; behaviour and the position of the individual in the state, that is, everything which comes under Common Law, must also be in the hands of the state, but this law must be evolved out of the established Islamic Law, and it must be Islamic in spirit. But—and this second limitation is more significant—the law relating to the basic part of human society, the family, must be left in the hands of each community. One may conclude that the Ottoman Moslem Turk was on the whole for man-made law. He was, nevertheless, fundamentally conservative, and his judicial and legal innovations were essentially Moslem in spirit.

The Young Turks went a step further. In 1916 they took over the Sheriat Courts from the Sheikh-ul-Islam and placed them under the Ministry of Justice. They also attempted to modify the family law, in the spirit if not within the letter of

Islam. By a legal ordinance they brought into existence a new family law. But they made it a matter of choice for the people, in their family affairs (marriage mainly), to make use of the new or the old law, for the old law was not abrogated. Of this we will speak in connection with women. These measures were annulled by the Sultan in 1919.

Outwardly the judicial reforms of the Republic and the separation of the state and religion are not different from the previous reforms. Considering the times, those of the nineteenth century were even more daring. But the adoption of the Swiss code, specially the family clauses, constitute a revolution in the spirit. The present schools not only demand man-made laws, but also insist that the Common Law, that which affects behaviour and even the family, need not be evolved from Islamic or from the established Turkish laws. This is a gigantic swing towards the West, which no Islamic society has so far ventured upon.

I am not a jurist or a doctor of law to discuss with confidence the comparative merits of the Ottoman Civil Code and the newly-adopted Swiss Code. But I will take up a question which I have been usually asked by my Western audiences. 'As Islam is Law as well as Religion, do not the Turks cease to be Moslems?' No. Whether one agrees with the other aspects of the policy of the dictatorship or not, one must say that it has restored religion to where it should belong, to the spirit, to the soul. The Turks are attached to their religion as deeply as any other people. Religion is a reality which no society dare ignore. Therefore if the state lets the Islamic community evolve its own moral and spiritual destiny, free from the corruptive influence of politics, I should not be surprised if Turkey became the cradle of a great movement of spiritual reform.

In the domain of economics the Republic has intensified state control by means of state monopolies and official or unofficial banks which centralise business and promote national industry. In its foreign policy it has shown decidedly pacifist tendencies and has contracted alliances with its former enemies. It has been an undeniable factor in the establishment of peace and stability in the Near East.

The conflict of East and West in the Ottoman State which continued for seven centuries has ended finally in a victory for the West. However unpleasant the admission of the fact may be, its truth cannot be challenged. But it is only in the externals, the state and its machinery and to a large extent the civilisation that the West has stamped itself ineffaceably. The culture, the soul of the people, that is a plant which can grow and thrive only on its native soil. We shall review this aspect of Turkish life in the next two lectures.

5

Literature and Culture—I

The Ottoman Turks are a race as mixed as the Americans. Greeks, Slavs, Italians, Hungarians, Albanians, especially Circassians and people of every possible race in the Near East have been as individuals or as groups assimilated, converted and Turkicised. Therefore, except in the nomads of Anatolia who wander and usually marry within their tribes, there is very little of the original Turkish race left. But be they of the city, of the rural districts or of the wanderers, one thing is common to them. It is a strong national consciousness, and that conscious unity comes to them from their language. For in spite of alien influences in the way of thought and of the large number of foreign words which have become current at different periods, the Turkish language has retained its structural uniqueness and its peculiarities.

The Turkish language belongs to the Ural-Altaic, or, as it is sometimes called, the Turanian group, which includes the Finnish, the Hungarian, the Tartar and probably the Japanese. Though one of the chief Semitic languages, that is, Arabic, has played a supreme part in forming its vocabulary, as it has in moulding the thought of the Turks; though Persian, one of the Indo-Aryan group, has given it many words, still Turkish has not been altered either in its grammar or in its very particular inner harmony. All these alien elements have added to it the richness, subtlety and variety which all mixed languages of the world have. Max Muller, the great linguist, who studied the Turkish language scientifically, declares in his *Science du Language*:

'We can say that it is a great pleasure to read a Turkish grammar, even if one does not intend in the least to speak or write the language. The ingenious manner in which the grammatical forms are produced, the regularity that dominates the entire system of declension and conjugation and the transparence of the whole construction impresses one with the marvellous force of the human intelligence revealed in this tongue.'

Turkish never acquired the geometrical logic of Arabic and French, but it has retained an equal clearness and native ingenuity in expressing thought and feeling in the tersest and shortest terms. It has none of the metaphysical complexity, the profound subjectiveness and the monumental floweriness of Persian, but it is a perfect instrument for expressing subtle mood and it is able to evoke nature with unique realism if not in the stylistic Persian manner. Therefore clearness and realism mixed with extreme sensitiveness are the characteristics of the language.

The language reached the climax of its development in the Ottoman period. But within the last twenty-five years the pre-Islamic, the earliest past has acquired such prominence in our thought and literature that it is necessary to make a very brief survey of the pre-Islamic period of Turkish history.

I have already mentioned the earliest discovered forms of writing in the Orkhon Inscriptions. Apart from them there is a vast number of myths, tales and epics which have been handed down and are told to the children in the cities and in Anatolia today. We will take the 'Oguz-Nameh' as one of the typical forms of legend and epic. It has preserved its original name and form: further, it contains the grey wolf legend of which we have heard so much in recent times.

'When Oguz was born his face was blue, his mouth was as red as fire, his eyes and hair and eyebrows were black and very beautiful. When he had sucked but once at the breasts of his mother, he talked and asked for food. In forty days he grew up and played. His feet were those of an ox, his body that of a wolf, his breast was that of a bear and hairy. He led the flocks of horses and hunted without permission.'

This is followed by the killing of dragons, and finally the story of his marriage with the heavenly maiden is told.

'When Oguz was praying to Tanri one day, the air became dark and a blue light fell from heaven, more dazzling than the sun and the moon. Oguz walked towards the light and he beheld a lovely maiden sitting in the midst of light. There was a halo on her head like that of the polar star, so beautiful was she that when she cried the blue heavens wept, and when she laughed the blue heavens laughed with her.'

Oguz had six sons called Day, Moon, Star, Sky, Mountain and Sea. From them great Turkish Kingdoms start. The names are quite fashionable now in Turkey.

Oguz was trapped in a war and a grey wolf descended from heaven and showed him the way to safety. This recurs in other legends. It is evident that the wolf is the racial emblem of the early Turks. They carried a golden wolf-head on their flag. The oldest legend about the grey wolf occurs in one of the Chinese annals.

'The Tokios used to live first on the shores of the Western Sea. A neighbouring people exterminated them all. Only a youth was left, but his feet and hands were cut off and he himself left in the marshes. A she-wolf looked after him and gave him food and saved his life. Soldiers of another people came, but with the help of the Gods the wolf took the youth to the eastern shores and ascended the mountains. She entered a cave with him and she bore him two sons. One of them was called "Asna". Being the more intelligent, he became the king. In remembrance of his origin, he had a flag with the head of a wolf on the door of his tent.'

The early music and literature of the Turks are both connected with certain rituals, some of which have come down to us, though in different forms. Bards sang during all these rituals to the accompaniment of an instrument called 'Kubuz'. This was a custom as early as the fifth century, when the Turks were still in Central Asia, and as late as the seventeenth century in the Balkans. It still exists in a modified form in Anatolia.

The first ritual is 'Sigir' (ox). This was the name given to the musical banquets held after big hunts where the bards sang. It came down to the Ottoman period, as the early Ottomans were great hunters.

Another important ritual is the 'Shulun', the sacrifice of animals, during which the gods were supposed to come down and commune with the people. This was abandoned in the Moslem period.

'Yug, or Mourning over the Dead', was another important ritual, in which bards sangs of the life of the dead hero or made him speak in the first person. In these compositions, nature played a great part, for mountains, rocks, clouds, all spoke and sang. This articulate nature dominated in the Ottoman tales and epic; the horse of the hero was very often as important a person as the hero himself. He was burnt and buried with his owner.

This form of literature, that is, elegy, is one in which the Turks have always excelled, and Islamised forms of mourning for the dead, with hymn-singing, Qur'an and Mevlud chanting have remained very important parts of Turkish communal and social life down to our own time.

Religion was evidently another subject which exercised the mind and imagination of the early Turks, and their religious literature is very remarkable. The cosmogony of the Altai Turks is, I believe, quite original.

'Before the Earth and the Heavens were created, everything was water. There was neither earth nor sun nor moon. The Beginner of all Life, the Father of Mankind, Tanri Kara Khan, created a being in his own image and called him Man. Tanri Kara Khan and Man flew over the face of the waters like two black swans. But Man rejoiced not in the happiness of quietude. He wanted to soar above, higher and higher, but losing his strength he fell into the limitless depths of the waters. In danger of being drowned, he implored the help of Tanri Kara Khan. Tanri Kara Khan commanded Man to rise to the surface of the waters and Man rose.'

'As Man could no longer fly, Tanri Kara Khan willed to create the Earth. He commanded Man to plunge into the depths of the waters and bring some earth from there. When Man brought up the earth in his mouth, he kept some of it in his mouth that he might create a separate world for himself. But the earth swelled up in his throat, so much so that Tanri Kara Khan ordered him to spit it out. Man would have choked, unable to breathe because of the earth that was in his mouth.

The Earth which Tanri Kara Khan created was all plain, but when the earth from the mouth of Man fell out, the Earth became covered with marshes and hills.

Tanri Kara Khan in his wrath at this named the disobedient man "Erlik Khan". He expelled him from the circle of Light.

Erlik Khan is the same as the Devil of other cosmogonies and it is an original departure to conceive of the Devil as the first man and not as a fallen angel.

'When Erlik Khan saw that the new dwellers of the Earth were beautiful and good, he asked Tanri Kara Khan to give them to him. Tanri Kara Khan refused, but Erlik Khan knew how to tempt them and take them by teaching them evil ways. Tanri Kara Khan was wrathful and decided to leave men alone henceforth. And cursing Erlik Khan once more, he expelled him to the third layer below the Earth, in the Abode of Darkness.'

The struggle between God and the Devil is picturesquely told and it ends with the triumph of God. Apart from its archaic beauty there is in it a subtle sense of humour and understanding of human weakness all through.

Potamine, a Russian scholar who has studied the Mongol and Turkish mythology and classified them as North Asiatic Mythology, states that these legends were early enough to have influenced the Jewish writers of the Old Testament, that the first epic forms among the Slavs, Finns and Germans were derived from Turkish and Mongol sources.

Apart from myths and legends, the Turks possessed a considerable number of didactic poems and proverbs.

The most striking feature of this folklore, which the Turks carried with them to the near East, is its originality and the mixture of fierceness and contrasting tenderness. We see clearly that, considering the time and the environment, the moral nature of the early Turks was highly developed. We are also struck by the outstanding communal character of the early productions. No name is connected with any epic, myth, legend or poem. The group rather than the individual always is in the foreground.

Everywhere we find the same virtues emphasised: hospitality, generosity, respect to parents and above all truthfulness. All these are, of course, human virtues rather than Turkish virtues. But there are two traits which have remained peculiar to the Turks down to our own day. The first is a natural impulse always to help the weaker side. The Ottomans were very particular about it; the legend of the creation of their early state is based on it; further, throughout their history, they have shown this tendency very strongly.[1] I do not know whether this admirable trait will remain. But their other peculiarity was very apparent during the national struggle. It is their Spartan endurance of every possible hardship and suffering.

After the conversion of the Turks to Islam, literature was naturally coloured by the new religion they had adopted, but it did not lose its fundamental characteristics. We must begin our study of the new phase with the Seljuk period, the starting point of all the intellectual movements and the literature of the Turks in the Near East. The literature and culture of the Seljuks attained its highest development in the thirteenth century, the time when the Seljuk State was declining. But great movements, especially the spiritual and philosophical, often coincide with the periods when states have ceased to be oppressively strong. This period is being specially studied by a few remarkable young Turkish scholars, but what we know of it is yet incomplete. This is a great pity, for the Seljuks were perhaps more remarkable than the Ottomans, in literature if not in state-building.

The court language of the Seljuks was Persian and that of learning was Arabic. But the masses spoke Turkish and the masterpieces were translated and interpreted, commented upon and propagated among the masses to an unprecedented degree by a host of secondary teachers and writers. The terms 'Ulema-i-Rusum' and 'Khalk Ulemasi', the official Ulema and the people's Ulema, belong to that period, and their use continued throughout Ottoman history. But it became less and less important towards the end.

We shall review the literary activities of the Seljuk age in the three aspects which seem to be the most important.

1. Religion dominated literature as well as other activites in the thirteenth century. Its influence was especially intense because the Turks of the Near East had to face the onslaught of the Crusades. The war-cry of the Turk, 'Ur ha !', — adopted by the English and turned into 'Hurrah !' — was dropped and 'Allah, Allah !' took its place. The Turkish epic became religious. The heroes of whom the people sang were those fighting the Christian forces. Among a vast number of epics there is one which is particularly noteworthy, *Battal Gazi*. It deals with the series of wars against the Byzantine Christians, and it was the epic on which the valour and the ambition of the Ottoman Janissaries was nurtured.

2. In non-religious literature the profusion of animal stores continued; the love-stories are reminiscent of the early days in which nature spoke and the number of heroines, a dominating characteristic of old Turkish literature, is still considerable. But towards the end of the Seljuk and during the early Ottoman period a new epic of a semi-political kind developed, which celebrated the struggle of individual heroes

against the state, very much in the spirit of Robin Hood, by championing the people's and the poor men's rights against the king and the rich. This sort of epic flourished mostly in the Smyrna region. Those who have been in Turkey probably know that the Smyrna highlander, called Zeibek or Effe, is a very characteristic person in life and in history. Not only have these highlanders always struggled against state tyranny in the Ottoman period; they were the first to take up arms against the Greek invaders in 1919. There is the grave of a girl highlander which is visited by Smyrna Turks as if it were the shrine of a saint. This girl was the head of a political band, fighting the government and the rich and protecting the poor.

The music and the dance of these Effes or Zeibeks is now becoming very fashionable. There is a ballad of the 'Fair Highlander', with very expressive music, which reminds one of the earliest Turkish ballad in which the horse shared the honour with the hero.

The Fair Highlander leans against the mountain. It rains and his ammunition rusts. His mad heart will be tamed one day. Shame on thee, O Golden Chestnut, see'st thou not the blood on his purple vest!

Clouds have gathered over yon mountains. Three hundred horsemen, five hundred men on foot are marching against him. The Fair Highlander was unique in this world. Shame on thee, O Golden Chestnut, see'st thou not the blood on his purple vest!

3. But the most valuable and enduring achievements of the thirteenth century literature are the writings of the mystics. The basis of mysticism are different verses of the Qur-an and the sayings of our Prophet. Like the mysticism of other peoples, it is pantheistic and believes in the transmigration of the soul and its final union with the Supreme Being. In its evolution it was affected directly by Nestorian Christianity, Manichaeism and Neo-Platonism; indirectly by Indian mystical thought translated into Arabic by Alberuni.

Three contemporary figures in the thirteenth century stand at the head of the movement. Ahmet Yesevi, Haji Bektash and Yunus Imre.

Ahmed Yesevi was a Turk of Samarkand who never came to Asia Minor. His principal book is *Divan-i-Hikmet*. It is believed that he is not the author of all that is written in the book, additions having been made at a later period. But the work was in simple Turkish, dealing more with human conduct than complex metaphysics, and so Ahmet Yesevi's teaching spread among the people very swiftly through his disciples and followers. Haji Bektash and Taptik Imre, or Yunus Imre, are among his best known disciples.

The Bektashi orders really established themselves a little later, during the Ottoman period. The Janissary organisation had Haji Bektash as its patron saint. It is often said that the force and the rigid organisation of the order was due to this mystic spirit as well as the democratic tendency which dominated it throughout. The curious part of it is that though connected with the state, the order has also been the greatest source of inspiration for those who fought against state tyranny. The teachings of the order were not popular in Anatolia only but also spread very rapidly in the Balkans. Albania was one of the Bektashi centres. Another reason for the strength of its appeal was the ruthless way in which it attacked the complex theology of the orthodox. It stood up for love and grace in religion against the conception of a God of Wrath and Vengeance. A great number of anonymous hymns, poems and religious songs originated from the order, and there can be no doubt that we owe to it the development of the critical faculty in the Turkish masses.

Yunus Imre, the other great disciple of Ahmet Yesevi, is regarded at the moment as the greatest Anatolian poet of his age. He wrote a great many hymns for children and simple people which remained in vogue for hundreds of years. He also very humorously and delicately satirised the theological and orthodox tenets of Islam. Here is one of the best known of his pieces.

What have I done to Thee, Oh Lord, that Thou shouldst decree my frailty ere I was born? Thou hast conceived me as a rebel, Thou hast been free to shape me according to Thy will. When I opened my eyes to this world, I found myself in a prison crammed with 'jins' and fiends, and boiling with lust.

Thou hast made a bridge like to a hair and said to me, "Cross, save thyself from thy doom foretold!" How should a man cross over a bridge like to hair? He will surely slip and fall headlong beneath. When Thy servants build a bridge, it is for the good. They build it that folk might safely cross the flood. They make it spacious and strong that those who cross may say, "Behold, this is the Right Way!"

Thou hast set a balance to weigh evil deeds; Thou hast designed to cast me into fire straightway; scales are meet for him that is a grocer, a merchant, a spice-vendor or a goldsmith. Thou art ever present and knowest all my ways.

'Sin is uncleanest of all thing unclean. Why shouldst Thou search and weight that filthiness? It would be seemlier if Thou didst cover it with Thy Grace!'

Many other mystic orders were established about this time whose names are known to you all. They no doubt played a great part in moulding thought and creating social solidarity in the age of Seljuk decline. But the one which has exercised the greatest influence on the literature, music and thought of the people is the order of Mevlevis.

Hazret Mevlana Jelal-eddin Rumi, the founder of the Mevlevi order in Anatolia, was one of the greatest figures of the Islamic world. He came as a boy with his father to Konia from Balkh, after a long journey through Persia, Syria and Eastern Anatolia. His father was from Balkh, but as to his real origin there is some difference of opinion between Persians and Turks. His mother was a descendant of the Khwarazm royal family and he and his father were well received by the Seljuk Sultan Alauddin Keykubad. I believe the discussion about the Mevlana's origin is due to the fact that he wrote his greatest work in Persian. But that seems natural, as both Persian and Arabic were classical languages and works of scholarship could be written in either of them; the Mevlana, besides his Persian works, wrote in Turkish, a little in Arabic and even in Greek. The Mevlevi order, though it had a popular side, was in Turkey the 'Tarikat'[2] of the intellectual, of the artist and of the elite. The Chelepi of Konia always belted the Sultan at the coronation ceremony and enjoyed a very high position in the Turkish social order.

Of all the common traits of Islamic and Eastern mysticism the Turks emphasised the moral and communal side, while the Persians dwelt altogether on the aesthetic and the philosophical. In that the Persian is, perhaps, nearer to the Indian. Though the Mevlana's teaching is of all Turkish mysticism the one nearest to the Persian conception, still he attaches great importance to social and moral conduct. There is a legend regarding this peculiarly Turkish trait that is told in Anatolia.

Sheikh Sa'adi, of *Gulistan* fame, sent his book to the Mevlana when he had finished it. The Mevlana wrote on the cover, 'Be namek est', and when Sheikh Sa'adi read it he answered, 'Velakin hulu est !'[3] The Mevlana cared for the salt, the substance, and Sa'adi for beauty and sweetness.

A contemporary of Hazret Mevlana was Muhiuddin Arabi. He was an Arab of Andalusia and came to Konia when the Moslems were being persecuted by the Spanish Church. Here he married a Turkish woman and his stepson, Sadreddi Konevi, became one of his disciples and commentators and spread abroad his teachings. Both the Mevlana and Muhiuddin Arabi are great artists besides being great teachers and philosophers. Muhiuddin Arabi is very much in the front page at the moment because Miguel Asin Palcinos, a modern Spanish writer, in a work published in 1919, declares that the *Divine Comedy* was inspired by his works and by the *Risalatul-Ghufran* of Abul 'Ala al-Ma'ari.

An anonymous religious poem which seems to have a great deal of the Mevlevi spirit is this:

'Come, O Dervish, wander not in desolation: whatever thou lookest for is, believe, in thee. If thou art in search of Ka'aba, Grace and Salvation is in thee.

Follow not the mirage, roaming in the deserts; if thou art in search of truth, do not look for it in the Book: if thou knowest how to read, the Qur-an is in thee.

With thy knowledge thou dividest a hair into forty. Whom art thou looking for? In thy dreams there is none but thee; the one who has built the empty arch over thy head is in thee.

Call not this good and the other evil; call not this true and the other a lie—none exists, the lie is in thee.

Enter the city of hearts, wander around. Compare the sun and the atom. Thou only art capable of good and evil. If thou inclinest to evil, Satan is in thee.

Think not of "I" and "Thou"; take no colour, white or black. the Creator of Light shines in thy heart; remain not in darkness; the Everlasting is in thee.

I have heard that thou art a son with no father, that thou wast born in Heaven and expelled thereform; that thou hast wanted in plenty and hast ended in want. Why blame Allah, the revolt is in thee.

Why look for help to others, if thou hast been exiled from Heaven, O Vagabond; the serpent that tempted Eve is in thee.

Though of low origins thy quality is great. If thou art a pagan thou canst worship all: if thou art drunk with the cup of love, thy Beloved is in thee.

'Oh ignorant one, worship not the externals as truth and light, a candle at each corner. The stream of events flows for ever, the Everlasting is in thee!'

Under the influence of this mystic ideology a very remarkable econnomic and social organisation, called the 'Ahiler',[4] came into existence during the age of Seljuk decline. They are said to have established a regular state in Angora, but this subject has not been properly studied yet. It was the organisation of guilds and corporations among small traders and originated with the association of tanners. It is an organisation symptomatic of the thirteenth century in general, if one considers the guilds and city corporations of Europe and similar corportate bodies in the Islamic world. But in Turkish Anatolia they seem to have been very firmly rooted and to have had a very particular complexion.

It is evident that political decline and anarchy must have been one of the reasons for creating associations which would ensure solidarity and at same time raise the moral standards. Ibn Batuta tells us a great deal about them in his book of travels.

'The Ahiler', he says, 'are against exploitation, they are against banditism from below and against tyranny from above. " In one of the *Futuwatnamehs*[5] one reads: "The 'Ahi' must not go begging at the doors of Beys, the Sultan and the Bey should not know of the existence of the "Ahi" or the Sheikh.'

When the apprentice or the novice donned his apron and joined a corporation, he had to take an oath to seek seven virtues and to eschew seven vices; he had, in the symbolic language of the 'Ahiler', to open seven doors and to close seven doors. The door of Meanness must be closed and that of Generosity must be opened; the door of Oppression and Tyranny must be closed and that of Gentleness and Kindness be opened; the door of Luxury and Self-indulgence must be closed and that of Restraint and Asceticism and Self-discipline must be opened; the door of Popularity must be closed and that of Justice must be opened; the door of 'Herze'[6] and 'Hezeyan'[7] must be closed and that of Learning and Knowledge must be opened; the door of Ambition must be closed and that of Contentment must be opened; the door of Falsehood must be closed and that of Truth must be opened.

There is given a list of those who are not to be admitted to the order: the atheist, the astrologer, the butcher, the surgeon, the tax-gatherer, the hunter, the money-lender.

It was a strict rule of the order that the 'Ahi' must be self-made. If he boasts of ancestry he cannot enter the doors of the brotherhood. 'Even if he be the son of a prophet,' they said, 'it means nothing when he himself is lacking in virtue.'

This of course denotes a supreme, a real democracy; not the democracy of the modern world with its mad competition and selfish individualism, but a democracy where contentment, a really equitable distribution of the necessaries of life and the good of the group are the supreme aim. A passionate desire to serve the people and to uplift them morally is evident throughout the teaching of the 'Ahiler'.

Yahya bin Khalil, the writer of the oldest *Futuwatnameh*, says in his book (*Futuwatnameh*, 901, Fatih Library), 'In my youth I knew not how to read and write. But I saw that "Ahi" organisations were getting lax and that they needed guidance. Allah in his Quran says that every people's prophet speaks in their language. To the Futuwat people I must teach in their own language. I learnt how to read and write and studied the principal books. Then I wrote this book.'

With the strengthening of the Ottoman State and the centralisation of authority all these guilds and corporations were placed under state protection.

In the Ottoman period Turkish became the court language, and then it really developed and came to its own. When the Seljuks passed away it was, in spite of some masterpieces, like the English of Chaucer compared to that of the post-Shakespearian period. It now acquired a matchless flexibility and harmony lacking in the other Turkish dialects. Probably the mixture of peoples led to the development of new vowels of a great and rich variety; and with time the harsh Arabic consonants 'K' (ق) and 'G' (غ) dropped out very much. The alien words the people adopted were Turkicised, treated according to Turkish grammatical forms and given peculiarly Turkish meanings. Thus alien words helped to enrich the popular language.

The writings of the Ottoman elite, on the other hand, took a different direction. The number of the alien words imported was greater and their original significance and grammatical form was preserved; subjects as well as words were freely and abundantly adopted, an artificiality was developed and an alien colour acquired which restricted the number of those who could be proficient in the language.

The written literature of the Ottomans may be divided into various groups.

Turkish Annals. I believe the Ottoman Turks have been greatest in their annals. Beginning with the fifteenth century, Ottoman Turkish history has been recorded by a court historian day by day. Though the language, specially during some periods, is heavy, still the writers themselves are blessed with that objectiveness and realism which makes their works of immense value both for the historical student and for the artist. They record life as it was, with character sketches of Sultans, Vezirs, the great in general as well as those of the man in the street. I know no other writing which has so faithfully recorded the acts of the mob in revolution as these annals. There is no attempt at criticism. Fortunately, as neither they nor the Ottomans of the period were afflicted with the inferiority complex which falsifies literature and thought, they could faithfully record life as it was, without being concerned as to how it would affect the foreign reader. Only two of the annalists have been translated into English, and they also in parts: Evlia, who was also a traveller and is often carried away by his own fantasy—which was that of a genius—and Naima.

The Ottoman classics consist of *Kassidas*, *Gazels* and *Merciehs*, as well as mystic poetry. As in India, those who excel in the former class of literature are called the authors of 'Divans'. Though as 'Gazel' and 'Mercieh' writers Turks have at times surpassed their original models, the poets of Persia, in the 'Kassida' they can be ranked only with second-rate Persians. Battles, Sultans, Vezirs are the topics if not the spring, the rose or the nightingale. At times in the description of horses or of certain battles they fall into a free strain and produce something worthwhile. Baki, who was one of the greatest in this line, composed a very remarkable elegy on the death of Soleyman the Magnificent. Though the rest of his 'Kassidas' are rarely if ever read, this one is still quoted. It is of course loaded with the inevitable imagery of the imperialist poet.

'Wherever thy noble steed has set its hoofs, the great from far and near have thronged around thee, to give their lives for thy glory. Across the face of the earth thou hast hurled forth from end to end thy iron-girdled world-champions.'

Mystical School. The two greatest poets of the Ottoman period belong to the Mevlevi order. Soleyman Dede, who lived in the fifteenth century, is the first. He was a simple Imam of the great Mosque at Broussa, where he used to teach the people and was a beloved figure. His greatest work—also the greatest in the Turkish tongue—is the *Birth-song of Mohammed*. Though other poets have written birth-songs, none has had the lasting hold of Soleyman Dede's. It has been chanted in every house as a Moslem requiem down to this day. Even those who profess to be rid of religion and affect a snobbish Western style of life go to this ceremony. The part relating to the Prophet's birth, as described by his mother, is a masterpiece of simple Turkish and deserves to be quoted.

'I beheld a light to which the sun was but a moth; it flashed from my dwelling like lightning, mounting the skies and illumining the world. Rank on rank, angles from heaven encircled my house. The Heavens opened and all gloom passed away ....'

She goes on to tell us about the celebration of the birth in that strange night when universal light irradiated all existence. It is a night when birds, beasts, men and *jin* and all creation dance with joy because of the revelation of the mercy and love of God.

'Creation had only joy, delight and mirth. Grief passed away and new life filled the earth. Every atom of the Universe took up the tale and raised its voice crying, Hail!

Hail, O Soul of Souls most tender, Hail!
Hail, O Sun of Love's Brotherhood, Hail!
Hail, O Pleader for the Fallen, Hail!
Hail, O Friend of the Portionless, Hail!'

Galib Dede was the next and last mystic poet. He lived in the late eighteenth and early nineteenth century. His great theme is love and beauty, mostly woven around the story of Leila and Mejnun. But his was a monumental genius. and I believe if a poet such a Fitzgerald translated his verse, he would delight the world as much as Omer Khayyam has done.

The Naturalist School. Towards the close of the eighteenth century, though the state was rapidly declining, refinement, beauty and enjoyment of life had reached their apogee. There was a revulsion against religious subjects and 'Kassidas', which had only Sultans as their theme. Turks became interested in life itself, and also desired to depict it as they saw it. From this desire sprang the naturalist school of the early nineteenth century. Though the writers are all secondary, yet, thanks to their works, there is no period in which the purely human side of Turkish society could be better studied. They widened the range of literature and produced remarkable character sketches.

There is a study of contemporary types by Vassif-i-Enderuni, parts of which I shall quote. It is the advice of a mother to a daughter and the daughter's answer. Its chief interest lies in the fact that it is in the colloquial Turkish spoken by the women of Istamboul, that it is the character sketch of a young woman and an old one who belonged to the class that cook their own food and wash their own clothes, that its subject and the human way it is treated makes of it a lasting and universally valid presentation of the struggle between two generations.

Listen girl, be sweet and true, be neither a hypocritical prude, nor bold. Do not wander about dragging thy skirts in mud and mire. Don't be a street-broom, be a womanly woman.

Do not flirt, you plague, you pest, do not run after every dandy and beau, do not pass thy time in feasts and entertainments. Learn how to embroider...(A list of a great many different stitches is here given.)

Pembe, my child, why do you buzz round me like a mosquito? Why dost thou shake thy belly like a dancer, you good-for-nothing girl, you baggage, you minx. What is this romping about, what is this chaffing with men from behind lattices? You are already thirteen, how can you think of tambourines and dances? Why deck your head with spangles? It will attract the eyes of drunken and worthless men.

Your elder sister is already married. Allow yourself to be chaperoned by her. You are no longer a child, although you are not tall. See how Attika is married. May her luck follow you.

I wish your dad would marry you to a judge with a villa by the sea, so that we could visit you. Already mothers come to inspect you every day. That old lady may bring an engagement ring today. Go, put on your jewels, hang your coins around your neck.

You stiff-necked girl ! Why do you draw yourself up and shower abuse on your mammy's head? Alas for the toil spent I have spent on you! Don't be a street-broom, be a womanly woman!

This flapper of a century ago answers very significantly. Part of the answer is what she thinks; the other is conversation.

If mammy preaches again, I will scratch her eyes out. I mean to act on my own. Did she stay at home when she was young? See how the neighbours are in coaches to ride and to roam.

Why do you drone like a spinning-wheel? Go and do your weaving, mammy! Why do you tell me this and that is to be my husband? May you and husbands wither like corn on the cob! Even if I were to sell every pot and pan in secret, as long as there is life in me, I'll seek a boy of fifteen and him my sweet-heart make.

Washing greasy rags in the kitchen will spoil my hands. Mammy makes me cook in the kitchen and entertain her friends. May my dad break her pate for it. She uses me as if I were a slave bought with her money. How can I spoil my soft, white hands? The fitting thing for them is to weave silken threads.

How summers and winter pass! Yet she wants me to sit in the house. I will be getting old at this rate before my wisdom-tooth cuts. I will seek a boy of fifteen and him my sweet-heart make.

Come, Esma Hanum, rouge my face, trim my locks; everybody praises my face. Let me give myself a touch in the glass. I will borrow Tutti Hanum's red trousers, wind her yellow shawl around my slender waist, I will deck my hair with spangles, I will step thus into coaches with coquettish airs, I will sit in pleasure boats with costly fans in my hand. I can always wheedle daddy, just let me pass my white fingers through his beard.

'I do not care for moustached bullies. If a husband refused to do what I wanted, I would kick him into a well. I only want frisky lads with jaunty cocked caps—I will seek a boy of fifteen and him my sweet-heart make.'

From an artist's point of view it is a pity that this naturalism was swept away too soon. But what took its place, though inspired both in form and ideas by the French, is still a turning point in the history of the Ottoman Turks.

Though in the Tanzimat period there is a departure from the earlier form and the subjects, still there is one thing in common with the earliest school : literature is used as a means to propagate ideas, just as by the thirteenth century mystics.

Till the Tanzimat era, Turkish writers and thinkers had not looked for ideas and sentiments outside of religion, and by trying to borrow or to create an ideology independently of religion the Tanzimat writers took a new step. Dr. Adnan, speaking of the Tanzimat in his (unpublished) history of science and religion, calls the Tanzimat the passage of the first group of Moslem writers from the medieval to the modern times.

The founder of the Tanzimat school of literature was Shinassi (1826–1871). He was also the political leader of the Young Turks. He began life as a simple clerk at the Arsenal at sixteen. It was fortunate for the school that he was a profound student of Turkish and Moslem classical literature. He knew the Turkish dictionary by heart at that age, which sounds absurd, but not in his case, for he was destined to study scientifically each Turkish word in all the stages of its development, from the earliest Turkish literature to his own day.

At the Arsenal Shinassi made friends with an officer who was a French aristocrat turned Moslem and married to a Turkish woman. From him Shinassi learnt French and began to read the new philosophical and scientific works. He attracted the attention of Mustafa Reshid Pasha, the Grand Vezir, and even of the young and liberal Sultan Abdul Mejid, and was sent to Paris to specialise in Finance.

The first years of his life in Paris were devoted to philosophical and scientific studies, nevertheless he found leisure for the persual of literature as well, for he was gifted with a colossal, almost unparalleled capacity for work. These rare gifts, coupled with simplicity of manner and dignity as well as extreme austerity, attracted the attention of the French intellectuals. He became an intimate friend of Lamartine, Littre, the philosopher and lexicographer, and of Ernest Renan.

On his return he was made a member of the newly-formed Turkish Academy and a member of the Finance

Council, controlling the expenditure on the army. He is also counted among the intimates of Sheikh Jemal-eddin Afgani. It looked as if he might easily become a Grand Vezir. But he was of an uncompromising nature and gave offence to the great. He was even involved in a plot against Abdul Mejid. Thanks to the angelic quality of Abdul Mejid's heart, he escaped punishment. But after Abdul Mejid's death he persisted in his uncompromising attitude towards absolutism. He caricatured 'Aali Pasha, the new Grand Vezir, who was almost fanatically opposed to the constitutional movement among the Young Turks. 'Aali Pasha dismissed him from all his offices in insulting terms.

Though disappointed in service, Shinassi was firm in his resolve. He took to journalism and laid the foundations of the modern press in Turkey. Up to his time there were only official papers. He published the *Terjuman* and later *Tasvir-i-Efkar*, which played a most important part in thought and life of new Turkey. Printing as an art, publications on a large scale to create and to educate public opinion, were all his work. His paper continued to be published except during Abdul Hamid's time and finally ceased in 1925.

When the first issue of the *Tasvir-i-Efkar* appeared, Abdul Aziz sent five hundred pounds as a token of his appreciation. Shinassi sent the money back with the laconic answer, 'I desire to buy nothing that costs five hundred pounds'. But with his uncompromising nature and his general reputation of being a republican and an atheist, Shinassi could not preserve both his personal liberty and his independent attitude. When his colleagues began to be persecuted and he himself constantly attacked, he left for Paris and lived most of his time there, paying only occasional visits to Turkey. During his last years he was in Istamboul, living in his printing-house and working at the same feverish pace which characterised his whole life. He died of brain fever.

His most cherished and ambitious work was his monumental Turkish dictionary, which was to be in 14 volumes of 1000 pages each. He compiled it up to the twentieth word—we have thirty-one—giving the derivation of each word and its use throughout the various stages in the development of Turkish literature. The MSS of the dictionary is partly in the library of the Asiatic Society in Paris and partly in the University Library of Budapest.

The translations given in Shinassi's paper of Corneille, Racine, La Fontaine and Fenelon are considerable. He evidently was a lover of animals and keen on natural history. He wrote several animal stories in verse. Though the Turkish folklore is rich in animal stories, Shinassi is the first and last, I believe, among the classical school who wrote of animals. He was also the author of a comedy, *The Marriage of a Poet*, in which he caricatured both the old school and his own. The bulk of his writings, articles on every conceivable subject, is to be found in the collections of the *Tasvir-i-Efkar*. The hard and bare life of an intellectual pioneer in Turkey is well represented in the words of Zia Pasha, the didactic and satirical poet of the age: 'Unfortunate is he who acquires knowledge and virtue only to suffer persecution at the hands of the ignorant.'

Namik Kemal took up the torch of new thought, both as the leader of the school in literature and in politics. The son of a high official who lived in different parts of the empire, his early education was also on purely Turkish and classical lines. He met Shinassi in early youth and became an admirer and a disciple.

Shinassi had laid the foundations of the new school, but he had been a cool intellectual and a rationalist, while Kemal was a great romantic. The ideas Shinassi advocated in a restrained and matter-of-fact style, Kemal turned into great epics. Hence the modern school reached its highest emotional level in the works of Namik Kemal. But the thing to be noticed in both is that they were not mere imitators. Both attacked the imitators as bitterly as the old school. They were out to build up a literature and a philosophy of life that would be fundamentally Turkish.

Kemal's life-work is as colossal as that of Shinassi. Though Shinassi might have been both an atheist and a republican, Namik Kemal was not. He was a loyalist who wanted a constitution. He was also a very devout Moslem, believing in the accumulated power of the thought and the art which the Turkish nation had inherited.

Both by way of translation and original composition he left a large number of works. He was more interested in history than in science, though he was an ardent admirer of Francis Bacon. He also made translations from Montesquieu, Condorcet and Jean-Jacques Rousseau. His principal works are his *Introduciton to Ottoman History, The Age of Conquest,* novels, poems, theatrical pieces, and a critical survey of Turkish literature under the title *Ruin of Ruins*. In every new form of literature he appears as a pioneer.

He crystallised and turned into a religious creed two great ideas of the middle nineteenth century West. But in spirit he was thoroughly Turkish.

Patriotism in the modern sense owes its inception to his ardent mind. He analysed and turned into poignant pictures the suffering of the land. His *Dream* and *Lamentations,* one in prose and the other in verse, are the works in which this idea is very emotionally worked out. He dreams of Turkish lands as a supernaturally great, wounded mother in a shroud, wandering about in pain, yet pressing her children to her breast. In *Lamentations* he asks the mother to put on black over her white shroud and stretch out her arms, one to Kerbela, the other to the tomb of our Prophet. 'Tell Allah that the battles fought in the Turkish lands are each a 'Bedr', a 'Hunein'.[8] He traces the trail of Turkish blood throughout the empire, telling about the vast number of martyrs whose blood has watered the Turkish lands. Though this imagery is somewhat worn out, it was then new and the writer felt its influence very strongly. The other work on this theme is a drama called *Fatherland*. When it was first played the emotion of the audience was uncontrollable. After the theatre the audience demonstrated throughout the night, lanterns in hand, in the unlit streets of Istamboul. The next day Namik Kemal was arrested, exiled and then imprisoned.

The second idea which he presented with equal force is that of the rights of man in the state. With this he did not mix any religious fantasy. 'No man is fit to govern another man without that other man's consent,' said Abraham Lincoln. Kemal went out to prove that all government not based on the consent of the governed ends in tyranny, and every individual should fight and suffer to the last for the sake of the rights of man.

Though each historic period has its own ideology, and freedom of the individual is not an important feature today, still Namik Kemal's lesson remains true and great. It was the teaching of sacrifice and uncompromising resistance, if necessary, martyrdom for the ideas that a man believes in. The emphasis on the rights of man outside the sphere of religion was a new thing in the East.

Namik Kemal's classic piece, which epitomises this idea of his is his *Kasside-i-Hurriet* (Ode to Freedom). There is here none of the lyric and overdone imagery of his other works. It is a dignified and magisterial statement of his creed, for the sake of which he prefers to suffer all his life, rather than bow to and flatter the great in the hope of a position. For Kemal also, like Shinassi, if he had stooped to compromise, would have been a Grand Vezir. I will give you the spirit of the *Kassida* in a short and free translation.

Seeing that the tide of events has deviated from honesty and truth, we have resigned power in the state with honour and glory. Man, worthy of the name, never tires in the service of men. He must always give his hand to the downtrodden, to the unjustly persecuted. The supporters of tyranny are only the villainous in heart and mind. Dogs only delight to fetch and carry for the bloody hunter. Let it be said of me that the least of all my sufferings for my cause has given me greater honour and joy than the position of a Vezir, nay, a Grand Vezir.

'Though the rope of the executioner is the hand of the dragon of death, a thousand times is it preferable to life with the chain of slavery around one's neck. Though the field of Freedom may be that of fire and hell, man will not forsake it for mere life. Let Fate call all its tools of oppression and attack me, I shall be a cad it I turn my face from the path of service and struggle. How magic art thou, Oh Freedom, that we have become thy slaves, though we have broken all other chains.'

Namik Kemal's life was a prolonged martyrdom. Sometimes in prison and sometimes in exile or in alien lands, in spirit he always remained the great and valiant fighter that he was to the end. He died in exile in one of the islands and is buried at Bulair.

But among all the Tanzimat or earlier figures who devoted their literary power to the service of cause, none has achieved his ends to the extent Namik Kemal has done. For over a quarter of a century during Abdul Hamid's reign, thousands and thousands of youths sacrificed their career, even their lives, for the sake of reading his works in secret and propagating his ideas. Steamer after steamer sailed from Istamboul to Yemen or to Tripoli, carrying hundreds of young men, often schoolboys, to the two classic places of exile—the Yemen and Fizan deserts.

As an artist, if not as a man and a teacher, Abdul Hak Hamid was the greatest of the Tanzimat school. He is even considered by some as the greatest poet of all Turkish literature. Most of his life he lived in London as our Charge d'Affaires, and his great gift to Turkish literature were dramas and theatrical pieces in the most tasteful and developed modern style, though his subjects also were taken from the heroes or events of Islamic history. Abdul Hak Hamid is our last great romantic. His work raised the literary standard of the modern school, and I believe he would be accepted as an international figure if he were translated. But apart from this, his writings are full of allusions to tyranny and injustice, which he condemns in very strong terms. Though the characters and events he depicts are historical, the hints at Abdul Hamid's tyranny are obvious and very significant. Tyranny, blindness to the change of the times, indifference to public welfare and education, lack of confidence and co-operation between the rulers and the ruled are the four evils which, according to him, lead to the downfall and the ruin of a country. As an illustration, both of his style and his views, I will give a free translation of parts of his *Monologue of Tarik Ibn-i-Ziad*, the conqueror of Spain.

You are in the treasury of the Spanish kings, Oh Tarik! From whence, and whither? From Syria to Toledo, from a hut to a royal treasury, finally to a grave. (Looking at the crowns and handling them.) What are these shining objects in your hands, which dazzle your eyes? The broken and the trampled crowns of great rulers. You hold them in your hands—twenty-five proofs, twenty-five witnesses of past glory and power. Yet, O victorious commander you are nothing but a keeper of graves.

Never follow the example of those who owned these crowns. They were ignorant and proud. Never had they the fear of the power of the Lord, never did they consider the helplessness of men and never did they see the changes in the times.

Now you are in their palace of splendour, you own their wealth, you have discovered their buried secrets.

Behold the change in the course of the river of Fate—behold the doom of the great nation rolling at your feet. All this because of the change you have wrought. Nevertheless, O Tarik Ibn-i-Ziad, you are nothing. You are a nought!

Read, Tarik Ibn-i-Ziad, read! Each of these crowns tells you the tale of the adventure of an unhappy king. Read, O slave of Ibn-Nassir!

Roderick tyrannised over his people, so much so that there was nothing but the fire of hatred and revenge in the heart of his nation. The wise shunned his company, he was surrounded by flatterers and his realms were ruled by the ignorant and the incapable. Not a school, not a hospital have I seen amid the monuments of this city—nothing but palaces, prisons and churches!

'Roderick never dreamt that a state whose ruler is a tyrant, whose inhabitants are ignorant and helpless, is doomed to be trampled over by alien states!'

---

1. Turkish solicitude for the Poles, from the early eighteenth century onwards, the hospitality shown at an enormous risk to Count Tekeh, the Hungarian Chief, to Charles XII of Sweden and the Hetman Mazeppa and above all to the Hungarian refugees in 1848 are convincing proofs of this chivalry being innate in the Turkish nature. Regarding the courteous protection given to the Hungarians in 1848, Sir Edward Creasy says:
   'While the Porte was thus wisely pacific and conciliatory in its general conduct towards foreign Powers, a memorable and noble proof was given in 1849, that Sultan Abdul Medjid had not degenerated from the high honour and chivalrous generosity of the ancient race of Othman and Ertoghrul, the "Right-hearted Man". When the united forces of Russia and Austria put an end to the Hungarian war of independence, many chiefs, who had been most active in the Magyar cause, escaped into Turkey, and received hospitable shelter in the Sultan's dominions. The Courts of Vienna and St. Petersburg peremptorily demanded, first, their extradition, and afterwards their expulsion from Turkey. Sultan Abdul Medjid met these demands and the threats with which they were accompanied, with a dignified and firm refusal to violate the laws of hospitality, and betray the old principles of his race and creed. The two Emperors menaced more and more loudly, but in vain.' *The History of the Ottoman Turks*, p. 533–34. This valuable work, published by Bentley in 1877, is now unfortunately out of print (*Ed.*).
2. The orthodox law and the way of life it prescribes is the 'Sheriat'; the mystic rule of life is by contrast called 'Tarikat' (*Ed*).
3. 'Be nemek est' means 'It is without salt', also, 'It is tasteless.' 'Velakin hulu est' means 'But it is sweet.' (*Ed.*)
4. Lit. 'Brethren'.
5. 'In the language of the Sufis "Futuwat" is the expression for a disposition which is manifested in different ways and therefore cannot be expressed by a single word. In general "Futuwa" is described as placing others above himself'... This finds expression in liberality, unselfishness, self-denial, self-effacement, superiority to disappointment, indulgence to the faults of others, etc. (*Encyclopaedia of Islam, Art 'Futuwa'*). A 'Futuwatnameh' is thus a book of rules and general moral guidance for the members of the order, here used with special reference to the 'Ahiler' (*Ed.*)
6. 'Foolish talk'.
7. 'Raving'.
8. Battles fought by the Prophet and his first followers against Arab tribes who were determined to exterminate them (*Ed.*).

6

Literature and Culture—II

Abul Hamid set out to destroy the Tanzimat literature—that is, the literature of ideas and ideals. Outwardly he succeeded. The works of the Tanzimat writers disappeared from circulation and the particular words which expressed their ideology—'Constitution,' 'Freedom,' 'Fatherland'—from the dictionary. To read a smuggled page of Tanzimat literature or to utter one of these tabooed words was an offence against the state and often punished with perpetual banishment. The press was reduced to official announcements and a strict censorship scrutinised every line before it was published. The daily news consisted of lists of promotions, praise of the Sultan and whatever else the censor allowed.

In spite of all these drawbacks a school of literature did flourish in Abdul Hamid's time. It was the 'Edebiyat-i-Jedide'. With all ideas excluded one would have expected the writers to turn to the simple naturalism of the early nineteenth century. But they were not that sort at all. With their inner frustration, their ideas developed into strong complexes. These complexes can be analysed into three different sentiments: an anti-religious feeling, due to the notion that Islam shackled the Moslem and frustrated his attempts the modernise his political and social life; an anti-past feeling, because in the past people saw their great adversary who stood between the East and the West; and, finally, a childish craze for Westernisation, for the West seemed to contain all that was perfect and good. The conception our writers had of the West was limited to certain of its aspects only: science, rationalism and extreme materialism. But they were for everything that was Western.

In technique and externals these writers reached a high level. The novel in its modern form was produced by Halid Zia Bey, the novelist of the school. The subjects of his novel were taken from a very limited milieu—that of the super-westernised Turkish society. But his short stories are masterpieces, for they depict what was more representative and real, not merely a second-hand copy of alien types. On the whole this school was as faithful an imitator of the West as the old 'Kassida' writers had been of the Persian poets. Because of this tendency to emphasise change in externals, because of this disregard of the realities of the past of man's soul, the school had very little root. That is perhaps why they were also called by some the 'Decadent School'.

The greatest figure of the school is Tewfik Fikret, the poet. He produced very little and with difficulty, and it was of very unequal value. There are some creations of his which will live for ever in Turkish literature, as they would in any literature, there are others which are already forgotten. He himself was a very dominant figure—a kind of apostolic character of rigid and uncompromising puritanism. Those works of his which have come down and remain as powerful influences in thought deserve analysing.

'Mist'. This is a picture of the moral degeneration and misery of the city of Istamboul. The poet looks at it through one of those beautiful white mists which fall over the city and over the Bosphorus at times. He sees the tyranny from above, the debauchery, the luxury of the rich around the seat of absolutism and the demoralisation and the destitution of those below seethe and boil and form contrasting pictures. Istamboul is to him the Byzantinised Turkey. The refrain of the poem is: 'Veil thou, O City, O Tragedy, veil thou and sleep forever.' Istamboul is the sinner of the age. Tewfik Fikret's stand for the higher moral values of Right against Might, of liberty against political slavery is heroic. The poem was written during Abdul Hamid's reign, and as it could not be published then, it was copied and passed from hand to hand. And it did play a part in the downfall of Abdul Hamid.

In 1908 Tewfik Fikret came forward and published the *Tanine*. In his early writings after the Constitutional Revolution there is an optimistic trend. But he was disillusioned by the autocratic tendency of the Union and Progress and retired from public life, his last position being that of President of the Galata Serai School. As an educator he was matchless. In spite of his retirement he continued to write and publish from time to time.

His most powerful and longest work in verse is called *Ancient History*. It is an uncompromising attack on religion primarily and against the past in general, which, to him, obstructs the progress and development of a people. Its effect was not unmixed. Its supreme defect was its indiscriminate anti-religiousness. Such men as Tewfik Fikret could be pure and great in character without religion. But in all countries the fundamental moral education of the people is based on religion. One may criticise the superstitious, the obscurantist part of it, but on the whole religion should be respected and used as the basis for the moral education of the youth of all countries. Tewfik Fikret's wholesale attack engendered an irreverent attitude towards sacred values in the minds of a certain group of young people. Further, it produced a wholesale hatred of the past, a feeling which has come down to our own time.

Apart from this, however, there are very excellent and enduring thoughts forcibly expressed in this poem. Tewfik Fikret is a pacifist, an internationalist, a believer in the brotherhood of man and in the supreme ascendancy and use of human reason in all spheres of life.

The poem begins with the appearance of the Spectre of the Past, a looming skeleton, blood trickling down its teeth, a spectre that prolongs the nights and delays the morning to which all humanity is looking forward. It is the most violent attack on violence one could find in literature.

'We want a morning—a good morning to those who have slept the long, dark nights. O Spectre, slinking away in the dark! You look as if you have handled bloody objects ... You have been the destroyer of my race!

'Heroism you say? Its basis is blood and barbarism. Victory—that is to trample over cities, destroy armies, cut, break, ruin, drag, crush, burn and demolish—knowing no mercy, heeding no sighs and tears. Wherever you pass there is death and agony, all the harvest gone, even the grass and moss withered; families uprooted, homes desolate, every hearth a tomb, every roof a heap of ruins over orphan heads.'

Fikret's ideal is, 'No Sultanate, no domination, no extortion, no exploitation, no persecution—you are you and I am I, no lord and no servant!'

This anarchist tendency in religion and established order softens and takes a constructive form in his *Credo of my Son*.

'There is a great Power, High and Unseen—with all my conscience, I believe.

'The devil and the *jin* is in us, there is no angel nor Satan. The world will be turned into Heaven by Man, I believe.

''Evolution towards perfection is innate in creation. In this perfection and evolution with Tevrat, Injil and Qur-an, I believe.

Man is man's brother—a dream you say... Let it be! With a thousand hearts in this dream I believe!'

Apart from this Tewfik Fikret, throughout all his poems, stands against tyranny as a symbol of destruction. The opening lines of one of his national hymns, which was sung in the early days of the Constitutional Revolution, is, 'If Tyranny has cannon, shells, fortresses—Right has an arm that cannot be twisted, a face that never turns!'

His best poem for me is his *The Head of the Camel*. He wrote it for children and in very simple and beautiful language. I believe that it ought to be translated and taught to every child in its early years.

'Once upon a time a big camel had a head. There is no camel without a head, but take this as a tale.

This brainless, this rotten head led the poor camel over hill and mount and rock, exhausting him for nothing. To whom could the poor heavy body complain but to a crow, who said, "God gave you the head, carry it."

His hump was bewildered, his tail wandered about. May Allah never take the power of leading from the head and give it to a tail. People at first listened to the camel's complaints a little, but by and by got tired and snubbed him. The poor camel at last quietly leaped into a ditch and laid down its head saying, 'To Hell with you, dirt!'

"The head that is unjust is broken off one day.'

Reading it through, the last line seems to contradict what has been said before. For he speaks of stupidity of the head all through and calls it unjust only in the last time. But from the point of view of an educator I believe it is just wonderful. For in the mind of the child injustice and stupidity remain identical. With a simple stroke the story does away with the glamour, the cleverness, which the popular mind attaches to wickedness, and which I believe is one of the causes which makes the lure of wickedness so strong.

Outside Fikret's school there are two strong figures in Turkish literature who still live and write.

Hussein Rahmi, the novelist, followed a line of his own. A satirist and a realist, he was drawn from every possible class and type of people in Istamboul. On the whole he is, I believe, the greatest novelist we have produced within the last thirty years.

Mehemmed Akif, the other great figure, is a poet and if anything stronger and more masterly than Fikret. He subjects are taken from the people's life and from realities, but realities which were out of fashion in his time. Though he and Fikret attacked each other uncompromisingly, both after all wanted the same thing—a better and more equitable world. Fikret thought that man could attain this end by denying the past and by developing his reasoning power, and that only. Akif believed that no nation which discarded its past could have a future and that only through a better conception of religion could man be better. But though a strong Moslem, he did not mean to flatter the Islamic world in the least. Here is an extract of a long poem of his, called the *East*.

'You have wandered a lot through the East, what have you seen?' they ask. 'I have seen from end to end ruins, nations with no leaders, broken bridges, closed canals, empty highways, sickly and wrinkled faces, bent backs, brainless heads, indifferent hearts, rusted judgments, tyrannies, slavery, misery, hypocrisy, disgusting vices, diverse diseases, burnt forests, cold chimneys, wild fields, dirty faces, lazy arms, Imams with no following, brother killing brother, days with no definite aims, nights that expects no definite morrow!".

During the Young, Turkish regime, the 'Edebiyat-i-Jedide' carried on one part at least of its campaign uncompromisingly: Westernisation at all costs. People at the time were very much interested in education, not only of the higher classes but still more of the masses. For that and also for further and closer unification with the West it advocated the adoption of Latin characters. The strongest protagonist of this innovation was Hussein Jahid, the journalist and writer of Fikret's school. The idea did not originate with him, but he was the first to make it a subject of discussion in the daily press. Hussein Jahid's proposal of introducing Latin characters was very fiercely opposed by more than one class of the intelligentsia, not to speak of the people in general.

Pan-Islamists were against it because they feared it would cut us away from the Islamic world. We could not write the Qur'an in Latin letters. The pan-Turanists argued that the cultural unity of the Turks would be destroyed. There were some thirty millions of Turkish-speaking Turks in Russia who used the Arabic script. Our culture had been more or less adopted by them. Lastly, it was contended that all our cultural wealth was treasured in literature in the Arabic script. The classical languages of the Turks were Persian and Arabic. The Arabic script in the hands of the Turks had developed in its own way and its spelling had been rendered more phonetic, so that with a little more attention to phonetics, the Arabic script could be easily taught to the people. This was the objection urged by the nationalists.

The proposition of the Latin script was by no means the only suggestion of the kind put forward. A man called Ismail Hakki evolved a new alphabet, more phonetic and more legible, and worked for its acceptance. Enver Pasha himself took up the question and devised a new way of writing the Arabic letters that would make the spelling easier and the writing more legible. But neither device was seriously considered.

In regard to the modernisation of Turkish thought and letters, Dr. Adnan, in his history of science and religion, affirms that if we had studied the ancient classics in the original, instead of taking them second-hand from Western literature, we might have produced something very unique and original, for we already had a culture enriched by the Eastern classics.

Besides the "Edebiyat-i-Jedide", there were three other schools of literature which came into existence during the Union and Progress regime.

The pan-Islamist school, whose most outstanding figure was Mehemmed Akif, published the *Sebil-ur-Reshad*, a weekly advocating their ideas. They were very much in favour of reviving Islam in its primitive purity. Any talk of social change or reform was like a red rag to them. The Union and Progress watched them with suspicion. To counteract their super-conservatism they themselves published the *Islamic Review*, under the guidance of Keuk Alp Zia, the only sociologist and to some extent the philosopher the Union and Progress regime produced. The *Islamic Review* is of great importance, for in it a critical study of Islam in its bearing on thought and society was attempted to some degree. It set out to translate the Qur'an into Turkish. Keuk Alp Zia himself strongly believed in the necessity of a complete reform, if not according to the letter, at least in keeping with the spirit of Islam.

The pan-Turanist school started their activities in Salonika after the Constitutional Revolution, Keuk Alp Zia being the most prominent in the group. They were purists in language, and opposed to the use of alien words. Keuk Alp Zia was a very able poet among other things, and he drew not only upon those pure Turkish words which were current and included in the Ottoman Turkish literary vocabulary, but even imported words from pre-Ottoman Turkish and Central Asiatic Turkish dialects, which did not mean anything to the people. This phase of his did not however, last long. But he and the school were rabid detractors of the Ottoman past, setting up against it their racial past. Keuk Alp Zia has defined Turkish nationhood and the Turkish land thus: 'Our "Fatherland" is neither Turkey nor Turkistan, it is an immaterial climate—Turan!' The best achievement of the school was its serious study of the Turks from a sociological point of view. Mehemmed Fuad Kuprullu, a young scholar and poet of the time, has been studying this subject and has produced very remarkable works within the last twenty years. At the moment he is the best known Turkish scholar in the Western and Russian academic world. Another valuable contribution of the school was its attempt to explain reforms as an outcome of the state of the Turkish soul rather than an imitation of the West. The motto of the school was, 'Our race is Turkish, our religion Moslem and our civilisation Western.'

The Nationalist school has no figure which can be called its founder or leader. It includes perhaps the greatest number of writers, publicists, critics, poets and scholars of all shades of political opinion. It is a more natural growth and belongs to the soil and from the artistic point of view its achievements are considerable.

It was as keenly a purist as the pan-Turanist school, but without being artificial, as its aim was to preserve all the alien words which had been Turkicised. But it also put an end to the intrusion of alien grammatical rules into the Turkish language. That is to say, it followed the genius of the people in their assimilation of alien words rather than the rule of the earlier classical writers. It accepted the reality of religion and was inclined to reform. Its difference with the pan-Turanist was in its conception of the past. It believed in studying the past critically and it believed that the Ottoman past was the real and the nearest patrimony of the Ottoman Turks.

I will here discuss only two authors, Refik Halid and Omer Seyfeddine, purely for their artistic significance.

The most remarkable thing about Refik Halid is his use of the colloquial Turkish in a way that makes it an extraordinary instrument of all thought. His is Istamboul Turkish, that is, the women's Turkish, so subtle and yet simple and so rich in idiom. He was a strong satirist, and like all satirists lacks comprehensiveness. His brilliant mind looks at an object through a crack, but it gives a most realistic picture of what its gaze lights on. He looks at the mean, at the detestable, at the absurd. A rabid enemy of the Young Turks, he wrote masterpieces in the form of character sketches or caricatured the events of the time. All that he produced during this period is included in a collection called, *What the Hedgehog Said*. Later, after the assassination of Mahmoud Shevket Pasha, he was exiled to an Anatolian city. From the point of view of Turkish literature it was good thing. He came out with a series of stories of small Anatolian towns and of some village figures which would be masterpieces in any literature. Here also he looks at the mean, at the sordid; therefore it is not an all-round realism. But within its narrow scope it can be termed a work of genius.

Omer Seyfeddine, instead of the limited power of satire, possessed that precious, that rare quality of the simple Turk—a sense of humour. This means he could see men and things from all sides, therefore he is of perhaps greater value for those who want to understand the Turkish soul. Even when he is exposing the defects of the Turk and his simplicity and inability to cope with the more shrewd and unscrupulous elements of the country, he does it in such a way that one understands and sympathises with everyone's point of view.

In the sphere of the novel the new figures were those of Yakub Kadri and Reshad Nury, both of whom have produced several remarkable works. Yakub Kadri's *Father Light*, as a study of the inner life of the Bektashis, and Reshad Nury's *Wren*, the study of a young schoolmistress in the provinces, are extremely good.

To review the Republican era from a purely literary point of view would not take long. There are only a few new figures who deserve notice, but there is no definite school of literature outside the writers belonging to different old schools, especially to the Nationalist school. Yet one could dwell on the intellectual movement of the present age at some length, for it is rich in possibilities and aims. I shall discuss the culture and literature of the age in its two aspects or divisions.

I have already said that throughout the history of Ottoman thought two distinct classes of thinkers and writers were recognised. The first were those whose learning and teaching possessed an official, orthodox character, and who were called the 'Ulema-i-Rusum'. We will call them the official Ulema all through. They were the ones in the beginning of the Ottoman Empire who created the Ottoman ideology, and in a semi-theocractic manner defined the position of the individual in the state and his relations to his fellow-creatures. What their system was I illustrated in a diagram. Their aim throughout the ages was the stability of the system, therefore they insisted on keeping it within a rigid frame. It was the business of the poets to idealise the regime.

The second class of the learned or the artist we called those of the people, 'Khalq-Ulemasi'. Their writings and ideas were based on observation and on tendencies derived from the people or from a group of people.

The official Ulema lost their position and influence because of intellectual stagnation and through changes which came about in spite of them. In the age of decline the Tanzimat thinkers and writers held a position between the two classes of intellectuals, official and popular. They never became exactly official, for the Turkish State never wholly took the form they wanted. However, their influence was telling enough to justify our calling them the pioneers of all thought and literature in the new Turkey.

The Young Turkish regime, after 1908 really created the nucleus of the official Ulema—those who were to interpret and propagate the philosophy and the ideology of their regime. Keuk Alp Zia is the founder and the most important figure of the new 'Ulema-i-Rusum'.

Now we will study literature of the present regime and its thoughts in the productions of these two classes, the writers who are out to teach and to establish its ideology, whom we will call the official intelligentsia, and the writers outside it, whom we will call the independents.

The official intelligentsia naturally forms the majority; some belong to it through conviction and some because it is more profitable. The group among them who must be carefully studied are in the 'Kadro' movement.

'Kadro' is the name of a periodical. It means a frame or a military or administrative formation. If a man is dismissed from government service, we say, 'He is out of the Kadro'. The name is enough to give one a clear-cut idea of the writers who belong to it. They are out to put all the ideas and the ideology of the present regime in a rigid frame. And what they are putting within the frame is very much like what Keuk Alp Zia believed in, with certain modifications.

In politics Keuk Alp Zia had expressed the state-ideal in this verse, 'There is no Individual, but only Society, there are no Rights, but only Duty.' This meant the end of democracy, or a new democracy. It meant in practice the rule of a minority, and that was a single-party government. The 'Kadro' writers accept this principle.

'I am of Turkish race,' was the first principle of Keuk Alp Zia's credo. Race with him meant culture and the nation-consciousness which has come down to us in the Turkish tongue and what it has produced. Keuk Alp Zia specified the past culture. He was anti-Ottoman and an upholder of the Central Asiatic culture. So are the writers of the 'Kadro'. But as all that has been left from the pre-Ottoman culture of Central Asia does not satisfy the philosophy and the need of the age, the 'Kadro' writers set out to interpret history in a new way. They declare that the earliest human culture and civilisation was Turkish, the earliest human species the Turks. I will omit the discussion whether it is really so or not. But one can say that it is more than sufficient compensation to offer the civilisation of Ancient Greece, of the Hittites and Sumer-Accad to a generation whose nearer and historic past is being taken away.

So much for culture.

'My civilisation is Western' is the second principle of Keuk Alp Zia. The 'Kadro' writers accept this also, taking civilisation to mean the externals, the machinery and the procedure of all social and economic activity.

'I am Moslem by religion' was Keuk Alp Zia's third principle. Needless to say that he meant by Islam a reformed Islam, one which could be adapted to the necessities of the age. The new official 'Kadro' writers and others outside this group leave this part of the credo out. Religion and the state have been separated, they would say, religion is out of our domain. If you ask them why a secular state keeps the direction of religious affairs under its control, I do not know what they would say, but I guess that some would answer, 'If we let Islam organise itself in society without control, it might endanger the young secular state by engendering some new reactionary force.' Some perhaps really wish to leave its religion to the Islamic community, without allowing the state to interfere.

Now all present-day literature, whether it be novels or short stories or merely essays or articles, is animated by these principles. Education, press and literature all co-operate most efficiently in teaching them. They have a unique chance and possibility to overcome their greatest difficulty, that of fighting the effects of the Ottoman past, an opportunity such as neither Russia nor Fascist Italy nor Nazi Germany possess. And they have this because of the change of script.

In speaking about the earlier movement in favour of the Latin script, I had said that there were three objections to it: first, that of pan-Islamists, who feared the loss of Islamic unity, religious and political. In that the new regime no longer believes. The second objections came from the pan-Turanists, who insisted that we would lose our cultural unity with the Turks in Russia. In 1926, a representative congress of Turkish-speaking peoples at Baku accepted the Latin characters. Cultural unity with the Turks outside Turkey in the future lies, therefore, in the adoption of the Latin alphabet. The nationalist fear that we would be cut off from the Ottoman past does not count with the official Ulema. Therefore the Latin script could be easily adopted in 1928.

I have said in an earlier lecture, that of all the reforms that have been carried through by the new regime, two may have the greatest effect on Turkish life, the adoption of the Swiss Family Law, from the social point of view and the adoption of the Latin alphabet, from the cultural point of view.

The Latin script can be considered both advantageous or otherwise according to how one is disposed towards it. I will only repeat the arguments of both sides.

Those who are favourable to it hold that it unifies the Turks culturally with the West; it is easier to teach, and already great work has been done in the spread of literacy and mass education; it is the only way of escaping from the domination of Arabic and Persian culture; it is the only way of cutting adrift the coming generation from the burdensome Ottoman past. Those who are hostile to the measure urge that cultural unity with the West cannot be attained just by a change of script, but rather by a realisation of the common sources of human culture. The study and the acceptance of Latin and Greek classics as their own by the Ottomans in the fifteenth century might have united us culturally with the West, but now it is too late for us to attempt it. The spread of literacy is not an absolute end in itself, for an increase in the number of those who can merely read is not an increase in the number of educated people. It is not desirable for us to disown the Persian and Arabic influences in our culture; we have neither been Persianised nor Arabicised by them. We are Moslems, and ours is the common culture of all Islamic peoples. Lastly, it is by no means desirable to cut adrift the coming generations from the Ottoman past. Our real roots are in the Ottoman culture. Without them we will be second-hand Europeans.

Whether one favours the change of script or not, it is certain that there will be a profound change in the mind of the coming generations, the form of which is incalculable.

Another noteworthy attempt of the official writers is in the direction of purification of the language. Here also they are following the lines laid down by Keuk Alp Zia, who used to borrow words from dialects outside Anatolia, though he discontinued the practice in his later years. The effect of this has been a little confusing, and I doubt the possibility of its success. For a language is a living thing and grows in the consciousness of the people as they learn more and more, feel more and more and create words (which are nothing more than thought or image symbols) to express them.

This is a short and objective presentation of their really very remarkable activity of the official writers. Outside it there are two prominent figures whom I will discuss briefly.

The first is Nazim Hikmet, a young Communist poet. I have selected him, for he is a very powerful writer. In his open attack on religion he goes much further than Tewfik Fikret. He has been trained in Moscow, therefore his methods and his style have been affected by the new and militant Russian thought. But he has considerable originality and possesses that sacred gift which comes very near to what one may call genius. It would interest Indians to know that his best work is on India. It is a play called *Why Banerji Killed Himself*. He does not know India beyond what he was read or what he has learnt from Indian Communists in Russia. So the characters are really Turkish, with Indian names. He thus achieves the double purpose of attacking Western Imperialism and criticising things in this own country. Though he is not very different from the 'Kadro' writers in the spirit which scorns the old liberal tendencies, by temperament he is against them.

Here are a few lines in which he describes a gathering in Calcutta (now Kolkata).

'A crowd in the open, brother, oh, such a crowd. Like a forest in a hurricane it roared, the terrible crowd.

Workers from Calcutta, workers from Kashmir and sailors from Bombay—like sand brought from seventy-seven seas, there assembled human beings.

Naked children hung in bunches on branches, old women sat on door-steps, and if you plucked out a hair from your beard and threw it, it could not reach the ground, let alone a pin.

A crowd in the open, brother, a terrible crowd. Like billowy and black waters it got hold of me, oh brother, the crowd, the terrible crowd!"

He is very much against the fantasy and strangeness of the East as conceived by certain Western writers. Here are a few lines addressed to Pierre Loti.'

'Mystery, contentment, 'kismet,' caravanserai, fountains; a princess dancing on a silver tray, maharaja, padishah and a thousand years old shah; a woman with henna-ed nose, weaving with her toes, a green-bearded Imam chanting on a windy minaret: There never was or is or will ever be such as East, the East is the land on which naked serfs toil and die, the earth which belongs to everybody except to the man of the East!'

The most symptomatic poem of this young poet is called, *To be a Machine I Want*. It expresses the almost mystic passion of the young Communist world for a mechanised, materialised, soulless order. One understands why the Communist Russian peasant carries an ikon with the picture of a machine on it with the same fervour as he used to carry an ikon with the picture of a saint.

'Tirrum, tirrum, tirrum, trak, tiki, tak, to be a machine I want!

In my brain, flesh and bone the longings rise, every dynamo I long to ride. My tongue licks every copper wire and in my veins auto-cars race with locomotives.

Tirrum, tirrum, tirrum, tiki, tiki, trak, to be a machine I want!

I shall only happy be, the day I can set a turbine on my navel and double propellers on my tail.

Tirrum, tirrum, tirrum, tiki, tiki, trak, to be a machine I want!'

Besides the extreme left Communist writers whose representative is Nazim Hikmet, and the classical and official writers represented in the 'Kadro' movement, there is another remarkable figure of the present era in Turkey. His name is Zia Hilmi. He is a highly cultured young scholar whose thought has taken a singularly new direction. The Turkish intelligentsia within the last hundred years of Westernisation concentrated on the nineteenth century West, the West whose achievements have consisted in mechanising life and in utilising the scientific discoveries of the preceding three centuries. That is a West which is entirely materialistic. Zia Hilmi is the first Eastern youth, to my knowledge, who has gone beyond that. Again, the Westernised Turkish intelligentsia of the last two generations have gone for inspiration to the prehistoric Turkish past, leaping over the Ottoman and the Near Eastern, that is, the Seljuk. Zia Hilmi goes for inspiration to the thirteenth century Anatolian-Turkish past, the age of the Seljuks. If one were to connect Zia Hilmi with any trend of thought in the West today, he would claim kinship with what is called the New Humanism. But he is not an imitator, he thinks that the forces and thoughts necessary to build up his philosophy are to be found in the Near Eastern Turkish past.

His best work is called *Morals of Love*. It is a daring and very clearly worked out political Utopia. Though the influence of Plato is undeniable, the author is original enough to make of it a very noteworthy achievement. It is a work that deserves to be translated into the language of every country involved in the conflict of Eastern and Western ideas and ideals.

No record of the literature of a people would be complete without some study of its histrionic art. I shall, therefore, give a brief account of this also.

Dramatic art among the Turks begins with story-telling. The 'Meddah', or the artist who tells stories, impersonates the characters in the story. This was also common among the Arabs and the Persians. The stories told or acted have both an entertaining and a moral quality. The artists entertained the sultans as well as the people in the coffee-houses or in market-places and fairs.

Dr. Konush, a Hungarian orientalist, the pioneer in the study and collection of old Turkish stories says: 'If I, your obedient servant, the son of a Magyar, had not heard and preserved these stories 43 years ago, they would have been lost. Thank God they have reached my ears. I pass them on to you as a sacred gift.' Apart from the work of Dr. Konush, to whom the Turkish people should be very grateful, we get a great deal of scattered information about the personality of the story-tellers in the Turkish annals, printed or still in MS. Some of the stories they have told are to found in the

Istamboul Library. The best and most complete story found there is that of the *Lady of the Dagger*. It is about the life of an heir to money, a class that has always been an object of scorn. The story is full of dramatic effect.

Story-tellers have come down to our time. Some are of modern appearance, such as one sees on the European stage. But old or new, they are very able impersonators. It is a real treat to hear a good story-teller impersonate one character after another, a peasant, a slave-girl, a pasha, a donkey, a dog or a cat with equal facility. There is no special decor: with a handkerchief or a piece of cloth which becomes a veil, a turban or anything else, the story-teller creates the character he wishes. Throughout the performance there are veiled attacks on social or political personalities and reflections on events.

In connection with story-telling there grew theatrical companies, and they became a very distinct feature of life, specially in the seventeenth century, when there were twelve recorded companies of importance. They consisted at times of 200 players, and were provided with an orchestra a ballet, an acrobatic section, mimics, story-tellers and actors.

The most famous company was that of Akide. Its director and manager was called 'Eyub Pehlivan' (Eyub the Wrestler), who was a poet, a traveller, a musician and a man of great distinction and charm as well as humour. His dancers were famous throughout the seventeenth century. In his repertoire quite a number of plays are mentioned: *Garden and Gardening, Cat and Rat, Rat and Squirrel, Geese, Hencrows, Ducks Life Among the Street-dogs, Life Among the Camels, Opium-smokers, Tobacco-smokers*. Tobacco-smoking was at the moment a tragic as well as comic actuality. The practice has just been started in Turkey, and Murad IV, one of the most ruthless tyrants of Turkish history, persecuted smokers just as Nero persecuted the Christians. He would go about in the street incognito, smell chimneys or unearth smokers who had concealed themselves in cemeteries. Akide was past master in reproducing all situations and events in their most comic aspect.

These companies also gave us what is called the open theatre. It was half low comedy mixed with reviews and also masterly studies of the customs and life of the masses in Turkey. Women's parts in these shows were played by men.

In addition to these theatrical forms there was and is the 'Hayal' or the 'Karageuz'. Dr. Jacobi, in his *Geschichte des Schattentheaters*, published in 1925, tells us that the art came to the Turks through the Mongols, who had taken it from the Chinese. Turkish writers dispute this theory, and I believe rightly. For the likelier theory is that Ottoman Turks learnt the art from the Arabs and the Persians, or that it developed simultaneously in all the three nations in the Near East. With the Arabs there is no doubt that it had mystical and philosophical significance. Muhiuddin Arabi made use of it in the thirteenth century in Damascus to explain his mystical teachings. For him the World of Shadows was the symbol of the Created Universe, the curtain was the symbol of the Creator's powers to conceal or reveal Himself. In Egypt also the art was used for didactic purposes.

Among the Turks we find the art fully cultivated at Broussa in the fourteenth century. But the Turkish shadow-play had none of the religious quality of the Arabian. There were always veiled allusions made to the politics of the time, and suspicious rulers like Abdul Hamid had them carefully watched. The legend of the foundation of this art has a great social significance. During the building of the Great Mosque there were two workers who constantly talked and joked and made the others laugh and stop work. They were executed. It is evident that the said characters and the legend prove a kind of early rebellion among the workers. Karageuz, the principal character, is still considered a popular saint in Broussa. He represents the Turk in the street, with all his commonsense, realism and matchless humour. He is always making fun at the expense of the great. Haji Eyvat, his friend, is the impersonation of an officially-learned man and also somewhat of an opportunist, always interpreting life so as to suit the great of the land.

Up to the nineteenth century histrionic art continued to express itself in these primitive forms. Though simple they had both creativeness and the naturalistic trend which characterises the Turkish mind when it is free of alien influence. The modern theatre began with the Tanzimat. Its first well-known playwright was Namik Kemal. A theatre was built at Gedik Pasha and a company, led by a very talented Armenian, Gulli Agop, began to give Namik Kemal's plays and other translated ones. The theatre became all of a sudden the instrument for the teaching of new ideas. It evoked tremendous enthusiasm. But the plays, though useful from a propagandist point of view, lacked the originality and the genuine art of the simpler popular theatre. Abdul Hamid naturally put an end to the utilitarian and political significance of the drama. Translated stuff continued to acted with more or less ability. In the early stage, specially when translated stuff was being produced, the actors and actresses were Armenian. Though some of them were undeniably good artistes, the drawback was their Turkish, for a people demands perfection in the language of its stage and its tribune. However, as the appearance of Turkish women on the stage was an inconceivable thing, the theatres continued to employ Armenian actresses.

Another centre of the theatre in Turkey was Broussa. A playhouse was established there by Ahmet Vefik Pasha, one of the governors, who was also one of the outstanding literary figures of Tanzimat period. His adaptation and translation of Moliere into Turkish is the best I know of in any language. His taste was more for the classical, but the theatre he founded became a purely Turkish centre of the histrionic art. The Turks have produced very remarkable Molierian actors, but the adaptations have very little of the original left in them. Vefik Pasha put on the Turkish stage really Turkish versions of clerical hypocrisy and social degeneration in its most realistic and devastating form.

Apart from these the open theatre, which also took cover during Abdul Hamid's rule, produced a few really great actors. But the moment any of them became a popular favourite, Abdul Hamid attached him to the palace, which was a way of removing the artist from the public eye.

In 1909 the Young Turks engaged Antoine, the famous French regisseur, to establish a conservatoire and a new theatre. With him the Turkish Conservatoire, under the name of 'Dar-il-Bedayi', came into existence and began to flourish. It also produced pretty good actors and writers took to representing actual Turkish life on the stage. The dramas staged up to the present time have been generally comedies, partly because Turkish histrionic talent is more effective in the comedy. After 1923, two events wrought a fundamental change in the theatre. First, Turkish women began to adopt the state as a profession and second, the theatre found in Ertogrul Muhsin a man with high ideals and an excellent artist and manager. Apart from a great natural talent for acting, he has studied his art in Paris, Germany and finally in Russia under Meyerhold and Stanislavski. In Russia he was even entrusted with the direction of a film. The theatre where Muhsin is the regisseur can now produce Western as well as Eastern classics very ably, and Shakespearian dramas are better produced there than in many other non-English countries. Very original comedies, written by a blind old man who specialises in the Ottoman period, are among the star features. Now not only Istamboul, which is the intellectual centre of Turkey, but also the provinces have become intensely interested in the drama, and the national theatre during certain months tours Symrna, Trebizond and other provinces, repeating its repertoire.

This is a brief review of the history of the Turkish theatre. In it also one sees the conflict of East and West as in politics and literature. But fortunately in this sphere the native soul has not been exterminated. Though the Turks now study the technique of the Western theatre–which they should—their dramatic art is still struggling to express itself in its own way.

7
Turkish Women

In Turkey we have a saying, 'Women are all one nation'. Experience has taught me to believe in the wisdom of this saying. Though men may belong to differentiated groups called races and nations, the female of the human species remains the same. A man from Turkey may not be able to understand Indian men, a woman from Turkey will understand Indian women, and vice versa. The fundamental problems which affect a woman's life and her duty to society have always been the same all over the world. The evolution of women in the earliest ages, according to the data available at present, has common characteristics, irrespective of race and climate. All over the world the female appears invariably as the pioneer who has built up human society as distinct from animal existence. There was a mother thousands of years before the father was recognised as having anything to do with the propagation or the care of the offspring. It was the mother who started agriculture and industry in their most primitive aspects, in order to feed and to clothe her young. She also created the family as the unit of human society. The rest has evolved around that. The woman must have had the time of her life endeavouring to induce man to settle down and tie himself to the family, for man is individualistic, militant, egotistic, which is as it should be, for these characteristics were evidently also essential to bring civilisation into being.

Since Nature appointed the mother to create the family, and since aggregations of families have inevitably grown into nations, Nature also endowed woman with two seemingly incompatible characteristics, extreme conservatism and extreme revolutionism. Customs, traditions, language, thought and literature evolve and accumulate around the family or group of families. Woman is conservative as long as those values are the ones which keep the given family or the group alive. But a small human unit is like a cell. In order to live it has to break, to multiply and to form larger and more complex units. Because of this necessity women also uphold great revolutions and great religions which supply the aging, the stagnating human society with new forces, spiritual or material. Christianity had women adherents. Islam's first recruit was a woman, so was the first martyr. There were a great many women who worked and died for the French and the Russian revolutions. They are rarely in the forefront in such upheavals, and strange to say the new forces called into play do not necessarily add to women's happiness, but they, or at least a considerable part of them, will stand by and suffer for anything that adds new life to a tired old society on the verge of decline. All these things I say are naturally about the average men and women. For there are also geniuses, mostly men, who are difficult to classify, and who are not always an unmixed blessing to human society. I am dealing with the average.

I believe that woman is the organic part of society. She is Nature's means of producing life and preventing its stagnation. Man is the abstract, the inorganic force. He imagines the new shapes, he sets out to conquer Nature and woman. He wants to stamp civilisation with his own personality. It has been so in the past ages. For the moment we will leave the future alone and review the part of man and woman in the past and present civilisations only.

Because civilisations in their more advanced forms have been more man-made then woman-made, the position of woman has differed according to the values each civilisation has emphasised. When the objective of a great civilisation has been great art, great philosophy, in short, beauty and thought, woman's position in that society has not been seriously considered. Such a society was that of Athens in ancient Greece.

In Athens the positions of women, or rather of the respectable women, was decidedly inferior. There were three classes of women, the slaves, whose status was like that of men-slaves; the citizen women, who were the only ones eligible for marriage, and whose children alone were considered legitimate and worthy of citizenship. They had no public rights, and they were confined to their upper apartments, where they occupied themselves with their household affairs. Their lack of education as well as the prevailing custom debarred them from being the companions of their highly-cultivated husbands; they left next to no trace in Athenian history. The third class were the hetairae, or the companion women. They had no marriage rights, but they had every public right. They were often women of great culture and education, and exercised great influence on the intellectual and artistic life of the city. Aspasia was a prominent figure in the age of Pericles, the golden age of Greece; Socrates mentions Diotima as his inspirer and teacher. They were all alien women and of the hetaira class.

Now there is no doubt that this sort of society was favourable to the breeding of geniuses. But was it a lasting or valuable society from a social point of view? Not by any means. The position of the companion women was the cause of very loose morals and promoted an official prostitution, and life in general at Athens was very unstable. To the student of old Athens two questions at once occur. Would it not have been better to educate the respectable women and make them the companions of their husbands? Did not this peculiar arrangement which led to loose morals hasten the downfall of Athens?

Some such questions must have arisen in Plato's mind when he studied Athenian society, and also another Grecian civilisation, which was based on different principles. For in his ideal state he advocated equality of the sexes, though their tasks may differ from each other.

The civilisation which struck Plato evidently as sound than the Athenian was the Spartan. It emphasised health, strength and stability rather than great art and great philosophy. In such a society each individual must be carefully trained, especially the mothers. They must be fully developed physically to bear healthy children; they must be trained and educated in order to the able to handle them; above all they must be morally elevated, to create character and morality in their offspring. Spartan society had a high standard of moral and physical virtue; each citizen, as the unit of such a society, had to be harmoniously developed in body and mind. Every strong nation or society which has this ideal before it invariably devoted much care and thought to the training of its women.

The Romans took a healthy and well-balanced view about women's position in society, dividing the basic social duties rationally between men and women. Men worked outside and women mostly at home, but they were equals and companions. The Roman matron was a superior being in character and mind, and has left a definite impress on Roman history. But though in practice there was equality between men and women, it was not so in the laws. Women were under the guardianship of their fathers or their husbands to the end of their lives, that is to say, in theory they were perpetual minors. When the early and robust ideal of Roman society began to lose its hold, husbands took advantage of their superior rights. They repudiated their wives with little reason, or ill-treated them. Women in their turn began to revolt. We have husband-poisonings on a large scale at first. Then, towards the end of the Republic, Livy, the historian, records feminist risings very much like the risings of militant suffragettes from 1906 to 1913. Towards the end the Republic was obliged to give women equal rights in marriage and in property, and marriage took the contractual form so much favoured by certain groups of feminists.

Because Rome also was out to create a healthy and enduring society, it is there that one sees very reasonable theories in regard to women's position in society. These theories came from a Stoic philosopher, Musonius Rufus by name. He said that women should have equal education and equal changes with men. As women and men were not alike, the tasks they undertook would and should differ, but no tasks should be exclusive, for there would always be a few men fitted for the lighter and a few women fitted for the harder. In reference to morals he demanded a single standard, a high and pure one, both for men and women. In marriage he advocated equality and brought marital relations to a standard of companionship and joint responsibility.

The Christianity of Christ made no difference between men and women. Its strong point in the early stages was the sacred character, the indissolubility of marriage, and its insistence on monogamy added great strength to Western society. But in the Middle Ages, when the Roman Church organised a new society according to the teachings of St. Paul and the Church Fathers, the position of women fell very low. Sex and marriage were declared evil things; the centre of society shifted from the home to the monastery. Women who lived as nuns and died as martyrs were respected, but the rest were the creatures of the devil. They were responsible for the original sin and the fall of man, and an oecumenical council even denied them a soul.

In the sixth century came Islam, with a very different attitude towards women. The supreme aim of Islam being social justice, it could not leave half of society out of consideration. In pre-Islamic Arabia the position of women was degraded to that of cattle. A man could take as many wives as he wished, he could kill them, even bury his infant daughters alive. Islam instituted marriage, limited the number of wives and in case of divorce bound the husband to pay alimony. It inculcated a chivalrous attitude towards women in general and meted out equal punishment in cases of immorality. But its greatest significance for the modern world is that it is the first system which accords property and economic rights to women and makes them independent of the guardianship of their men. 'Men shall have the benefit of what they earn and women shall have the benefit of what they earn and women shall have the benefit of what they earn,' says the Qur'an (Sura IV, verse 32). I believe this verse contains the two greatest and most enduring truths without which no decent society can exist. It recognises woman as a free human being, responsible for what she does—more than twelve centuries before the West recognised the principle. The second significance of this verse goes far beyond women's rights and far beyond the Islamic world. It establishes a principle of universal validity, which must and shall be the foundation-stone of the future human society. One can receive the benefit only of what one earns: that and only that. There can be no toiling and starving masses with individuals receiving phenomenal wages. Put in a nutshell this verse means, 'You shall not exploit your fellow creatures, by they men or women.'

Nevertheless Islamic society adopted two customs which are regarded by the civilised world in general and by modern Moslems in particular as the causes of its decline, the seclusion of women and polygamy.

We do not find seclusion of women among the first Moslems. If one studies the life of the Prophet, one sees that from the very beginning he fought against the uncivilised habits of the Arabia of his days, where men and women went about nearly naked. Decency was one of his great passions. His nurse tells the story that as a baby he cried whenever he was undressed. Now, we know that there are two distinctly human characteristics which create civilised society, decency and disgust—disgust for material dirt and insensateness, disgust for moral filth and unseemliness. Both these characteristics of civilised life Mohammed tried to develop in the men of his age. It is not by mere chance that in Islam good and evil are expressed as 'Beauty' and 'Ugliness' ('Husn' and 'Kubah').

The Qur'an (Sura XXIV, verse 31) commands women to pay due regard to their dress, enjoining them to wear veils that will cover the sides of their head, their bosom and their ornaments; there is no order to cover their faces, still less are they expected to shut themselves up and abstain from social activities. The Prophet's own wife was one of the most remarkable women, with a great social reputation. In this commandment we see two things, first, that women should be decently dressed, even if they desire to make themselves beautiful, and secondly, what is more significant, they are asked not to use their beauty and sex to exploit their fellow creatures. This is just what a modern feminist or any healthy society aims at. With this very reasonable beginning, we see in the early days of Islam a host of women working as teachers, poets and preachers, some even enlisting as soldiers. But when Moslems came into contact with old and socially decadent civilisations, their ideas underwent a change. Women were not only veiled; they were shut up and debarred from social service. This seclusion did immense harm to Islamic society. Women gradually lost their health, they were not carefully educated and the perverted belief that women are the property of men also crept in.

Polygamy existed in pre-Islamic Arabia. Islam tolerated it in a restricted form. 'Take three and four, but if you fear that you will not do justice between them, then marry only one,' (Sura IV, verse 3). This is the condition under which polygamy is permitted by the Qur'an. The four Imams of the Faith, who interpreted and codified the law in the ninth century, could very well have construed this verse on polygamy differently; they could have even made polygamy a penal offence. They did not. Both seclusion and polygamy continued as institutions. The former cannot be defended from any point of view. It meant the gradual deterioration of half of the Islamic world. The second, that is, polygamy, has something to be said in its favour. It restricted prostitution, it legalised the children of the second life. But it also undermined the unity, the strength of the Moslem family. While women in the Christian world suffered from lack of economic equality the women of the Moslem East never became full partners of their husbands in that basic unit of human society, the family.

In the West, chivalry first raised the status of women. The Renaissance restored the family to its rightful position. The French Revolution went further and advocated equal rights for women. Condorcet, the French philosopher, disapproved of disabling half of the human race from taking part in the formation of the laws. 'The rights of men,' he said, 'result solely from the fact that they are sensible beings, susceptible of acquiring moral ideas and reasoning on these ideas.' Olympe de Gouge said in her declaration of the Rights of Women, 'The sovereignty of a nation is nothing but the reunion of its men and women.' And again, 'As a woman has the right to mount the scaffold, she should also have the right to the tribune.'

A world-wide movement in favour of women's rights began after 1848. Finland gave full parliamentary suffrage to its women in 1906, Iceland in 1907, Denmark and Norway in 1910 and 1915. These countries are considered the most civilised from a social point of view all over the world.

Space and the fear of becoming tedious forbid my dwelling on the historical development of feminism in the West. But in order to understand the agitation and the changes demanded in the East, I will briefly go over the important phases of Western feminism.

The first phase was democratic. It was an outcome of the French Revolution. Its aims were educational, social and political. Its finest vindication is to be found in the masterpiece of John Stuart Mill, *The Subjection of Women*. The movement began and developed through its striving for equal educational facilities. When this object had been nearly attained, women took up the social aspect. They not only obtained better marriage rights, a thing which concerns primarily their own sex, they also became very useful organisers and efficient workers in the cause of social uplift. Thanks to women, social welfare has become a scientific process in the West. America, England, France and especially Belgium have been training women to raise the social status of the more unfortunate section of their society. Women, children, the sick and the criminal have become objects of study for the women of the West, and they are guided towards a healthier and fuller life. The last phase of the emancipation of women is the political. I cannot say they have made any useful contribution to political life, and they may not in the future. Democracies are themselves at the cross-roads.

The second phase of women's emancipation in the West is the industrial and the economic. While the democratic aspirations of women involved a struggle of one sex against another, here it was that of men and women as a class against each other. The mechanical progress and the industrialisation which changed the constitution of Western society towards the middle of the nineteenth century, also shifted the centre of social gravity from the home to the factory. The home was no longer the unit of the social organism. The important part of the question which concerns women in the world of labour is that in the highly industrialised countries it is impossible to send them back to the home. America is perhaps the most typical example of this contingency, for there women have very little they can do at home. In the earlier stages of human life woman was saved from parasitism by her work at home. Now even the bringing up of the child has gone into the hands of the expert and the kindergarten teacher. Therefore, if women remained at home they would be nothing more than parasites. Half of mankind, especially mothers, turning parasite would mean a degeneration of the human species which cannot be suffered. This new problem in the West has become very complicated and might have incalculable effects if industrialisation and mechanisation continue to be as swift and all-pervading as at present. Fortunately, the East is not facing that sort of a dilemma. So we shall leave it at that, and turn to the question of Turkish women and try to find out the result of the conflict of West and East in their life.

It is neither fair not scientifically correct to generalise, but from all the data available at the present we are obliged to classify Turkish society with the Spartan type rather than with the Athenian. From the literature as well as from the political characteristics of the Turks, the reader might have gathered that they emphasise social rather than individual values. Their aim was to build a healthy, strong and lasting society rather than a highly intellectual or artistic one. Such a society naturally demands an equal share of service and labour from its women.

Fortunately for us, we can study the simplest form of Turkish society in the Turkey of today. There are tribes still in a nomadic state who must have entered the Near East before or after the Ottoman Turks. We call a large portion of them the 'Yuruks'. They preserve their early customs and they are as purely Turkish as it is possible to be. Unlike the city-dwellers and the peasantry, they have not intermarried. The language and what belongs to the language also has remained pure. I was told by a Russian Turkologist in New York that there are words in their vocabulary which are found in the Orkhon inscriptions. They are also Moslem, though mostly Shiites. The position of women among them is such that in certain aspects it would appeal greatly to Western feminists. There is absolute equality; work is shared; though women have veils over their heads their faces are open. For beauty they can beat anything I have seen so far. Yet they associate with men freely within and outside their tribes and remain strictly faithful to the high moral code of their tribe. Marriage is contracted between the young without any interference of the parents. The youth of both sexes work together and play together. When they are once married there is no divorce and I have not come across any case of polygamy. Divorce is only allowed in case of adultery, which is extremely rare, and both parties are punished very severely and equally. An equal standard of morality applies to both men and women.

From this we may rightly deduce that the early Ottomans, who also came as a handful of nomadic people, led more or less the same sort of life. Some of the earliest tribes mentioned in connection with the early Ottomans, such as Black Goat, Black Mutton, White Goat and White Mutton still exist, though they are half or wholly settled. They also preserve a great many of their early customs. The woman is the manly type. That is, her virtues are those of strength of character and straightforwardness. Women are praised by the masses in Turkey generally with some such remark, 'She is like a man.' No one says, 'She is very beautiful.' In the consciousness of the race the moral virtues have retained their higher place for men as well as for women.

The Ottoman Turks first built their state in Broussa. In the early stages of that simple but very lovely and lovable civilisation and culture one sees that they adhered faithfully to their early family virtues. Ibn Batuta, the Arab traveller of the fourteenth century, visited Broussa. There he went to call on the Sultan, who was not at home. The Sultan's wife received him and discussed state affairs with him. Equality, freedom and simplicity were virtues that adorned the palace as well as the hut. Ibn Batuta complains of the freedom of Turkish women, especially in the Crimea, where he saw them going about in the streets, buying and selling. It evidently shocked him, for that section of Moslem society to which he belonged had different views on women and different customs.

The Ottoman Turks who began their civilisation and state on such simple and admirable lines began to alter gradually. There were first intermarriages of Sultans and Beys and I suppose of the people too with women of other races. But this by itself did not affect the state of affairs much, for the women were assimilated. But there were other causes, such as conquest and intimate contact with other civilisations, specially with Byzantine manners and customs, which led to profound changes.

After the conquest of Istamboul, Turkish society split definitely into two classes. The Sultan and the high officials modelled their households on the Byzantine idea of seclusion, the harem and the eunuch guards. Not only did polygamy increase, but the habit of keeping concubines, which is an even more pernicious custom, became prevalent. The Sultans had so far married alien princesses; now they married only slaves. Their women existed for their pleasure and not for their society.

The middle and the lower classes, however, retained some of their old customs. Though veiled, their women went about freely, but intercourse with men outside the family circle was, with very few exceptions, prohibited. Though there was slavery, concubinage was not frequent, nor was polygamy. Turkish women of the middle class, if their husbands took another woman as wife, made life impossible for the men. At times even the two women combined to punish the husband. All that meant great unhappiness and was very bad for the children.

One class of women throughout all conditions of society retained their privileges. They were the mothers. Though love and honour for the mother is a universal feeling, with the Turks the instinct was and is very deep-rooted. It was not always very comfortable for the daughters-in-law, but before the old lady of the house passed away there was no possibility of escape from her iron rule.

There is a period in Ottoman history, roughly between the seventeenth and eighteenth centuries, which we call '*Women's Sultanate*'. And it coincides with the worst era of decline. The Sultan's harem was not, as is usually believed, a pell-mell herding of ignorant women. It was extremely well-organised and its members received an education according to their capacity. But women living only in their own society, cut off from the outside world, become morbid if not actually hysteric. When Soleymen the Magnificent's wife, Hurrem Sultan, managed to create the 'cage system' for the princes of the royal family, she condemned the future rulers to a very special, morbid and sex-conscious society. The Sultans became mere toys in the hands of the palace women.

Though there have been some intelligent and able women who have managed to do good, still the interference of the harem in politics, especially under such conditions, was a great evil. The worst of it was that the Valideh Sultan (dowager Sultana) automatically enjoyed political authority. Mothers always shared the power of their sons to some degree, but the dowager Sultana acted on her own initiative. The unwritten law of the realm gave her that right. But the wives and royal concubines had no such rights. They worked through the Sultan, there was no end of intrigue, and corruption raged as it had never raged before. Offices were sold and bought through these fair ladies; for their whims the treasury was plundered, the people of the bazaars robbed of their jewels or silks at all times of the day and night. On top of these wives there were also women story-tellers or entertainers who entered the palace and joined in the intrigues. 'The Sable Period', eight years of wickedness, owes its name to the imagination of one of these women. Sultan Ibrahim, a monster of cruelty and madness and immorality, was told in a story that some ancient king had his palace walls lined with sables. He at once ordered the provincial governors and the well-to-do the supply him with sables. He would build such a palace for a favourite.

Though the political domination of the place women was disastrous, women in general exercised a very beneficent influence in promoting public welfare and education even under such adverse conditions. That not a few of the architectural glories of Turkey were erected in memory of some mother and wife goes without saying. What is more important is that they themselves were great builders of mosques, inns, fountains, bridges and other foundations of public utility. In or out of the palace, partly through religious feeling and partly because it was the custom, a woman did almost always devote her means to some good work. The majority of public buildings were built and endowed by women. One who goes through the archives of the 'Evkaff' will be profoundly impressed by their spirit of service, their thoughtfulners and their generosity. Health was one of their supreme cares. Most if not all the hospitals have been built by women and very wisely and richly endowed. Among the most important and best hospitals left over are the 'Gureba', a huge hospital for the poor, and 'Nisa', another very large hospital for women. Thanks to the endowments both are very up-to-date and extremely useful institutions.

The care of the insane, which is considered one of the signs of higher civilisation, reached a remarkably high level in Turkey owing to the public spirit of women. When, in the seventeenth century, Europe was treating its insane by putting them into straitjackets, Turkey could boast of a hospital in Magnissa where the insane were looked after very kindly and music used for their cure.

At least one woman in the seventeenth century was intensely interested in prisons. It was Kussem Sultan, the mother of Ibrahim. She used to visit prisons yearly and buy the freedom of those imprisoned for inability to pay their debts. As she had a personal interview with the head of the prison and studied the log-books, it must have had beneficial effect on the treatment of the prisoners. Nor was her charity restricted to prisons. Every year she had twelve young girls and twelve young boys taught some trade and found them work. Every year twelve marriages took place in Istamboul between her protegees and adopted children.

'Imarets', or Soup-kitchens, were another institution women endowed on a large scale. No one need have starved in those days; and yet this kind of philanthropy did not lead to pauperism in the earlier days, for it was considered contrary to human dignity to accept alms when one could work. I think it of supreme importance to establish such 'imarets' in countries where famine or unemployment prevails, but to run them on more scientific methods.

Education was the sphere of our social service in which women displayed the most passionate concern. Most of the higher schools in Turkey have been founded by women and richly donated. Primary schools attached to mosques were also mostly of women's creation. Those who could not afford to open schools invariably undertook to educate some of the poor children of their quarter or street. I have gone over some of the most interesting 'Vakfnamehs', or trust-deeds, of these institutions founded by women. They show that it was not only money that was devoted to the purpose but intelligence, forethought and careful study of educational requirements. Instructions are given regarding cleanliness and the care of the children, even the diet had been thought out, but the best feature is the insistence on giving children the opportunity to play in the open air. Quite a number of the deeds have a separate endowment fund for the purpose, and contain clauses which make it incumbent on the teacher to take the children to the country regularly.

Apart from these institutions there were also private schools for body and girls conducted by women teachers. They existed even thirty years back and they were better managed than the mosque schools. The education of the women of fifty or sixty years ago was due to these schools, and judging from the number of women poets and writers throughout Ottoman Turkish history, it would be correct to say that the well-to-do educated their daughters carefully in their own old-fashioned way. During the age of decline the only defect in these institutions was their inability to take into consideration the change in the times and adjust themselves to the new thought which had come to the Western world.

It might be said generally of Turkish women that they were very self-willed and both the government and their menfolk found them hard to handle. In the early eighteenth century there were several royal decrees regulating women's dresses. One understands that as late as the early nineteenth century the bulk of women outside the palace were not veiled as their menfolk or the Sultan wished them to be. Dress regulations never could be imposed on them. Abdul Hamid himself would issue a royal 'Irade' or ordinance every Ramazan and the police got busy in the streets cutting the dresses of the women who were not attired according to regulations. But the enforcement of the 'Irade' was never attempted for more than three days.

Selim the Third, the great reformer, was also the first feminist. He had a remarkable sister, Hadije Sultan, who evidently tried to awaken women and make them aware of the progress the world had made. The women of the palace were won over to the ideas of reform. But work in this field really began with the Tanzimat. Namik Kemal particularly and his school generally advocated with their usual passion and indignation the education and social emancipation of women. Although the school was undoubtedly influenced by Condorcet and the French writers, they regarded the subject from an Islamic point of view. They argued that Islam itself required all its followers to be well-educated. So far the old classic literature had tabooed all reference to women. The Tanzimat took them up seriously. In the tragedies of Abdul Hak Hamid especially, Islamic women are given a most important part. His saying that 'The measure of a people's civilisation is the standard of their women,' is the motto of the Women's Training College now.

About 1860 the state opened a normal school to train women as teachers and founded primary schools for girls.

In the principal provincial cities there were such schools. Women teachers became state officials. These schools were attended mostly by the children of the masses and the teachers were also recruited from the poorer classes, for unfortunately the women of the richer class were still strictly confined to their home duties. Foreign schools also multiplied and in the later part of the nineteenth century the foreign governess, especially the English governess, became an institution. There was a deeply-rooted idea in Turkey that the English women was serious and manly and must therefore be the model for the modern Turkish woman.

In Abdul Hamid's time there was a remarkable group of women writers who published a weekly paper, *The World of Women*, which did very useful work, for it had a large circulation among both sexes. Its contributors and editorial staff were all women. Women writers were no longer mere poets singing of love, of nightingales and nature; they studied deeply the social and educational questions which affected their lives.

Women got their real chance in 1908. The Young Turkish or the Constitutional Revolution brought forward men who meant business. Their political and social creed laid strong emphasis on education, and especially in women's education they accomplished something very memorable and great. The very atmosphere became freer for women and it was fully realised that a new Turkey could never be created without their collaboration. Women themselves began in the earliest days to create organisations. Their first club, the 'Taali Nisvan', invited men of different professions to deliver lectures for women. They also created a small centre for teaching women to look after children. Quite a number of social organisations was started all over Istamboul, the most useful being the joint organisation of men and women teachers, who opened night or day schools to teach the adult population to read and write. Education became the motto of women and for the first time women of the richer classes also threw themselves into the work. When the Balkan war broke out and tragedy followed tragedy, women did their full share of duty of organising protest meetings, nursing, establishing centres where the orphans and the widows of the Balkan refugees could learn some craft and thereby earn their bread. I personally believe that the nursing of common soldiers by Turkish women served more than anything else to educate the masses in the new outlook about women.

On the other hand the state took a very energetic step. It modernised the entire educational system of Turkey and equalised educational rights. The normal schools were multiplied and conducted on better and modern lines; women's colleges sprang up all over the country. The finest building of the period is the Women's Training College in Istamboul. I can say with some degree of certitude that it is as good as any one could find elsewhere. They Young Turkish regime began also to send woman students to European universities and colleges; in 1916 the Istamboul University opened its doors to women. In 1921 there were two lady doctors practising.

The pressure of the Great War urged women forward to many an indispensable service and sacrifice. Turkey's manhood was on the frontiers. The country was nearly blockaded. From end to end the only producers were women. They army had to create women's battalions to do the work behind the lines. The needs of the army, its food and clothing, were supplied entirely by women. Further, the governmental departments had to recruit employees from among women. By 1916 women had really reached a stage in education and experience when they could take considerable part in the work administration.

Perhaps more remarkable than the education of women in principal cities and the labour of the agricultural regions was the activity of the women of smaller towns. The care of the family had fallen entirely on their shoulders. They became the intermediaries, travelling all over the country, buying and selling and carrying on the entire small trading for the sake of keeping alive their children. Without the activity and the enormous service of women, Turkey would have collapsed internally during the Great War.

In acquiring their new position and learning to fulfil their new duties women were helped enormously the nationalist institutions which we called 'Turk Ojagi' (Turkish Hearths). They were founded by the Turkish intelligentsia and the students of all shades of political opinion, and they enabled men and women to co-operate in order that they may better understand the needs of the nation and the conditions of progress.

The activities of the Ojaks would take a chapter by itself. I shall leave them alone. But the important thing about them is that they gave a national as well as a religious sanction to women's equality in educational and social matter. The Tanzimat had given a religions sanction, but it had been limited. Keuk Alp Zia, the pan-Turanist sociologist now proved in a large number of works that in their pre-Islamic stage also the Turks gave equal rights to women, and that only had made them great and enduring as a race. Owing to his activity and his influence both as a writer and as a member of the central Young Turkish Council, he managed to have the new family law promulgated in 1916. It did not do away with the old regulations, but it gave men and women the right to choose between the two forms. The new law was also based on Islamic principles, at least in the spirit if not in the letter. In Islam marriage is based on mutual consent; therefore the new regulation created a kind of contractual marriage. A woman could demand the right to divorce or prevent polygamy or make any other condition she liked.

This new regulation was not regarded with favour by the majority of women or men, although quite a number made use of it. What Turkish women wanted was not easy divorce, but a firmer and more indissoluble marriage. They did not look at marriage from a selfish, individualistic point of view, but as the organic bond of society. What they wanted was to abolish polygamy and to take away the right of divorce from the individual and give it to society, that is, to the court of law.

Such was the situation of Turkish women in 1918, when the Armistice was signed. The most salient feature of the gradual emancipation of Turkish women and their evolution as useful and beneficial social units, features in which it differs from Western feminism in its democratic aspect, are, first, that it was not the revolt of one sex against the other's domination. It was a part, and an integral part of Turkish reform and accepted as such by all progressive parties in Turkey. In whatever else they might have disagreed, they all believed in that. Secondly, as against other reforms, the conflict of East and West has in this one played only a minor part. It was considered a natural revival of the best, both in Islam and in the racial culture and tradition of the Turks. This, I believe, gave it its greatest force. There is only one point which brings the service of Turkish women in the economic field into line with universal conditions. Their education and present social position are due to deliberate work and effort, but the wide scope of their activities from an economic point of view is the outcome of the present world situation, mostly created after the Great War.

The national calamity, which reached its apogee in the foreign occupation in 1918, made everyone in Turkey realise what a country really meant to its women. They were struck and bereaved to an unimaginable degree. Beginning with the Balkan wars, they had slaved for their country and sacrificed their best and dearest, and it all looked as if their supreme sacrifice had been in vain. Therefore if any human beings at the time were really exhausted and drained of all life and energy, it was the Turkish women. But one saw at the same time that a country was a big home for its women—their collective home. For its honour as well as for its security and well being they felt themselves responsible to the last.

In innumerable private meetings of political organisations, young women in black with their note-books on their knees sat discussing with men the ways and means to deliver the country from its stupendous adversity. In public protest meetings of thousands and thousands women also predominated; not only the young and the educated, but the old, those who had looked on the change in the life of women as something absurd. In villages they gathered in the evenings around fires, knitting and talking. No man can want peace as passionately as a woman. For order and peace is a necessity for the happiness of the home and the little ones. But this time there would be neither home nor country without a last and supreme struggle. And they threw themselves into that supreme struggle. It caused us no wonder or even surprise to hear that women in the Smyrna mountains or in Cilicia were actually fighting or helping their soldiers.

When the government of Angora was established and the irregular forces incorporated in the regular army, women ceased to be active fighters. But still nothing could be accomplished without them. In every city and town women's associations of 'Defence of National Rights' were organised to help the Red Crescent and other associations. But the most impressive and perhaps the most essential part of service was rendered by the peasant women. Once more they had to sow and reap and produce all the means of livelihood all alone. Once more one saw them bare-footed, clad in rags, marching from one end of the country to the other carrying ammunition on their backs or leading ox-carts. Some of this service was obligatory, but there was also a host of volunteers. I remember a transport unit composed entirely of women, consisting of eleven ox-carts and eleven women. Their leader was Sergeant Fatima, an old woman of about seventy, six feet tall and straight-backed, with a face as strong as a rock. She had come with all the rest, holding her dumb and blind grandson by the hand. One of the drivers was in the family way. They worked in silence and dignity, leading their carts not only through mud and mire but also up to the firing line.

However falling and brave the men, no country can preserve its independence under such conditions as of the Turkish lands in 1918, unless its women are attached to the values which create a state and a country. I met an old woman in a Smyrna town, or rather on the rests and ruins of a town, who had emigrated five times since the Balkan war because she did not want to die under a foreign flag. What is there in a red piece of cloth with a crescent on it ? It is the symbol which matters and the symbol meant more than life. I will not multiply instances of women's sacrifice in those days. They are beyond number. Fikret says that 'a country rises only on the shoulders of the brave,' and New Turkey rose on the shoulders of its brave children, men and women. But there is one thing I must say in regard to the women. Great as the material part of their service was, the moral part of it was still greater. For once they had thrown themselves into the struggle, I never saw a woman lose heart. That had an incalculable value in such a struggle as we went through.

The Republic started its reforms after the Lausanne Conference. The scope of women's education was widened. If there were only three Turkish women doctors in 1921, there are something like fifty now. There is a considerable number of women working as assistants in hospitals all over the country and as officials in the hygiene department. The number of women with University qualifications, both Turkish and foreign, has increased, the University has several women as assistant professors. All the public departments employ women on a considerable scale. They are taking great interest in the study of law, in the provinces there are even woman judges, and some important positions in the police department are occupied by women. Everyone takes all these things as a natural consequence of the changes which have been going on very slowly since the Tanzimat period and a little more swiftly since 1908.

Two important measures have been passed in regard to women in society under the Republican regime. A new civil code has been promulgated which abolishes polygamy, equalises inheritance and entrusts the right of divorce to a court. This is a copy of the Swiss Civil Code. Secondly, women have been given the municipal vote and are eligible to the councils. There are in important provincial towns woman members at the moment. This perhaps is more important than the political vote, for municipalities are after all the domestic sections of the city, and the city is a big home. Its care, hygienic, aesthetic and general would be best understood by women. Whether they will have the legislative vote in a near or far future does not matter so much.[1]

8

Review and Future Outlook

We have traced the conflict of East and West in Turkey in the last seven lectures. At the moment the West seems triumphant on the surface. But the East is still there all the same in the soul of the Turk as an undercurrent, and its force is undeniable. It has been so whipped that only the finest and purest essence of it is left. When this Eastern element in the Turkish soul develops freely, the future blend of East and West in the Near East might present a model solution for turning what has so far been a conflict into co-operation.

Let us now in conclusion review this conflict from the original standpoint, the emphasis on matter (or the seen) and the emphasis on the spirit (or the unseen), which are the distinctive features of the Western and the Eastern mind.

My simple definition of West and East has evoked considerable written and spoken criticism. Some have thought me unjust to the West because of my assertion that the dominant characteristic of Western civilisation is materialism. They have replied by giving instances of the great social work accomplished by Western men and women. I want to repeat what I have already said before, that materialism as a philosophy is not necessarily a selfish one. It is a belief in the betterment of the material world and the material condition of men. It is not immoral either. It has its own strict code of human behaviour and relationship.

Among those who have objected to my definition is Dr. Iqbal. His criticism, which appeared in the *Civil and Military Gazette*, is a brilliant piece of reasoning and shows the serious study the great poet has made of the subject. I shall refer to the Western and Eastern aspects of his objections respectively as I deal with each. But I think I may state without any fear of contradiction that 'emphasis on matter', however vague and crude the term may be, is accepted by most Western scholars as the dominant characteristic of Western civilisation. Dr. Iqbal states that Plato, the first European philosopher, was also the thinker who invented the idea of pure spirit, and that idea has affected both the West and the East. This is perfectly true. But that does not change our objective observation that the Western civilisation—such as it stands—is materialistic. We are not looking at all at certain phases of its thought. We are looking at the results.

I propose to review the Western civilisation of today according to the interpretation of it by Dr. Haas, a German scholar who has published, in the form of a small book, three lectures which he delivered at Geneva on 'What is European Civilisation?' I choose him because the belongs to that set of Western thinkers who deny every Eastern influence in the making of their civilisation. He is proud of its uniqueness, but he is also honest about its sorry results. I take the stages as he presents them, and as they are generally presented, and work them into the same sort of diagram as that of the Ottoman Empire.

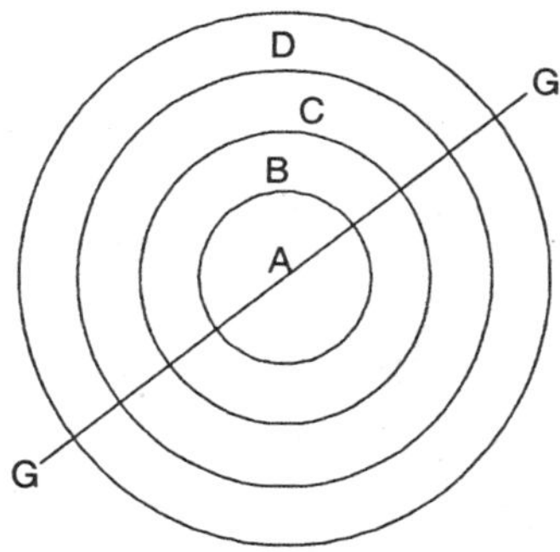

A–Ancient Greece. The aim here was to develop man harmoniously in all his faculties. The supreme measure was the beautiful body. It clearly emphasised the seen. The physical education—games and dancing—and the mental education—poetry and music, drama, philosophy, even the sciences—were kept in proportion so as not to develop the mind at the expense of the body. Its religion had no spirituality, no theology, no priestly caste, no mysticism. The mystical aspects of Greek life, such as the Orphic Mysteries, Dr. Haas deems as Eastern and he does not include them in the culture of ancient Greece.

B–Rome. After the making of man as such the West set out to build society and state. It regulated and organised all human relationships. But it still remained materialistic, still emphasised the life of man on earth as the most important.

C–Christianity. At this stage the West shifted its attention from the visible to the invisible. One can safely affirm that the monastic period of early Christianity is Eastern. But the author of 'What is European Civilisation?' dwells more especially on the over-recurring characteristic of the European mind. 'The European mind, in the philosophy and faith of the Middle Ages, shapes the supernatural and the physical according to the image of the living organism.' 'In all Christian speculation about the mysteries, the image of the living body is continually being used in order to make clear the truths of faith and the relations between them,' he says.[1] Because of this he does not consider Western Christianity as Eastern. For him, whatever its origins, it has become a Western institution.

D–Study of Nature. The Western mind, according to Dr. Haas, sought scientific knowledge with absolute disinterestedness and pure idealism. It looked on nature from a purely mathematical and intellectual angle. And to look at it from such an angle demanded the banishment of life, soul and meaning from it. This was a great sacrifice. For to think of nature as merely matter with no soul and purpose behind it naturally leads man to think of himself also as a being with no soul. But the sacrifice was necessary at the time and the

Western man made it. For Dr. Haas the attitude of the Western mind in its early study of nature is its most unique phase.

E—The results—probably the unforeseen results—of such a study with its extraordinary scientific discoveries have been the following: First, it gave a mechanical interpretation of life. Soul was explained by sensations, which, like atoms, form complexes and integrate according to the laws of cause and effect. A nature without a soul means life without a soul or purpose. Secondly, history began to be interpreted as a purely material process and to be explained as a play of economic interests, which religion and spiritual or moral values only served to further or conceal. Thirdly, the Western mind lost its belief in the creative faculty of man. He was controlling nature through the knowledge and discoveries of the great minds of an earlier age. He had nothing to do with it. He could no longer believe in his own creativeness. Fourthly, this phase led some Western scholars, specially in Germany, to a very pessimistic attitude of mind in regard to Western civilisation. For them Western civilisation seemed to have said its last word and was doomed to pass away.

G—is the unfailing organising power of the Western mind, which runs through all the cycles or phases of Western civilisation.

The author of 'What is European Civilisation?', after presenting it in these four cycles, refuses to believe that the Western mind has touched the limit of its creativeness. He predicts that after having gone through its past phases of organisation of Man, Society, Nature, it will begin over again with man and evolve through another series of cycles.

An Eastern scholar may well ask—'What sort of new cycles? How will the organising power of the Western mind manifest itself? Will it again take material values as standards or will it adopt the unseen, the spiritual as its measure?' The forces in action in the West are so confused that it is difficult to foretell the future Western world. However, we may attempt to feel our way through certain aspects of European thought and speculate a little on their possible results.

There are two decidedly opposite directions in which we may venture:

1. The new scientific discoveries of our century. They have been destroying slowly but surely the materialism and the determinism of the nineteenth century. No philosopher can any longer explain with any degree of confidence the living organism in terms of physical and chemical processes. Science is no longer so cock-sure. The incalculable, the Unseen has been entering its domain. There is space and room for a belief in the unseen force in creation. Owing to this there is a revival of interest in the philosophies and religions of Asia. There is a considerable number of scientists who show definite mystic tendencies.

Among the people in the West also there is an obvious curiosity for the Unseen. In the Anglo-Saxon world quack religions and revivalist phenomena are frequent. In France the pilgrimages to Lourdes have increased and a considerable number of French actresses have been retiring to convents. Even Devil-worship and Black Magic have more adepts than one would imagine.[2]

These are tendencies which lead one to speculate on the possibility of a spiritual revival in the West. And to the question: 'On what line is the Western mind going to organise life?' one may give the same answer as Steinmatz, the electrical genius. He was asked by Roger Robson, the business magnate, what line research would see the greatest development in the next fifty years. Instead of mentioning some line concerned with electrical experiments, he said the greatest discovery would be made along spiritual lines.

'Here is a force which history clearly teaches and which has been the greatest power in the development of men and history. Yet we have merely been playing with it and have never seriously studied it as we have the physical forces. Some day people will learn that material things do not bring happiness and are of little use in making men and women powerful and creative. Then the scientists of the world will turn their laboratories to the study of God and prayer and the spiritual forces which as yet have hardly been touched. When this day comes the world will see more advancement in one generation than it has in the past four.'

Although in a considerable part of the world of science, philosophy and even of art as well as in society itself there is this unmistakble urge towards adopting a spiritual basis, it is by no means certain that such a development will take place in the West in any near future. For philosophical thought takes some time before it can penetrate and shape human activities, although it does and always has shaped human society within a certain period. But side by side with this spiritual force which has the blessing of science, at least a considerable part to it, we see other forces in action. And to get some idea about them we have to look to another field of activity in the West.

2. **Economic and Political life**. Here the forces still at work are the product of nineteenth century materialism. The old politicians are as strongly under the thumb of the old capitalism as they were in the pre-war years. They are decidedly materialistic. Their opponents, the communist politicians, are also materialist. Admirable as their desire is to do away with the abuses of capitalism and to distribute wealth on a more equitable basis, their disregard, nay, their hostility to all spiritual forces threatens to eradicate every value which is not in the domain of the seen. Will the West reorganise itself on a more thoroughly materialistic or on a more spiritual basis? That is the problem of the future West. But as to the continuation of the conflict between the two worlds or the possibility of co-operation, we can speculate only after reviewing the East and at least some of the forces at work in it.

My simple definition of the East as overemphasis on spirit has met with opposition from various sources. Quite a number of Hindu and Moslem intellectuals said to me in almost exactly these terms—'We are not spiritual, we have the technique of it; our incessant talk of religion is a sort of religiosity and not religion; quite a number among us, both Moslem and Hindu, use spirituality for the purpose of exploitation.' But it is impossible to have the technique of a thing without having possessed the thing itself some time or other. We cannot exploit a non-existent sentiment. The Western leaders use or abuse, in short, exploit economic and political beliefs because they are realities in the West. If the Eastern politician or the leader of another sort exploits religion and spiritual ideals, it is because they are realities in the Eastern world.

Dr. Iqbal objects also to the assumption that the East emphasises spirit as the basis of its philosophy. He cites Mani, the ancient Persian poet, who taught dualism, and Buddha, who denied the existence of pure spirit as a substance. Those are facts just as Plato's philosophy of pure spirit in the West is a fact.[3] But in dealing with the civilisations we are only considering their final results. The final results of Eastern civilisations, such as we see them today, are that they have in the main failed to organise material existence, and that they are not masters of their own parts of the material world—their land and economic resources—while the West is not only master in the West but very much so in the East. The other argument which I constantly hear, that Hindus are good business men and merchants is no argument at all. For even spiritual people are not disembodied spirits and must live somehow.

Let us now proceed to work out the East in the same way from the starting-point, just as we have worked out the West. What is its starting-point? The essence of the Western mind we have found in ancient Greece—the human body as its symbol. The essence of the Eastern mind is in ancient Hindu India. For all other cultures of the East are adulterated with some emphasis on matter, while the Hindu mind remains solely bent on the unseen and the psychic. If the laws of the psychic are to be discovered and used for the benefit of mankind—as the laws of nature were discovered and used for the benefit of mankind in the West—the Hindu mind holds the key. This is one point on which Dr. Iqbal would agree with me. For he says, 'In ancient India the whole structure of thought was built on a conception of free spirit.'

Mahatma Gandhi also admits the over-emphasis on the spirit, ascribing it to a wrong interpretation of early Hindu writings. We shall return to this point later. In the meantime, to understand this emphasis on the spirit throughout all Eastern cultures, Hindu, Moslem, Persian, let us consider certain passage from *The Essential Unity of all Religions* by Dr. Bhagvandas. All religions came from the East, and Dr. Bhagvandas makes comparative quotations from most of the sacred books.

'The proclaimers who proclaim the Truth use many varying forms to put it in, but yet the Truth implied in all is one.'

(*Upanishads*)

'Let the names differ, beloved!
All truths are only one,
In the sea-wave and the bubble
Shines the lustre of one Sun.' (SUFI)

'But to one Goal are marching everywhere all human beings, though they seem to walk on paths divergent; and that Goal is I—the Universal Self—Self-Consciousness.'

(*Gita*)

'One of the fundamentals of Maulana Jelaleddin Rumi's teachings also is derived from that verse of the Qur-an which tells us that we all return unto *Him*.'

'Teachers are sent to each race that they may teach it in its own tongue, so there may be no doubt as to the meaning of their mind.'

(Qur'an)

'This that I am uttering now unto you, the Holy Qur'an–it is to be found within the ancient *seer's writings too.*'

'For teachers have been sent to every race.'

'And aught of difference we do not make—for disagreement there is none betwixt them.'

(Qur'an)

This insistence in all the sacred books of the East on the oneness of spiritual truth has been an essential feature of old Turkish mysticism. Two of the quotations I have selected from the Qur'an are connected with the lives of two very important figures in the history of our mystic thought. The first I quoted when speaking of Yahya bin Khalil, the leader of the 'Ahiler' in the thirteenth century, who was among those aiming to organise the economic forces of Turkish society on a spiritual basis. The second, to which the two that follow are closely related in spirit, has a legendary significance in the life of Soleyman Dede, the writer of the *Mevlud* that great human masterpiece of the fifteenth century. Soleyman Dede was teaching in the mosque at Broussa and he read the second of these quotations. A Persian, who was an orthodox Moslem, objected to his interpretation of the verse and declared him a 'Kaffir'. The people of Broussa backed Soleyman Dede. The man went to Egypt and Aleppo and obtained 'Fetvas' from the Moslem Ulema pronouncing Soleyman Dede a 'Kaffir'. The people refused to recognise those 'Fetvas'. The legend is that Soleyman Dede was assassinated in the street by the same man.

We may thus conclude that a belief in spiritual unity underlies much of Eastern thought, and the emphasis laid on it has been real and undeniable. Only the emphasis has varied in different parts of the East, being strongest in Hindu India. Therefore we may take this over-emphasis of spirit as the starting-point and trace around it the different cycles of the development of Eastern peoples. But, curiously enough, the cycles do not work out into a diagram of the same kind as has been drawn when representing the development of

Western civilisation. Eastern civilisations do not follow each other, each emphasising a particular phase of life, such as ancient Greece, Rome and the medieval and modern West. They appear in parallel lines, longer or shorter, but each beginning and ending in itself. And through them all runs this over-emphasis on the Unseen.

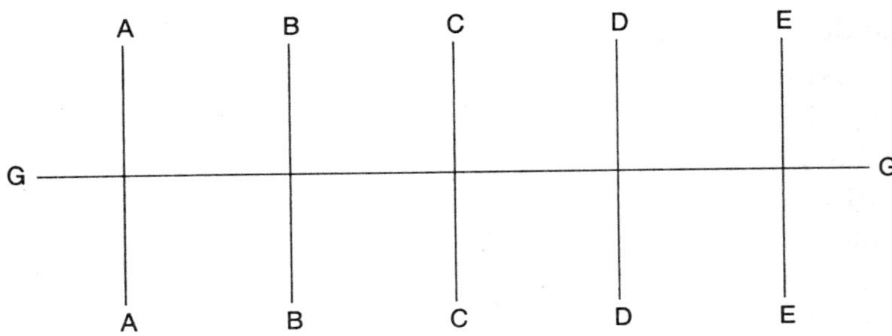

Let A, B, C, D, E, each represent any Eastern civilisation at random. We find that they all rise and pass away in their own particular area, like beads strung on the threads of time, connected with each other no doubt, but not formed into a composite unity by any social or political purpose that survived their physical existence. In those which we see today, the inability to organise material existence on any solid and durable basis is glaringly evident. It would be difficult to find a better definition for their common characte-ristic—represented by the line G in the diagram—than that of over-emphasis on the spirit.

These civilisations have not been able to work out their material problems in a synthetic way. Just as the West, specially in the last century, found its over-emphasis on matter fatal, so has the East found its over-emphasis on spirit fatal. Just as the technical age in the West has used the earlier scientific discoveries to exploit men and to enslave them through its material power and organisation, so the rulers and the priesthood of the decadent East exploited religion and spirituality to acquire power or riches. M. Akif, the Turkish poet, is right when he says of the East:

'I have seen from end to end ruins, nations with no leaders, broken bridges, closed canals, empty highways, sickly and wrinkled faces, bent backs, brainless heads, indifferent hearts, rusted judgements, tyrannies, slavery, misery, hypocrisy, disgusting vices, divers diseases, burnt forests, cold chimneys, wild fields, dirty faces, lazy arms, Imams with no following, brother killing brother, days with no definite aims, nights that expect no definite morrow!'

Although we are not able to discuss the evolution of all the Eastern civilisations, we can say that most of them claim to have started with some sort of synthesis and to have taken sufficient account of the material necessities of life. Dr. Iqbal states that Islam, among all civilisations, Eastern and Western, has achieved the highest synthesis. I agree. Islam left the relation of man and his Creator in his own hands. There was no priesthood, no complicated and rigid theology, in its early stages. It worked out the synthesis of spirit and matter, of soul and body logically and completely, in all the aspects of human life. It gave a code to the Moslems which aimed at forming both the individual and the society. Health, cleanliness, bodily training, diet, moral and physical restraint are all given their due importance in the teachings of Islam. Its principles of social justice and equality will always be indispensable principles for every human state or society which aims at continuity and stability.

The degeneration of Moslems and their subjection are ascribed to two different causes by two different sets of critics: The penetration of mysticism, which over-emphasises the spiritual, and develops man's soul at the expense of his body. To this set Dr. Iqbal belongs. To this set quite an important part of the Turkish intelligentsia also belonged. The abolition of all mystical orders in Turkey is the psychological and practical result of such a belief and The rigidity of the 'Sheriat', which left no margin for adaptation to a changing world. Turkey is the only Moslem country where this belief had a stronghold and a large following.

The practical consequence of this has been separation of religion and the state.

These two points concern only Moslems. But there are three more criticisms which concern the East as a whole.

1. Owing to the fanaticism and unreasoning conservatism of the priesthood in the East (including our mullahs), their desire to keep the power in their hands, and their co-operation with selfish and incapable tyrants, the development of the East was always stopped at a certain stage, beyond which some peoples have not passed even now.

2. Added to these was a general malaise–the failure of the intelligentsia of the East to study both East and West in any objective or comparative way. Those who studied the West specialised in its last, that is, the mechanical age. Dazzled by its power and superficial splendour, they did not understand the more important historical phases which gave Western society its strength, its inner moral and social organisation and stability. They have either remained fundamentalists, denying all necessity of re-adaptation, or they have fallen into a superficially critical attitude of mind, trying to demolish all historic forces in the East, without seeing any possibility of revival and rejuvenation. For a long time in the East, therefore, the intelligentsia have been divided between the fanatical and the ignorant and apish imitators who believe that a wholesale adoption of the mechanical civilisation will give the indispensable inner organisation, the strength and the stability to the passive and inert Eastern masses. The result has been that the Eastern masses have remained devoid of all new thought or idealism, and enslaved by foreign powers or by their own despotic rulers.

3. This shortcoming in the intelligentsia of the East has prevented the formation of a definite philosophy, system or plan to reorganise Eastern society.

In the nineteenth century, however, the Eastern intelligentsia began bit by bit to realise that their disregard of their moral responsibility was suicidal, if not criminal. In every part of the East there was some sort of awakening. Turkey was the country in which reform movements started soonest. I have described in my early lectures our struggle for change. The final phase of the Turkish movement is the conviction of the necessity of adopting the methods and the organisation of the West in economic and political life. That is one solution of our common problem. Since coming to India I observe that here another method is being followed, a synthetic method. This may be as good, or even better than ours. The verdict belongs to the future. It would be interesting to hear other Eastern scholars tell us how they are working out their solution. And I hope that the Jamia Millia will be the platform where scholars from all parts of the East will communicate their views on the evolution of new life in their people. And I also sincerely hope that Western scholars as well will be asked to give their views, both in regard to what they are doing in the West and in regard to the relation of the West to the East. From such an exchange there may arise a better understanding between the Eastern countries and a more effective effort may be made to turn the conflict of East and West into co-operation.

When and how can the East co-operate with the West? It can do so only when it feels itself equal with the West, when it wants to do it in all freedom. Those who co-operate must not be only equals but must also possess mutually valuable things to exchange. A restricted class in the West is taking a step forward by a tardy recognition of the superiority of Eastern philosophy and thought. The East, by recognising that hitherto its material life has lacked organisation—while the West is very ably organised—is taking another step forward. With this in mind and with all deference to the oldest and wisest East, a member of a comparatively younger Eastern nation may be allowed to give a general verdict.

To the casual observer the crying need of the East in general and of India in particular seems to be inner organisation. From time to time strong men and rulers have done dazzling things in the East. But a nation organised on principles which will give it the strength to hold its own at critical moments has been rare. A nation cannot be organised from above. It must develop from within, according to its own laws of growth. With extremely few exceptions, nationhood in the East has not been a crystallised and powerful conception. I say nationhood and not nationalism, for the former brings into play and harmonises inner forces in all their variety from a utilitarian and aesthetic point of view, while the latter may cause inner disintegration and create conflict with the surrounding peoples.

The fundamental and simplest elements of nationhood being race, religion and language, let us analyse these briefly in regard to India.

The race theory cannot stand on its feet here the moment a historical analysis is made. Race understood as culture is there, but as blood it takes us nowhere. Many Moslems are of Hindu origins, many foreign tribes have become Hindus by adopting the religion and customs of the land during the great racial immigrations. It is fortunate for India the Islam (one of its principal cultures and religions) is against race, that the Arya Samaj has valiantly tried to break the castes which were originally meant to preserve the purity of race, and that Mahatma Gandhi is working to bring about a unity on more universal principles.

Religion being the greatest reality everywhere, but specially in India, it would have been a blessing if Indian nationhood rested on the unity of faith. But that cannot be. Not only is India composed of different religious communities, but each religion has no end of sects. A universal religion such as Akbar tried to impose was and is an impossibility, for religion cannot be imposed by a ruler. It is best to leave religion alone. But between all religions it is possible to create a tie by adding a new article of faith. 'Love of country is a part of Faith,' is the teaching of Islam. There may be such a principle in Hinduism as well. Each religious community could perhaps make it a part of its dogma to teach all children their oneness as Indians. This, I believe, will one day remove friction, if it does nothing else.

That each group should be free to preserve and develop its culture in a nation with varied cultures goes without saying. But that a common language is a necessity also goes without saying. A country may have a hundred languages, but it must have one adopted by its educational system throughout, a language which every child must be obliged to learn no matter to what school it goes for education.

Yet supposing that all these problems were solved in India, would that establish a nationhood? Not by any means. The standard of living of the Eastern masses is far below that of the most miserable slum-dweller of the West. I am saying this after having seen the inside of Indian village huts. The percentage of the slum-dwellers in the West does not exceed ten per cent, while the percentage of the peasants in the East is ninety. Neither do the industrial workers in the East fare better. The natural result of this is that though the poor man in the East may stick to his religion for comfort, he cannot ever afford the luxury of devotion and service to any abstract idea such as nationhood voluntarily or intelligently. Though man does not live by bread alone, he cannot exist without it and he needs something more than bread. There is a minimum standard of living below which man is bound to turn into a mere drudge, dragging through his life and hoping for a better state in the coming world. Such a man can never by made to think of any part of the earth as his country—his country is where he can find better comfort. And so when a believer in the materialistic interpretation of history tells me that religion or spirituality in the East was invented to deceive the masses into accepting their miserable destiny, I may not agree with him entirely but I have to bow to his logic.

Because ninety per cent of all Eastern populations are peasants (with the possible exception of Japan), the East in its internal organisation is forced to turn to the village at once. The social, the economic and the moral regeneration of the East depends on the development of its village life. It is fortunate indeed for Indians that Mahatma Gandhi has turned his attention to this vital question.

Mahatma Gandhi's attempt is an enterprise which should interest the whole East. For he is trying to regenerate the Eastern villager economically and morally, while he is fighting against a too rapid industrialisation. Whether he will succeed or not is another question. As it is, considering the time he has given, he has succeeded in a very large area. He is evidently quite aware of the fact that a swift, mechanised industry among such primitive masses may enslave them further to Western industry and capitalism. So far they have been the slaves of misery due to the wretched social and economic conditions. He is trying to make of them men who are both free and productive and self-supporting. He is trying to make the Indian villagers organic units of the Indian nation and not its passive slaves. Further, he is working out the problem synthetically. He firmly believes that the body and the spirit cannot be taken as separate things.[4] The regeneration of one is not possible without the regeneration of the other. They must co-operate and stimulate each other. Mahatma Gandhi's effort reminds me very much of the economic and moral organisation of the Turkish society by the mystico-economic orders called the 'Ahiler' in Anatolia in the thirteenth century.

All Hindu Indians should support him and serve him in this work, for he is the only person capable of using the best in Hinduism and of sorting out the superstitious, the degenerative elements which have crept into it. All Moslem Indians should also support him and further his cause, for his synthesis is dominated in its fundamentals by the everlasting principles of Islam. He seems to me—if I may be permitted to say so—an ideal neo-Moslem, with his cleanliness of body and mind, his self-restraint, his readiness to co-operate and love, his respect for bodily labour, education, truth and peace.

Both the Eastern and the Western world should study him seriously, for he is offering one of the ways which may lead to the salvation, not only the East but also of the West, by enabling it to co-operate with a free, strong, moral and peaceful East. I will say in conclusion: 'The key of the future will belong to that nation which knows how to blend material and the spiritual in as near and equal a proportion as it is possible to do.'

NOTE ON 'AHILER'

When this book was in the press the author sent an article for *The Jamia* on the Order of the 'Ahiler,' which contains a considerable amount of fresh data and the most up-to-date information on the subject, in the light of which a few corrections and additions to what is said of the Order on p. 107 ff. seem necessary. The name 'Ahi' is not derived from the Arabic word meaning 'brother', as in the footnote on p. 107, but it is of Turkish origin. The earliest 'Ahiler' or 'People of the Futuwat' as they were also called, were an order of knights. They played an important part in the establishment of the Ottoman State, the great Osman himself being an 'Ahi'. The early Janissaries were 'Ahis' or 'Bektashis', the Spahis, or cavalry consisting of the landed gentry, were also 'Ahis'. The sign of the Order was a 'shalvar' (trousers) of a special kind.

After absorbing the fighting element of the 'Ahiler,' and when the system of 'Blood Tribute' has been adopted, the Ottoman State began to look with disfavour on the political power of the 'Ahiler'. But wherever the power of the central state was weak, as in Angora and Kirshehir, the 'Ahiler' or the 'People of the Futuwat' continued to rule. When the Ottomans conquered Angora in the middle of the fourteenth century the political power of the Ahiler in Middle Anatolia ceased to be of importance. As an economic force and organisation, however, they continued to be supreme up to the eighteenth century, and existed till as late as after the Great War (*Ed*).

---

1. An Englishman once said to me, 'Christianity was Eastern in essence (because of its emphasis on the soul), we have Westernised it; Islam was Western in essence (because of its emphasis on society), you have Easternised it.'
2. How the lack of soul or of belief in the Unseen—not only among the artists but among the people in general—has killed art is seen in the writings of a considerable number of intellectuals and artists. One could take no end of examples from contemporary literature. I have chosen what I believe to be both a representative and beautiful passage from an article entitled, 'Art without God, or Vain Idols' by Herman Gregoire, a young French dramatist: "There is no art where there is no Faith. Our epoch because of this truth produces artists but leaves them without work. . . . Deprived of these bases and of this order all things lose their direction, evil turns into good, vice into virtue, pleasure into boredom. Oh, world without a soul! Led by what sort of a whim of vengeance has the Divine Dramatist composed the Contemporary Comedy acted only by moving corpses?"
3. Dr. Bhagvandas, whom I revere and admire, says in a letter which he sent before I left India, 'In your lecture at the Jamia you expressed the idea that while the East had rightly striven for the things of the spirit, it had not taken sufficient and rational account of the things of matter. This view is no doubt true of the later centuries, but I believe it does not apply quite to the earlier times, when ideals of social organisation were more genuinely pursued . . . .'
4. It would be interesting here to cite Aldous Huxley, the most prominent English novelist, in his double and contradictory reaction to the East and West—that is, to an over-emphasis on spirit and an over-emphasis on matter. During his visit to India he noted this over-emphasis on spirit and reached wildly against it. 'If the Western civilisation is unsatisfactory, it is because we are not interested enough in the actual world. We are not materialistic enough,' he wrote in *Jesting Pilate*, his book of travels. But when he visited America and came face to face with most typical result of Western civilisation, he changed his views at once. He says in the same book—'My own losses, as I have said, were enormous (this was because of the great number of convictions and beliefs he lost on the voyage). But. . . . I acquired two new convictions: that it takes all sorts to make a world, and that the established spiritual values are fundamentally correct and should be maintained.'

Biographical Notes

'Aali Pasha (1815–1871): Full name Mehmed Emin 'Aali Pasha; he was an Ottoman statesman and Grand Vizir for an extensive period.

Adnan Adivar, Abdul Hak (1881–1955): A medical doctor, Istanbul deputy to last Ottoman Parliament, minister of health for government of Great National Assembly, exiled from Turkey with wife Halidé Edib (1884–1964).

Afghani, Sheikh Jamaluddin (1838–1897): Of Persian or Arabic origin, was a Muslim political activist in Iran, Afghanistan, Egypt, and the Ottoman Empire during the 19th century. One of the founders of Islamic modernism, and advocate of pan-Islamic unity. He was the roving pan-Islamist who came to India from Egypt and stayed in Hyderabad for nearly two years, and later at Calcutta (now Kolkata).

Akbar (1542–1660): Jalaluddin Mohammad Akbar, was the Emperor of Hindustan during 1556 and 1605. Built Fatehpur Sikri as his capital (1570-85) and adopted the policy of *sulh-I kul* (peace with all).

Akif, Mehemed (1873–1936): Surname 'Ersoy'; a Turk-ish poet, and the author and writer of the lyrics of the Turkish National Anthem, *Istiklal Marshi* (*The March of Independence*). Born in Istanbul; a semi-Albanian by birth and deeply religious, and is held as a nationalist figure in Turkey and considered by Turks as their 'National Poet'. His real allegiance was somewhere in between Turkish and Islamic identities. After the abolition of the Khilafat, he left Turkey for Cairo to teach Turkish language, and returned only shortly before his death in 1936.

al-Ma'ari, Abul 'Ala (973–1057): A blind Arab philosopher, poet and writer. He was a rationalist of his time. His major work *Rislatul-Ghufran,* meaning 'The Epistle of Forgiveness' is a famous Arabic book from the 10th century.

Alberuni (970–1039): Born in Khwarizm, near present-day Khiva, he rose to become a well-known astronomer, author, mathematician and philosopher. The English translation of his book on India, referred to by Halide Edib, was published in 1888.

Ali, Mehemed: Name of two persons, (i) Mehemed Ali (1769–1849), the governor of Egypt, revolted against the Ottoman Empire, is regarded as the 'founder of modern Egypt'. The dynasty he established would rule Egypt and Sudan until the Egyptian Revolution in 1952. (ii) Mehemed Ali (1741–1822), the governor of Janina, the Ottoman Empire's European territory, revolted against the Empire during Mahmud II. He was later assassinated.

Ansari, Mukhtar Ahmad (1880–1936): Educated at Benaras, Allahabad, and Hyderabad. Went to England in 1901, where he was the first Indian house surgeon in the Charring Cross Hospital, London. Began practice at Delhi in 1910. Led the Indian Medical Mission to Turkey in 1912-13, for which he received a special award from the Ottoman Consul-General. President, Home Rule League, Delhi (1917). Chairman, Reception Committee, Muslim League, Delhi (1918). Played a leading part in the Khilafat movement. President, Muslim League, Nagpur (1920), and All-India Khilafat Conference, Gaya (1922). Member, Congress Civil Disobedience Enquiry Committee (1922).

Arabi, Muhiuddin or **Ibn Arabi** (1165–1240): Arab Sufi mystic and philosopher. Born in Medinat Mursiya in Andalus. In A.D. 1200, at the age of thirty-five, he left Spain and stayed near Mecca for three years, where he began writing his *Al-Futuhat al-Makkiyya* (*The Meccan Illuminations*).

Aristotle (384–322 B.C.): A Greek philosopher and scientist; a pupil of Plato and teacher of Alexander the Great. Aristotle (together with Socrates and Plato) wrote on many different subjects, including politics, government, metaphysics, physics, logic, ethics, theatre, music, etc.

Aspasia (c. 470–400 B.C.): A Milesian woman who was famous for her involvement with the Athenian statesman Pericles (c. 495–429 B.C.). She spent most of her adult life in Athens, and she may have influenced Pericles and Athenian politics.

Aziz, Abdul (1830–76): Thirty-second Ottoman sultan, son of Mahmud II. Ruled from 1861 to 1876; was deposed after a coup d'etat. First continued the policies of his predecessor, Abdul Mejid, supporting the Westernising reforms. After 1871, sided with the conservatives; committed suicide after being deposed.

Bacon, Francis (1561–1626): An English philosopher, statesman, and essayist. Also known as a proponent of the scientific revolution. He was knighted in 1603, created Baron Verulam in 1618.

Baki (1526–1600): The pen name of the Ottoman Turkish poet Mahmud Abdulbaki; considered to be one of the greatest contributors to Turkish literature, and came to be known as *Sultan-us-shuara*, or 'Sultan of poets'.

Bektash, Haji: Persian mystic, humanist and philosopher from Khorasan, Iran, who lived approximately from 1209 to 1271 in Anatolia. He is the eponym of the Bektashi Sufi order and is considered one of the principal teachers of Alevism. He is also a renowned figure in the history and culture of both the Ottoman Empire and modern Turkey. The Bektashi order spread from Anatolia through the Ottomans primarily into the Balkans. This order became the official order of the elite Janissary corps after their establishment.

Bey, Cochi: An Albanian *devshirme* convert and the close advisor of Murad IV (r. 1623–1640), had presented a perceptive reform package (*Risale* or Treatise) to the latter, highlighting the causes for decline of the Ottoman army.

Bey, Evranos: A convert from Christianity and of Greek origin, was the commander of the Ottomans during the conquest of the Macedonia in the Balkan Peninsula during the 14th century.

Bey, Halid Zia or Halid Zia Ushakligil (1867–1945): A Turkish author. His first literary works were translations of French novels, which played an important role in the Europeanization of Turkish literature. He founded the newspaper *Hikmet* in 1886. After his novel *Kirik Hayatlar* (*Broken Lives*) was censored, Halid Zia paused, and later ceased, writing novels, turning instead to short stories, dramas, and memoirs after 1923. His style is based closely on French romantism and most of his novels dealt with unfulfilled love.

Buddha or Siddhartha Gautam (c. 563–483 B.C.): A spiritual teacher from ancient India and the founder of Buddhism.

Catherine the Great or **Catherine II** (1729–1796): Empress of Russia; reigned for 34 years, from 1762 until her death.

Charlemagne (742/747–814): Also called Charles the Great, was King of the Franks from 768 to his death. His kingdom incorporated much of Western and Central Europe. After he conquered Italy, he was crowned *Imperator Augustus* by Pope Leo III in 800 as a rival of the Byzantine Empire of Constantinople.

Condorcet (1743–1794): French philosopher, mathematician, and early political scientist who devised the concept of a *Condorcet method*.

Corneille: Pierre Corneille (1606–1684) was a French tragedian who was one of the three great 17th century French dramatists, along with Moliere and Racin. Thomas Corneille

(1625–1709), the brother of Pierre Corneille, was also a great dramatist.

Das, Bhagvan (1869–1959): Started his career as a *tehsildar* (1890) but resigned from government service (1899). Took keen interest in national education. Headed the Kashi Vidyapeeth (1921–26). President, UP Political Conference (1920), and Hindi Sahitya Academy (1921). Social reformer and author of many books, including *The Essential Unity of All Religions*.

de Gouges, Olympe (1748–1793): A playwright and journalist whose feminist writings reached a large audience. In her *Declaration of the Rights of Women and the Female Citizen* (1791), she challenged the practice of male authority and the notion of male-female inequality. She was executed by guillotine during the Reign of Terror for her revolutionary ideas.

Dede, Galib: One of the greatest Ottoman poets who belonged to the Mevlana order, lived during the late 18th and early 19th century during Selim III (r. 1789–1807).

Dede, Soleyman: Lived in the 15th century. He was an Imam (cleric) of the Great Mosque at Broussa, and the writer of *Mevlud* (the birth-song of Mohammed), a great human masterpiece of fifteenth century.

Diotima: In Greek, Diotima means a complete woman and also the Greek Goddess of Love. Diotima (of Mantinea) was an ancient female philosopher and tutor of Socrates. Diotima of Mantinea plays an important role in Plato's *Symposium*, a philosophical dialogue.

Durkheim, Émile (1858–1917): A French sociologist whose contributions were instrumental in the formation of sociology and anthropology. Considered one of the founding fathers of sociology and an early proponent of solidarism. His work and editorship of the first journal of sociology (*L'Année Sociologique*) helped establish sociology within academia as an accepted social science.

Edward VII (1841–1910): King of the United Kingdom and the British Dominions and Emperor of India from 1901 until his death.

Effendi, Abdul Mejid or **Abdul Mejid II** (1868–1944): The 37th Head of the Ottoman Imperial House; reigned from 19 November 1922 to 3 March 1924; he was the last Khalifa.

Effendi, Fahim: The *Sheikh-ul-Islam* of the Ottoman Empire during the reign of Abdul Aziz (r. 1861–1876). He was among the *ulema* who vehemently criticised Sheikh Jamaluddin Afghani (1838–1897) and declared his teaching orthodox when the latter gave a lecture in 1870, possibly in Istanbul.

Effendi, Hairi: The *Sheikh-ul-Islam* of the Ottoman Empire some time during the early 20th century when Young Turks were in power; contributed immensely in the field of educational reforms.

Effendi, Jemali, The *Sheikh-ul Islam*, during the reign of Selim I (1465–1520). He had objected to the Sultan's proposal of forced conversion of Christians of the Empire.

Ertugrul (1198–1281): Also called Ertugrul Gazi, was the father of Osman I (the founder of the Ottoman Empire). He was the leader of the Kayi clan of the Oghuz Turks. In 1227, he inherited the command of the Kayi tribe following the death of his father, Soleyman Shah. He was given the lands of Karaja mountain near Angora (Ankara), by Alauddin Keykubad I, the Seljuk Sultan. Later, he was also given the village of Soygeut with the surrounding lands. That village became the Ottoman capital in 1299 under Ertugrul's son Osman I.

George, David Lloyd (1863–1945): British Prime Minister throughout the latter half of First World War and the first four years of the subsequent peace.

Fenelon, François (1651–1715): French Roman Catholic theologician, poet and writer. He is remembered mostly as one of the main advocates of 'quietism' and as the author of *The Adventures of Telemachus*, a scabrous attack on the French monarchy, first published in 1699.

Fikret, Tewfik (1867–1915): The pseudonym of Turkish poet Mehmed Tewfik. Born in Istanbul; educated at the prestigious Galatasaray Lycee, where he later became Principal. His works were deeply influenced by the French Symbolists, many of whose works he translated into Turkish. Along with many of his avant-garde contemporaries, he contributed to the literary magazine *Sarwet-i-Funun* ('the Wealth of Knowledge') until it was censored by the Ottoman government in 1901. Fikret's volumes of verse include *Rubab-i-Sikeste* ('The Broken Lute') from 1900 and *Haluk-un-Defteri* ('Haluk's Notebook') from 1911.

Gandhi, Mahatma (1869–1948): Complete name Mohandas Karamchand Gandhi; a major political leader of the Indian independence movement. He was the pioneer of *Satyagraha*—a philosophy that is largely concerned with truth and 'resistance to evil through active, non-violent resistence'—which led India to independence and inspired movements for civil rights and freedom across the world.

Hadije Sultan or **Turhan Hadije** (1628?–1683): One of the favourite concubines of the Ottoman Sultan Ibrahim I (r.1640–1648) and the mother of his successor, Mehemed IV (r.1648–1687). She was prominent for the regency of her young son and her building patronage. *Turhan Hatice* was considered to be of Russian origin. She was brought to the Ottoman palace at the age of twelve as a gift to the mother of Sultan Ibrahim, Kussem Sultan. The latter gave Hatice to Ibrahim as a concubine, from whom the future sultan Mehmed IV was born.

Hamid, Abdul Hak (1851–1937): Surname Tarhan; an early 20th century Turkish poet and playwright; considered one of the greatest Turkish Romantic writers. He was instrumental in introducing Western influences into Turkish literature. He is known in Turkish literature as 'Sair-i Azam' (The Grand Poet) and 'Dahi-i Azam' (The Grand Genius). His works include a prose *Macera-yý Aþk* (Love Affair), *Zeynep*, a play *Nesteren*, etc. The latter depicted a rebellion against a tyrannical ruler, and the actual ruler of Turkey at that time, Sultan Abdul Hamid II. He was entrusted with the service of foreign affairs of the Ottoman government in several places including in Bombay from 1883 to 1885.

Hamid I, Abdul (1725–1789): The 27th Sultan of the Ottoman Empire. He was the son of Sultan Ahmed III (1703–30) and succeeded his brother Mustafa III (1757–74). He concluded the war with Russia by signing the humiliating Treaty of Kutchuk Kaynarja (signed on 21 July 1774).

Hamid II, Abdul (1842–1918): The 34th Ottoman sultan (r.1876–1909); second son of Sultan Abdul Mejid. In 1876 he succeeded his brother Murad V when the later was declared insane. Introduced constitution and parliament (1876), but suspended both within a very short period. Established autocratic rule, which became gradually more oppressive from the 1880s onwards. Supported the pan-Islamist movement. He was deposed after the failure of the counter-revolution (Young Turk revolution) of April 1909.

Hikmet, Nazim (1901–1963): A poet, playwright, novelist and memoirist who is acclaimed in Turkey as the first and foremost modern Turkish poet; one of the greatest international poets of the 20th century. Referred to as a 'romantic communist' or a 'romantic revolutionary'; he was repeatedly arrested for his political beliefs and spent much of his adult life in prison or in exile. His poems depicting the people of the countryside, villages, towns and cities of his homeland as well as the Turkish War of Independence and the Turkish revolutionaries are considered among the greatest patriotic literary works in Turkey.

Hurrem Sultan or Roxalane (c. 1510–1558): The wife of Soleyman the Magnificent. She enjoyed a prime position in the palace and had an influence upon affairs of the state and foreign relations. She was allegedly involved in several intriguing activities against the heir apparent, Prince Mustafa, and his mother, Sultan Soleyman's concubine Mahidevran (also called 'Gul Bahar'), and eventually led to one of her sons, Selim the Grim (1465–1520), inheriting the empire.

Husain, Zakir (1897–1969): Educated in Etawah and Aligarh (Uttar Pradesh, India), and Berlin. Joined Jamia Millia Islamia in 1926, and was appointed Vice-Chancellor (1926–1948). Vice-President of India (1962–67), and President (1967–69).

Hussein Jahid: A Turkish journalist and writer (of Fikret's school); a Young Turk who supported the Westernisation movement in education during the 'Edebiyat-i-Jedide'. He advocated the adoption of Latin alphabets for Turkish language.

Ibn Batuta (1304–1368/1377?): A Moroccan scholar and jusrisprudent; best known as a traveller and explorer, whose account documents his travels and excursions over a period of almost thirty years, covering some 73,000 miles (117,000 km). These journeys covered almost the entirety of the known Islamic world and beyond, extending from North and West Africa, Southern and Eastern Europe, South-West and Central Asia, Indian subcontinent and China, a distance readily surpassing that of his predecessors and his near-contemporary Marco Polo (1254–1324).

Ibn-Khaldun (1332–1406): A famous historian, scholar, theologician, and statesman born in present-day Tunisia. He is considered the forerunner of several social scientific disciplines: demography, historiography, cultural history, sociology and modern economics. He is best known for his *Muqaddimah*.

Ibn-Nassir or **Musa Ibn-Nassir** (640–716): A Yemeni Muslim who served as a governor and general under the Umayyad Khalifa Al-Walid I (668–715).

Ibrahim I (1615–1648): Sultan of the Ottoman Empire from 1640 until 1648.

Imre, Yunus (1238?–1320?): Turkish poet and Sufi mystic. He has exercised immense influence on Turkish literature, from his own day until the present. One of the first known Turkish poets besides Ahmet Yesevi and Sultan Walid. Following the Mongol invasion of Anatolia, Islamic mystic literature thrived in Anatolia, and Yunus Imre became one of its most distinguished poets. He is one of the first poets known by name to have composed extensively in the Turkish language.

Iqbal, Mohammad (1876–1938): Educated at the Scotch Mission College, Sialkot; Government College, Lahore; Cambridge, and Munich. Returned from Europe in July 1908. Secretary of the Punjab Khilafat Committee in 1919. Resigned from both the Muslim League and the Khilafat Committee after the Non-Cooperation resolution was passed in September 1920. Presided over the annual session of the All-India Muslim League (1930) and called for the establishment of an autonomous state in the northwest of British India. Iqbal's fame rests in his collection of Urdu and Persian poems and in his lectures on the reconstruction of religious thought in Islam.

Ismail Hakki: An important figure of Turkish language reform movement; evolved and suggested a new alphabet from Arabic/Persian with more phonetic.

Iswolski (1856–1919): Complete name Alexander Petrovich Iswolski or Izvolsky; a Russian diplomat remembered as a major architect of Russia's alliance with the British Empire during the years leading to the outbreak of the World War I. He was Russia's ambassador in various European capitals and served as Imperial Foreign Minister (1906–1910).

Kadri, Yakup (1889–1974): A Turkish novelist, journalist and diplomat.

Kemal, Namik (1840–1888): The renowned Turkish nationalist poet, journalist, translator and social reformer. Influenced by the growing nationalist sentiment of his day, published a politically controversial newspaper. After the government cracked down on the newspaper, he fled to Western Europe and worked there as a translator. When he returned, his most famous work, a play named '*Vatan Yahut Silistre*', promoted nationalism and liberalism, and was considered dangerous by the Ottoman government. Immediately afterward, he was sent into exile to Cyprus in 1873. He was pardoned by Murat V in 1876; later became the governor of Sakiz (now Chios), Greece, where he died in 1888.

Keykubad I, Alauddin (d. 1237): The Seljuk sultan; reigned from 1220 to 1237. Considered to be the most illustrious prince of the dynasty; under whose rule, Seljuk Anatolia reached its apogee. He sponsored a large-scale building campaign across Anatolia. Apart from reconstructing towns and fortresses, he built many mosques, medresses, caravansarais, bridges, hospitals, etc. mainly in Konya and Kayseri. Because of his qualities as a ruler, he became a legendary figure and is referred to as 'Keykubad the Great'. He was favourable to both Maulana Jalaluddin Rumi and his father.

Khan, Bilke (683or 684–734): One of the most powerful emperors of the Gokturk Empire. His name literally means 'wise chieftain'; and his personal name was Ashina Mojilian.

Khan II, Bilke: Ruler of the Gokturk Empire after the killing of Meto Khan, a tyrant who ruled sometime after Bilke Khan (683or 684–734).

Khan, Erlik: The god of death and evil according to the Turkic shamanic traditions. In Turkic mythology, Erlik was the deity of evil, darkness, lord of the lower world and judge of the dead.

Khan, Meto: Ruled the Gokturk Empire sometime after Bilke Khan (683 or 684–734), was a tyrant. During his tyrannical rule a great many Turks had immigrated to China.

Khan, Tanri Kara ('Black King God'): The first 'being' in the universe, according to the Khanty and Mansi mythologies. He was the creator-god of those pantheons and may be compared to Bai Ulgan, a Turkic and Mongolian creator-deity.

Khayyam, Umar (1048–1131): A Persian poet, philosopher, mathematician and astronomer who lived in Persia.

Konevi, Sadreddin (1210–1274): The stepson and the most influential disciple of Muhiuddin Arabi (1165–1240).

Kul-Tegin (685–731 or AD 732): A famous general of the Second Turkic Kaganate. He was a second son of Iltermish Shad and the younger brother of Bilke Khan.

Kuprullu, Mehemmed Fuad (1890–1966): A Turkish historian and politician, known for his contributions to Ottoman history, Turkish folklore and language. As a historian his works included *Origins Of the Ottoman Empire*, *The Saljuqs of Anatolia: Their History and Culture According to Local Muslim Sources* and *Islam in Anatolia after the Turkish Invasion: Prolegomena*.

Kussem Sultan (c. 1589–1651): A consort of Sultan Ahmed I; the mother of Sultans Murad IV and Ibrahim I, and a prominent Valideh Sultan; became the most powerful woman in Ottoman history.

La Fontaine, Jean de (1621–1695): Probably the most widely read French poet of the 17th century.

Lamartine (1790–1869): Full name Alphonse-Marie-Louis de Prat de Lamartine; a French writer, poet and politician. Famous for his partly autobiographical poem, '*Le Lac*' ('The Lake'), which describes in retrospect the fervent love shared by a couple from the point of view of the bereaved man. He was one of very few French literary figures to combine his writing with a political career.

Littré, Émile Maximilien Paul (1801–1881): A French lexicographer and philosopher, best known for his *Dictionnaire de la langue française*, commonly called 'the Littré'.

Loti, Pierre (1850–1923): The pseudonym of Louis Marie-Julien Viaud; a French sailor and writer.

Mahmud II (1785–1839): Son of Sultan Abdul Hamid I; the 30th Sultan of the Ottoman Empire from 1808 until his death. His reign is notable mostly for the extensive legal and military reforms he instituted, for which he is called the 'Peter the Great of the Turks'. In 1808, Mahmud II's predecessor (and half-brother) Mustafa IV (1807–08) ordered his execution along with his cousin, the deposed Sultan Selim III (1789–1807), in order to defuse a rebellion. Selim III was killed, but Mahmud was safely kept hidden by his mother and was placed on the throne after the rebels deposed Mustafa IV. His reign marked the first breakaway from the Ottoman Empire, with Greece gaining its independence following a rebellion that started in 1821. Among Mahmoud II's most notable achievements, the Janissary corps was abolished in 1826, permitting the establishment of a modern Ottoman Army; Mahmud was also responsible for the subjugation of the Iraqi Mamluks in 1831 and the preparation of the Tanzimat reforms in 1839.

Mani: Born of Iranian (Parthian) parentage in Assuristan (modern-day Iraq) which was a part of Persian Empire about about AD 210–276. He was a religious preacher and the founder of Manichaenism, an ancient Persian Gnostic religion that was once prolific but is now extinct.

Mejid, Abdul (1823–1861): The 31st Ottoman sultan; and ruled from 1839 to 1861. He continued his father Mahmut II's Westernising (Tanzimat) reforms. During his rule the Sublime Porte replaced the Palace as the main centre of power.

Meyerhold, Vsevolod Emilevich (1874–1940): A Russian theatrical producer, director and actor whose provocative experiments dealing with physical being and symbolism in an unconventional theatre setting made him one of the seminal forces in modern theatre.

Mill, John Stuart (1806–1873): The British philosopher, political economist, and civil servant; an influential liberal thinker of the 19th century. An exponent of utilitarianism (an ethical theory) developed by Jermy Bentahm (1748–1832), although his conception of it was very different from Bentham's.

Mohammed the Conqueror or **Mohammed** II (1432–1481): The seventh Ottoman Sultan; reigned twice (1444–1446, & 1451–1481). At the age of 21, he conquered Constantinople, bringing an end to the Byzantine Empire. After the conquest of Constantinople the Ottoman state was internationally recognized as an Empire for the first time. The conquest of Constantinople allowed Mohammed II to bring more areas of Anatolia and eastern Europe under the Ottoman rule. He amalgamated the old Byzantine administration into the Ottoman state. Mohammed II's reign is also well-known for the religious tolerance with which he treated his subjects. He spoke seven languages, including Turkish, Greek, Hebrew, Arabic, Persian and Latin by the time when he conquered Constantinople.

Montesquieu (1689–1755): A French social commentator and political thinker. He is famous for his articulation of the 'theory of separation of powers'.

Mujeeb, Mohammad (1902–1985): Educated in Oxford (1922). Studied printing in Germany (1922–24). Joined Jamia Millia Islamia (1926) as Vice-Chancellor. Author of *Indian Muslims* (1967). His father Mohammad Nasim (1859–1953) was a famous lawyer, closely associated with political activities in Lucknow. Brother, Mohammad Wasim (b. 1885), went to Pakistan after the partition of India.

Osman (1258–1326): Also called Osman Gazi or Osman I, a descendant of the Kayi branch of the Oguz, was the leader and ruler of a principality in north-western Anatolia, and is regarded as the founder of the Ottoman Empire. Osman, the son of Ertugrul, declared the independence of his own small kingdom from the Seljuk Turks in 1299. The westward drive of the Mongol invasions had pushed scores of Muslims toward Osman's Anatolian principality, a power base that Osman was quick to consolidate.

Pasha, Ahmet Vefik (1823–1891): A famous statesman, diplomat, playwright and translator of the Tanzimat period during the Ottoman period. He was a pioneer of the pan-Turkism movement; considered to be the first Turkist of the Ottoman Turks. He wrote the first Turkish dictionary. Vefik also initiated the first Western style theatre plays in Bursa and translated Moliere's major works.

Pasha, Alemdar Mustafa (1765–1808): A military commander and an ayan (provincial notable) of Ruschuk province of the Ottoman Empire, became Grand Vizir for a brief period in 1808; helped defended in reinstating Selim III and Mustafa IV (1779–1808) and the former's reform agenda.

Pasha, Ali Fuat (1882–1968): A Turkish officer, politician and statesman. During World War I, he served as a commander of division, army corps and army of the Ottoman Empire. He organized the resistance in Western Turkey against the Greek invasion and thus actually started the Turkish War of Independence.

Pasha, Damad Ferid (1853–1923): Full name Damad Mehmed Adil Ferid Pasha; an Ottoman statesman who held the office of Grand Vizir during two periods under the reign of the last Ottoman Sultan Mehemmed VI Vahdeddin, during 1919-1920.

Pasha, Enver or **Enver Bey** (1881–1922): Earlier name Ismail Enver; a soldier and politician in the Ottoman Empire. He was a Turkish military officer and one of the leaders of the Young Turk revolution who deposed the Ottoman Sultan Abdul Hamid II in 1908. He was the main leader of the Ottomans in both Balkan Wars and minister of war during World War I (1914–18). A rival of Mustafa Kemal Pasha in the post-war period, he unsuccessfully sought Soviet help to overthrow him (1920). The Soviets permitted him to help organize the Turkic and Muslim Central Asian republics, but he joined Basmachi rebels against the Soviet Union and was killed fighting the Red Army.

Pasha, Fevzi (1876–1950): A professional military officer, fought in Dardanelles, Caucasus, and Syrian campaigns in World War I, chief of General Staff and Minister of War in Istanbul (1919–1920), minister of defence and head of council of ministers for Ankara government (1921–1922), led troops at battles of Inn-enunu and Sakarya, first chief of general staff of Turkish Republic (1923–1944).

Pasha, Gedik Ahmet (d. 1482): A distinguished Ottoman Grand Vizir as well as an army and navy commander during the reigns of Sultans Mohammed the Conqueror and Beyazid II. Leading the Ottoman Army, he defeated (in 1471) the last principality resisting Ottoman expansion in Anatolia, the Karamanids (who had been the strongest principality in Anatolia for nearly 200 years). Gedik Pasha's victory proved crucial for the future of the Ottomans. He led several campaigns in Crimea, Circassia, Mediterranean region and other fronts. During the struggle for who would succeed the Sultan, he sided with Beyazid II. However, the latter did not fully trust Gedik Pasha and had him imprisoned and later killed in 1482 at Adrianople.

Pasha, Ismet or **Mustafa Ismet Pasha** (1884–1973): Later became Ismet Inn-eunu (Ýnönü); a Turkish Brigadier General, statesman and the second President of Turkey. He commanded his greatest battles as a general at a Central

Anatolian town called Inn-Eunu, known as the First and Second Battles of Inn-Eunu which played an important role in the Turkish victory at the Turkish War of Independence. Served in the Ottoman army; later joined the Committee of Union and Progress. He won his first military victories by suppressing two major revolts against the struggling Ottoman Empire, first in Rumelia and later in Yemen; served as a military officer during the Balkan Wars and the World War I, and also worked together with Mustafa Kemal Pasha. He was the chief negotiator of the Turkish delegation at the Treaty of Lausanne. He served as the Prime Minister of Turkey for several terms and succeeded Mustafa Kemal as President after the latter's death.

Pasha, Izzet or **Ahmed Izzet Pasha**: One of the last Grand Vizirs of the Ottoman Empire, under the reign of the last Ottoman Sultan Mehemmed VI Vahideddine, between 14 October 1918 and 8 November 1918. Although his period of office was of short duration, he was notable by being the signatory of the Armistice of Mudros on behalf the Ottoman Empire on 30 October 1918, thus putting an end to the World War I for Turkey. He was decommissioned on 8 November 1918.

Pasha, Kiamil (1833–1913): Also known as Mehmed Kamil Pasha the Cypriot, was an Ottoman statesman in the late 19th and early 20th centuries, who became, as aside regional or international posts within the Ottoman state structure, Grand Vizir of the Empire during four different periods. After the Young Turk Revolution of 1908, Kiamil initially had supported the new men in power; but soon afterwards opposed the Young Turk Regime and became a figurehead of the so-called 'liberal' opposition. During the First Balkan War he had to return to Cyprus where he died in 1913.

Pasha, Kiazim Kara Bekir (1882–1948): A Turkish general and politician. He was the commander of the Eastern Army in the Ottoman Empire at the end of World War I and served as Speaker of the Great National Assembly before his death. According to the Treaty of Sevres, which ended the World War I, Ottoman Sultan Mehhemed Vahededdine gave order to Kara Bekir to surrender to Entente powers, which he refused. He stayed in the region and, on the eve of the Erzurum Congress when Mustafa Kemal had just arrived in Erzurum, secured the city with a Cavalry Brigade in his command to protect him and the congressmen. He pledged with Mustafa Kemal to join the Turkish national movement and subsequently took the command of the Eastern front of the Turkish War of Independence by the Kuvayi Milliye.

Pasha, Mahmoud Shevket (1856–1913): Ottoman officer of the Arabian descent. Commanded the Third (Macedonian) Army after the Young Turk constitutional revolution of 1908. After the suppression of the 1909 counter-revolution he became the war minister and commander of the First, Second and Third Armies. Replaced by the Liberals in 1912, he became Grand Vizir after the Unionist coup of 1913. Six months later he was murdered.

Pasha, Midhat (1822–1883): Full name Ahmed Shefik Midhat Pasha; a dynamic, pro-Western, enlightened Turkish reformer and statesman. He was the son of a civil judge and a declared partisan of reform, was trained in administrative career, and undertook several assignments in the Ottoman administration. Entered office of imperial council as apprentice scribe in 1836; made his name as efficient and progressive provincial administrator. Appointed president of the state council in 1868, but fell out with Ali Pasha. Grand vizir for three months in 1872. One of the initiators of the coup of 1876, which made him Grand Vizir again. Main author of the 1876 Ottoman constitution. Exiled to Taif in Arabia by Sultan Abdul Hamid II in 1877 and killed there on the Sultan's orders in 1884.

Pasha, Mustafa Kemal (1881–1938): Later became famous as Mustafa Kemal Ataturk, was an army officer, revolutionary statesman, and founder of the Republic of Turkey as well as its first President. Born in Salonica, then within the Ottoman Empire, he established himself as a successful and extremely capable military commander while serving as a division commander at the Battle of Gallipoli (1915–16). He later fought with distinction on the eastern Anatolian and Palestinian fronts, making a name for himself during First World War. Following the defeat of the Ottoman Empire at the hands of the Allies, and the subsequent plans for its partition, Mustafa Kemal Pasha led the Turkish national movement. Having established a provisional government in Angora, he defeated the forces sent by the Entente powers. His successful military campaigns led to the liberation of the country and to the establishment of the Republic of Turkey. As the first President of Turkey, Mustafa Kemal embarked upon a major programme of political, economic and cultural reforms.

Pasha, Mustafa Reshid (1799–1857): Son of a scribe; started his career in the chancery as a protégé of his brother-in-law, Syed Ali Pasha. Ottoman ambassador in Paris and London. Minsiter of foreign affairs in 1836. Led the pro-British faction at the Porte and took the initiative for the trade treaty of 1838 and the reforms of 1840s and early 1850s.

Pasha, Raouf/Raouf Bey (1881–1964): Complete name Huseyin Rauf Orbay; a Turkish sailor and statesman; he took active part in the Turkish War of Independence. Born in Istanbul; served as a naval officer in the Ottoman Navy; and he was the captain of the cruiser *Hamidiye* during the Balkan War. As the Minister of Navy, he signed the Mondros ceasefire treaty (1918); later resigned from his position and collaborated with Mustafa Kemal Pasha during the War of Independence. After the Sivas Congress, he along with Mustafa Kemal and others signed Amassia protocol with the Ottoman administration in 1919. When the War of Independence ended he became the first Prime Minister of the new Republic of Turkey in 1922.

Pasha, Refet: One of the signatories, along with Mustafa Kemal, Rauf and Kiazim Kara Bekir Pashas of the 'Amassia Agreement' (1919), which gave the first call to the Turkish national independence movement against the occupying powers.

Pasha, Said (1830–1914): Also called Kuchuk Mehemmed Said Pasha (literally Mehemmed Said Pasha the Small) was a statesman in the Ottoman Empire and editor of the Turkish newspaper *Jerid-i-Havadis*. He was the Grand Vizir during Abdul Hamid II and his successor Mehemmed V's time. He was known for his opposition to the extension of foreign influence in Turkey.

Pasha, Tal'at or **Mehmed Tal'at** (1874–1921): One of the first important members of the Committee of Union and Progress (CUP). Played an increasingly important part in Ottoman politics becoming deputy for Edirne, minister and finally in 1917 as Grand Vizir. He left the empire with Enver and Jemal Pashas in 1918. Tal'at Pasha, along with Enver Pasha and Jemal Pasha formed a group called *The Three Pashas*. These men formed the triumvirate of the Ottoman government until the end of World War I in October 1918. He as an Interior Minister is blamed for the Armenian deportation and massacre cases during the first world war. He was assassinated in Berlin 1921.

Pasha, Zia (1829–1880): An Ottoman poet and reformist.

Pericles (c. 495–429 B.C.): A prominent and influential statesman, orator, and general of Athens during the city's Golden Age—specifically, the time between the Persian and Peloponnesian wars.

Peter I the Great (1672–1725): Ruled the Russian Empire from 1682 until his death, jointly ruling before 1696 with his weak and sickly half-brother, Ivan V. Peter (1666–1696) carried out a policy of Westernisation and expansion that transformed the Tsardom of Russia into the Russian Empire, a major European power.

Plato (428/427–348/347 B.C.): The ancient Greek philosopher, disciple of Socrates, and teacher of Aristotle. His famous work is the *Republic*. Building on the life and thought of Socrates, Plato developed a profound and wide-ranging system of philosophy. His thought has logical, epistemological, and metaphysical aspects, with underlying motivation of ethics.

Prince Mustafa (1515–1553): The firstborn son of Soleyman the Magnificent (1494–1566) and his concubine Gulbahar Sultan, an heir apparent to the Ottoman throne before he was murdered; served as the prince of Manisa (1533 to 1541) and of Amassia (1541 to 1553).

Racine, Jean (1639–1699): A French dramatist, one of the 'big three' of 17th century France (along with Molière and Corneille), and one of the most important literary figures in the Western tradition.

Rahmi, Hussein (1864–1944): A Turkish writer and politician. The son of a family close to the Ottoman court was born in Istanbul. He became a civil servant, then a writer and journalist, and later served as a member of parliament, Great National Assembly between 1935–1943.

Refik Halid: A satirist of the late Ottoman period; a rabid enemy of the Young Turks; he used colloquial Turkish. He wrote masterpieces in the form of character sketches or caricatured the events of the time. His works is included in a collection called *What the Hedgehog Said*. After Mahmoud Shevket Pasha's (1856–1913) assassination, he was exiled to an Anatolian city.

Renan, Ernest (1823–1892): A French philosopher and writer, deeply attached to his native province of Brittany. He is best known for his influential historical works on early Christianity and his political theories.

Reshad Nury: A Turkish novelist. His best work, *Wren*, is the study of a young schoolmistress in the provinces.

Roderick (died 711 or 712): The Visigothic King of Hispania for a brief period between 710 and 712. He is famous in legend as 'the last king of the Goths'. During his period Muslims conquered the Visigothic Hispania under the commandership of Tarik Ibn-i-Ziad (d. 720).

Rousseau, Jean-Jacques (1712–1778): A great French philosopher, literary figure, and composer of the Enlightenment whose political philosophy influenced the French Revolution (1789–1799), and the development of liberal and socialist theory.

Rufus, Musonius (b. AD 20–30): A Roman Stoic philosopher of the first century A.D. He fell under the ban of Nero owing to his ethical teachings, and was exiled to an island on a trumped-up charge of participation in Piso's conspiracy.

Rumi, Maulana Jalaluddin (1207–1273): A 13th-century Islamic mystic, jurist, theologician and Persian poet. Rumi is a descriptive name meaning 'the Roman' since he lived most parts of his life in Anatolia or 'Rum', which had been part of the Byzantine (or Eastern Roman) Empire until the Seljuq conquest two centuries earlier. He lived most of his life under the Sultanate of Rum, where he produced his works and died in 1273 CE. He was buried in Konya and his shrine became a place of pilgrimage. Following his death, his followers founded an order widely known as the order of the *Whirling Dervishes*, famous for its Sufi dance known as the 'sema' ceremony.

Selim the Grim or **Selim I** (1465–1520): The eleventh Sultan of the Ottoman Empire; reigned from 1512 to 1520. He is referred to as 'the Grim' or 'the Brave', (in Turkish *Yavuz).*

Selim III (1761–1808): The 28th Sultan of the Ottoman Empire; ruled from 1789 to 1807. He undertook a programme of Westernization and his reign felt the intellectual and political ferment created by the French Revolution.

Seyfeddine, Omer (1884–1920): A Turkish nationalist writer from the late 19th and early 20th centuries; considered to be one of the greatest modern Turkish authors. He immensely contributed for simplifying the Turkish language by removing the Persian and Arabic words and phrases that were common at the time. Born to a Circassian family in Balikesir and was a son of a military official. He graduated from a military veterinary academy in 1896, followed by a prolonged military education that lasted until the 1903 events in Macedonia.

Shakespeare (baptized April 26, 1564–1616): A great English poet, dramatist, and actor, often called the English national poet and considered by many to be the greatest dramatist of all time.

Sheikh Saadi (1184–1283/1291?): One of the major Persian poets of the medieval period. A native of Shiraz, Persia; lived in Baghdad for quite some time (1195–1226) and studied Arabic. He is recognised both for the quality of his writing as well as for the depth of his social thought.

Sherif of Mecca, or **Sayyid Hussein bin Ali** (1854–1931): Born in Istanbul; the last of the Hashemite rulers over the Hejaz to be appointed by the Ottoman Empire. Sharif Hussein rebelled against the rule of the Ottomans during the Arab Revolt of 1916. He was the Sherif of Mecca, and Emir of Mecca from 1908 until 1917, when he proclaimed himself king of Hejaz.

Shinassi (1826–1871): One of the political leaders of the Young Turk, was the founder of the Tanzimat school of literature. He published the papers *Tejuman* and *Tasvir-i-Efkar*.

Socrates (c. 470–399 B.C.): An ancient Greek philosopher; one of the founders of Western philosophy; strongly influenced Plato, who was his student, and Aristotle, whom Plato taught.

Soleyman the Magnificent or **Suleiman I** (1494–1566): Also called 'Kanuni Sultan Soleyman', was the tenth and longest-reigning Ottoman Sultan, who reigned from 1520 till his death in 1566.

Stalin, Joseph (1878–1953): General Secretary of the Communist Party of the Soviet Union's Central Committee from 1922 until his death.

Stanislavski, Constantin Sergeyevich (1863–1938): A Russian actor and theatre director.

Tarik Ibn-i-Ziad (d. 720): Known in Spanish history and legend as *Taric el Tuerto* (Taric the one-eyed), was a Berber Muslim and Umayyad general who led the conquest of Visigothic Hispania in 711 under the orders of the Umayyad Caliph Al-Walid I (668–715). Tariq ibn Ziyad is considered to be one of the most important military commanders in Iberian history.

Tsar Nicholas or **Nicholas II** (1868–1918): The last Tsar of Russia.

Vahideddine, Mehemmed or **Mehemmed** VI (1861–1926): The 36th and last Sultan of the Ottoman Empire, reigning from 1918 to 1922. The brother of Mehemmed V, he succeeded to the throne as the eldest male member of the House of Osman after the 1916 suicide of Abdul Aziz's son Yusuf Izzeddin, the heir to the throne.

Valideh Sultan (or **Sultan Valideh**): The term which can be translated as Queen Mother, was the title conferred to the mother of a ruling sultan in the Ottoman Empire. Because the position was the most important after the Sultan himself, the Valideh Sultan(s) used to have a significant influence on the affairs of the Empire; in particular, during the 17th century, in a period known as the Sultanate of women, a series of incompetent or child sultans raised the role of the Valideh Sultan to new heights. Hurrem Sultan, Kussem Sultan, and a host of others were most influential Valideh Sultans.

von Aehrenthal, Count Alois Lexa (1854–1912): An Austrian diplomat (Foreign Minister of Austria-Hungary) who engineered the Bosnian crisis of 1908.

Wilson, Thomas Woodrow (1856–1924): The 28th President of the US. He led his country into World War I and became the creator and leading advocate of the League of Nations.

Yahya bin Khalil: The leader of the 'Ahiler' in the 13th century and the writer of the oldest *Futuhatnameh,* was among the 'akhis' aiming to organise the economic forces of Turkish society on a spiritual basis.

Yesevi, Ahmet (1106–1166): Was a Turkic poet and famous Sufi. He founded the first Turkic *tariqah* (order), the Yasaviyya or Yeseviye, which spread over the Turkic-speaking areas. The earliest known Turkic poet who composed poetry in a Turkic dialect; his poems created a new genre of religious folk poetry in Central Asian Turkic literature.

Zia, Keuk Alp (1876–1924): Childhood name Mehmed Zia, adopted the penname Gökalp; he was a sociologist, writer, and poet. He was influential in the overhaul of religious perceptions and evolving of Turkish nationalism. His work has proved particularly influential in shaping reforms of Mustafa Kemal Pasha; his influence figured prominently in the development of Kemalism, and its legacy in modern Turkey.

Zia Hilmi : A Turkish writer of Communist inclinations; one of the classical and official writers represented in the 'Kadro' movement. His best work is called *Morals of Love.*

Notes on Events

The **Amassia Protocol**, signed on 22 October 1919 just after Sivas Congress between Mustafa Kemal Pasha, Rauf Bey and Bekir Sami Bey on the one side and the Ottoman Minister of Marine (later Grand Vizier himself) Khulusi Salih Pasha who had come to Amasya to represent the short-lived Ottoman government of Ali Riza Pasha on the other side. The Amasya Protocol was an MoU between the Ottoman government in Istanbul and the Turkish revolutionaries aimed at seeking ways to preserve national independence and unity through joint efforts. It also signified a recognition by the Ottoman government of the rising Turkish revolutionary forces in Anatotia.

Balkan Wars: The two wars in south-eastern Europe in 1912-1913 in the course of which the Balkan League (Bulgaria, Montenegro, Greece, and Serbia) first conquered Ottoman-held Macedonia, Albania and most of Thrace and then fell out over the division of the spoils. These two military conflicts deprived the Ottoman Empire of almost all its remaining territory in Europe. In the First Balkan War, the Balkan League defeated the Ottoman Empire, which, under the terms of the peace treaty (1913), lost Macedonia and Albania. The Second Balkan War broke out after Serbia, Greece, and Romania quarrelled with Bulgaria over the division of their joint conquests in Macedonia. Bulgaria was defeated, and Greece and Serbia divided up most of Macedonia between themselves. The wars heightened tensions in the Balkans and helped spark World War I.

Capitulations (of the Ottoman Empire) were contracts between the Ottoman Empire and European powers, particularly France. Turkish capitulations, or *ahadnamehs*, were generally bilateral acts whereby definite arrangements were entered into by each contracting party towards the other, not mere concessions. The capitulations were grants made by successive Sultans to Christian nations, conferring rights and privileges in favour of their subjects resident or trading in the Ottoman dominions, following the policy towards European states of the Byzantine Empire.

The **Congress of Berlin** (13 June–13 July 1878) was a meeting of the European Great Powers and the Ottoman Empire's leading statesmen in Berlin in 1878. In the wake of the Russo-Turkish War (1877-78), the meeting's aim was to reorganize the countries of the Balkans. Otto von Bismarck, who led the Congress, undertook to balance the distinct interests of Britain, Russia and Austria-Hungary. As a consequence, however, differences between Russia and Austria-Hungary intensified, as did the nationality question in the Balkans. The Congress was aimed at the revision of the Treaty of San Stefano and at keeping Istanbul in Ottoman hands. It effectively disavowed Russia's victory over the decaying Ottoman Empire in the Russo-Turkish War (1877-78). The Congress of Berlin redistributed back to the Ottoman Empire certain Bulgarian territories that the previous treaty had given to the Principality of Bulgaria, most notably Macedonia.

The **Constitutional Movement** in the Ottoman Empire spread over two phases: The First Constitutional Era was the period of constitutional monarchy from the promulgation of the *Kanun-i-Esasi* (meaning 'Basic Law'), written by members of the Young Ottomans, on 23 November 1876 until 13 February 1878. The era ended with the suspension of the Ottoman parliament by Sultan Abdul Hamid II. The first constitutional era did not include any party system. The Second Constitutional Era began shortly after Sultan Abdul Hamid II restored the constitutional monarchy after the 1908 Young Turk Revolution. The period established many political groups. A series of elections during this period resulted in the gradual ascendance of the Union and Progress Committee (CUP)'s domination in politics.

The **Constantinople Agreement** (March 18, 1915) was a set of secret assurances made by the Triple Entente during the First World War. France and Great Britain promised to give Constantinople/Istamboul and the Dardanelles (land on either coast in Thrace and Asia Minor), which at the time were occupied by the Ottoman Empire, to the Russians in the event of victory. The city of Constantinople was intended to be a free port. It was never carried out due to the failure of the Dardanelles campaign and the threat Britain saw in Russia after the former finally reached the city in 1918. The agreement was revealed by the Bolsheviks in 1917, making public the British diplomatic intentions and encouraging the passing of the Balfour Declaration (1917). Knowledge of the agreement was used by Mustafa Kemal Pasha to regain Constantinople for the Turkish Republic, risking war with the Allies.

The **Crusades** were a series of military conflicts of a religious nature waged by much of Christian Europe against Muslims and others who who posed threats from external and internal fronts. The Crusades originally had the goal of recapturing Jerusalem and the Holy Land from Muslim rule and were originally launched in response to a call from the Byzantine rulers against the expansion of the Muslim Seljuk Turks into Anatolia. Rivalries among both Christian and Muslim powers led also to alliances between religious factions against their opponents, such as the Christian alliance with the Sultanate of Rum during the Fifth Crusade. The Crusades had far-reaching political, economic, and social impacts, some of which have lasted into contemporary times.

The **Eastern Question**, in European history, encompasses the diplomatic and political problems posed by the decay of the Ottoman Empire. The Eastern Question is normally dated to 1774, when the Russo-Turkish War, (1768–1774) ended in defeat for the Ottoman Turks. As the dissolution of the Ottoman Empire was believed to be imminent, the European powers engaged in a power struggle to safeguard their military, strategic and commercial interests in the Turkish domains. Imperial Russia stood to benefit from the decline of the Ottoman Empire; on the other hand, Austria and the Britain deemed the preservation of Turkey to be in their best interests. The Eastern Question was put to rest after the First World War, one of whose outcomes was the collapse of the Ottoman Empire.

The **Entente Powers** or the Allied Powers of World War I were the countries at war with the Central Powers which included the Ottoman Empire during World War I. The main allies were France, the Russia, the Britain, Italy and the US. France, Russia, the Britain (and, by default, its empire), entered World War I in 1914, as a result of their Triple Entente alliance.

The **French Revolution** (1789–1799) was a period of political and social upheaval in the political history of France and Europe as a whole.

The **Graeco-Turkish War** of 1897, also called the Thirty Days' War, was a war between the Ottoman Empire and Greece, during the reign of Sultan Abdul Hamid II. Its immediate cause was Greek concern over the situation in Crete, where the Greek population was still under Ottoman control. This war was the only conflict between Greeks and Turks in the century, where Greece was forced to cede land to Turkey.

Gulhane-hatti-Humayun or the Edict of the Rose Chamber was an 1839 proclamation by Ottoman Sultan Abdul Mejid I, that launched the Tanzimat period of reforms and reorganization. The proclamation was issued at the behest of reformist Grand Vizir Mustafa Reshid Pasha. It promised reforms such as the abolition of tax farming, reform of conscriptions, and greater equality of religion. The goal of the decree was to help modernize the empire militarily and socially so that it could compete with the Great Powers of Europe. It also was hoped the reforms would win over the disaffected parts of the empire, especially in the Ottomancontrolled parts of Europe, which were largely Christian.

The **Khilafat Movement** (1919–1924) was a campaign launched mainly by Muslims in the Indian sub-continent to influence the British government and to protect the Ottoman Empire during and aftermath of World War I.

The **Lausanne Treaty** (24 July 1923) was a peace treaty signed in the city of Lausanne that settled the Anatolian part of the partitioning of the Ottoman Empire by annulment of the Treaty of Sevres signed by the Ottoman Sultan as the consequences of the Turkish War of Independence between the Allied Powers of World War I and Great National Assembly created by the Mustafa Kemal and others during the Turkish national movemnet. This treaty was signed after the newly-founded Turkish government rejected the Treaty of Sevres. Ismet Pasha was the main negotiator from the Turkish side during the Conference of Lausanne and Eleftherios Venizelos was his Greek counterpart. The treaty is composed of 141 articles with major sections like; (a) Convention on the Turkish straits; (b) Abolition of Capitulations (Trade); (c) Exchange of populations between Greece and Turkey, etc. The treaty provided for the independence of the Republic of Turkey but also for the protection of the ethnic Greek minority in Turkey and the mainly ethnically Turkish Muslim minority in Greece.

The **London Pact** or more correctly the Treaty of London, 1915, was a secret pact between Italy and the Triple Entente, signed in London on April 26, 1915 by the Kingdom of Italy, the UK, France and Russia. According to the pact, Italy was to leave the Triple Alliance and join Triple Entente, as already stated in a secret agreement signed in London, on 4-5 September 1914. Furthermore, Italy was to declare war against Germany and Austria-Hungary within a month. In exchange, Italy was to obtain some territorial gains at the end of the war.

A **Medical Mission** from India went to Turkey during the Balkan Wars (1912-13). It was led by M.A. Ansari (1880–1936), a medical practitioner and statesman, for which Ottoman Consul-General conferred a special award upon him.

The **Mudros Armistice** (30 October 1918) ended the hostilities in the West Asian theatre between the Ottoman Empire and the Allies of the First World War. It was signed by the Minister of Marine Affairs, Rauf Bey and the British Admiral Somerset Arthur Gough-Calthorpe, on board the *HMS Agamemnon* in Mudros harbour on the Greek island of Lemnos. The Ottomans surrendered their remaining garrisons outside Anatolia, granted the Allies the right to occupy forts controlling the Straits of the Dardanelles and the Bosphorous; and the right to occupy 'in case of disorder' any territory in case of a threat to security. The Ottoman army was demobilized, and ports, railways, and other strategic points were made available for use by the Allies. In the Caucasus, Turkey had to retreat to within its pre-war borders. The Armistice was followed with the occupation of Istanbul and subsequent partitioning of the Ottoman Empire. The Sevres Treaty (1920) followed the Armistice, but this treaty was not enacted due to the outbreak of the Turkish War of Independence.

The **National Pact** or *Misak-i Millî* is the set of six important decisions made by the last term of the Ottoman Parliament in 1920. These decisions resulted in the occupation of Istanbul by the British on February 16, 1920 and the establishment of a new parliament, the Great National Assembly in Angora. Decisions taken by this parliament were used as the basis for the new Turkish Republic's claims in the Treaty of Lausanne.

The **Orkhon Inscriptions**, oldest extant Turkish writings, discovered in the valley of Orhon River, northern Mongolia, in 1889 and deciphered in 1893 by Danish philologist Vilhelm

Thomsen. These Old Turkic script, also called Gokturk script are the alphabets used by the Gokturk from the 8th century to record the Old Turkci language. The alphabet was usually written from right to left.

The **Sèvres Treaty** of 10 August 1920 was the peace treaty of World War I between the Ottoman Empire and Allies. The Treaty of Versailles was signed with Germany before this treaty to annul the German concessions including the economic rights and enterprises. Also, France, Great Britain and Italy signed a secret 'Tripartite Agreement' at the same date. The Tripartite Agreement confirmed Britain's oil and commercial concessions and turned the former German enterprises in the Ottoman Empire over to a Tripartite corporation. The open negotiations which covered a period of more than fifteen months began at the Paris Peace Conference, continued at the Conference of London and took definite shape only after the Premiers conference at San Remo conference in April 1920. France, Italy and Great Britain, however, had secretly begun the partitioning of the Ottoman Empire as early as 1915. The delay was due to the fact that the powers could not come to an agreement which, in turn, hinged on the outcome of the Turkish national movemnet. The Treaty of Sèvres was annulled in the course of the Turkish War of Independence and the parties signed and ratified the superseding Treaty of Lausanne in 1923.

The **Sublime Porte** was the name of the open court of the sultan, led by the Grand Vizir in the Ottoman Empire. It was used in the context of diplomacy by the western states, as their diplomats were received at 'porte' (French term meaning 'gate').

The **Sykes-Picot Agreement** of 1916 was a secret agreement between the governments of United Kingdom and France, with the assent of Russia, defining their respective spheres of influence and control in west Asia after the expected downfall of the Ottoman Empire during the First World War.

The agreement was concluded on May 16, 1916 by the French diplomat Francois Georges-Picot and Briton Mark Sykes.

The **Tanzimat**, meaning *reorganization* (of the Ottoman Empire), was a period of reformation that began in 1839 and ended with the First Constitutional Period in 1876. The Tanzimat reform era was characterized by various attempts to modernize the Ottoman Empire, to secure its territorial integrity against nationalist movements and aggressive powers.

The **Treaty of Berlin** (1878) was the final Act of the Congress of Berlin (13 June–13 July, 1878) by which the United Kingdom, Austria-Hungary, France, Germany, Italy, Russia and the Ottoman Empire under Sultan Abdul Hamid II revised the Treaty of San Stefano (signed on 3 March of the same year).

The **Treaty of Kutchuk Kaynarja** was signed on 21 July 1774, in Kutchuk Kaynarca (or modern Kaynardzha, now in Bulgaria) between the Ottoman Empire and Russia after the former was defeated in the Russo-Turkish War of 1768-1774. The treaty was by far the most humiliating blow to the once-mighty Ottoman realm.

The **Treaty of St. Jean du Maurienne** (April 1917): The fourth set of secret negotiation made by the Triple Entente during the First World War with other powers to divide the Ottoman territories. Through this treaty Italy was promised Western Anatolia and Smyrna.

The **Tripolitan Wars** or the Barbary Wars were two wars between the USA and Barbary States in North Africa in the early 19th century. The first Tripolitan War was fought during 1801 and 1805 and the Second Tripolitan War in 1815.

INDEX*

*I have retained the inconsistency in spellings. Dr. Abid Husain and M. Mujeeb did not know Turkish to get the spellings right.